METAPHOR AND RELIGIOUS LANGUAGE

METAPHOR AND RELIGIOUS LANGUAGE

JANET MARTIN SOSKICE

CLARENDON PRESS · OXFORD

Oxford University Press, Walton Street, Oxford OX2 6DP

Oxford New York Toronto
Delhi Bombay Calcutta Madras Karachi
Petaling Jaya Singapore Hong Kong Tokyo
Nairobi Dar es Salaam Cape Town
Melbourne Auckland

and associated companies in
Berlin Ibadan

Oxford is a trade mark of Oxford University Press

Published in the United States by
Oxford University Press, New York

First published 1985
Reprinted (new as paperback) 1987, 1988, 1989

British Library Cataloguing in Publcation Data

Soskice, Janet Martin
Metaphor and religious language.
1. Theology.   2. Metaphor
I. Title
230'.014 BR118
ISBN 0–19–824727–3
ISBN 0–19–824982–9 (pbk)

Printed in Great Britain by
Biddles Ltd, Guildford & King's Lynn

Tantum ergo Sacramentum
Veneremur cernui:
Et antiquum documentum
Novo cedat ritui:
Praestet fides supplementum
Sensuum defectui.

Therefore we, before him bending,
this great Sacrament revere;
types and shadows have their ending,
for the newer rite is here;
faith our outward sense befriending,
makes the inward vision clear.

ACKNOWLEDGEMENTS

Thanks are due to many people who have helped me in preparing this book and I can here mention only a few: the Revd Dr A. C. Thiselton for encouraging me into it, Professor Basil Mitchell and Mr Rom Harré for seeing me through it, and Fr. Fergus Kerr, OP, Mr Ian Crombie, Dr Teresa Iglesias, and Dr Adrian Moore for assisting in its completion.

I would also like to thank the Trustees of the Gordon Milburn Junior Research Fellowship for their support of my project, and the Fellows of Somerville College, Oxford whose comments and encouragements were of great help during my time as a research fellow among them.

Finally, I would like to thank my parents, Mr and Mrs A. M. Martin, for their encouragement and my husband, Oliver, for his patient assistance and editorial skill from first to last.

CONTENTS

INTRODUCTION

THE title of this book, *Metaphor and Religious Language*, marks two interests of its writer. The first five chapters deal with metaphor and how metaphor works, the last three turn to problems of 'reality depiction' and attempt to show, on the basis of arguments from the philosophy of language and philosophy of science, what a theological realism *vis-à-vis* metaphorical terms would look like.

Some readers may be more interested in one of the book's foci than in the other. Those most interested in religious language, and especially in the question of how we can claim to speak of God at all, may wonder if we need to consider what seem like niceties in arguments native to the philosophy of language. I would say we do, not only because these arguments, or ones based loosely and sometimes carelessly upon them, will be introduced in theological discussion, but also because of the intimacy between what we can say and what we can know.

Those whose primary interest is in metaphor itself, whether literary or from the perspective of philosophy of language, semantics, philosophy of science or other—for indeed the followers of metaphor are legion—will not, I hope, find the philosophy of religion too obtrusive. Indeed the line that the theologians, or at least those of a more orthodox variety, want to walk is a most difficult and compelling one for, on the one hand, they must acknowledge, with the literary critic, that the metaphors which concern them are allusive and embedded in particular traditions of interpretation and belief, and, on the other hand, they must argue that this affective element is not the whole, that somehow this language can claim to be descriptive of a God who cannot be named, except in tropes and figures.

Metaphor, recognized since antiquity as chief amongst the tropes, has a long and noble involvement with Christianity, yet in the past three hundred years Christianity's reliance on metaphor has increasingly come to be regarded as a liability, particularly by those sceptical of Christian claims. For the most part critics have no objection to the occasional metaphor, what disturbs them is that, when speaking of God, Christians move from one metaphor to the next, always indicating that their comments must be qualified, yet never

CRITICAL
DEMAND for
NON-METAPHOR-
ICAL
THEOLOGICAL
LANGUAGE

speaking in a strictly straightforward way. The critic argues that at some point the Christian must break out of this circle of imagery and speak unequivocally of God, for otherwise we cannot know that his utterances have any sense at all.

Metaphor is, then, a pressing topic for theology and it is one often mentioned in doctrinal, philosophical, and exegetical studies —rarely, however, is it discussed in any detail. Attempts to defend the Christian's reliance on metaphor have tended to suffer two main defects; a terminological imprecision wherein terms such as 'metaphor', 'model', 'analogy', and 'myth' are used as equivalents, and a tendency to regard the problems of metaphor as problems exclusive to religious language. This we take as indicating the need for a more systematic study of metaphor, and one which gives a thorough treatment of metaphor in its own right before turning to its specifically religious applications.

COGNITIVE
POTENTIALITIES
OF
METAPHOR

Ours is not a study of particular metaphors used in the Bible or elsewhere in the Christian corpus (a task, in any case, for the Biblical scholar or systematic theologian)[1] but a study of the cognitive potentialities of metaphor, especially when speaking of God. Throughout the study, however, we have kept in mind the needs and interests of theologians and exegetes and attempted to make distinctions useful to their endeavours. In particular we have tried to systematize, for their consideration, the profusion of literature on the subject, a task made difficult because not only do comments arise from different philosophical schools but, even where writers are of the same school, there are not the standard uses of terms and developed debates that there are on more established topics of philosophical interest.

In view of the Christian's insistence that he will not or cannot transpose his concept of God into supposedly imageless speech, attacks on the meaningfulness of his metaphorical language are, in fact, attacks on any of his attempts to speak of a transcendent God. It is our hope that a defence of metaphor and of its use as a conceptual vehicle will support the Christian in his seemingly paradoxical conviction that, despite his utter inability to comprehend God, he is justified in speaking of God and that metaphor is the principal means by which he does so.

I

CLASSICAL ACCOUNTS OF METAPHOR

SO readily did interest in metaphor obtrude itself upon even the earliest philosophical and grammatical analyses of language that one can say that the study of metaphor begins with the study of language itself. Amongst Greek grammarians of the classical period, *metaphora* (which literally means 'transfer': *meta* 'trans' + *pherein* 'to carry') was recognized as a means by which language was both ornamented and extended. By such transfer of a word from an original to a secondary application one spoke not only of the neck of a man but of the 'neck' of a bottle, and not only of a man's mouth but of the 'mouth' of a river.[1]

Credit is customarily given to Aristotle for the first discussion of metaphor as an explicit subject matter, but because of its use in providing new 'names' by which language was extended, metaphor implicitly had a place in one of the earliest-known controversies concerning the nature of language: whether language is grounded in nature or in convention.

We know that this debate between nature, *phýsis*, and convention, *nómos* or *thésis*, first arose in the fifth century BC and was a principal topic amongst the Presocratic philosophers and later Sophists. It appears, too, in the Platonic dialogues, most particularly in the *Cratylus*.[2] Extreme naturalists, like Plato's Cratylus, argued that words were 'naturally' appropriate to that which they signified; for example, that 'hoot' arose naturally to signify the cry of the owl.[3] They supported their case not only by citing onomatopoeia and sound symbolism but also by providing somewhat unlikely histories for words in order to "trace them back to an allegedly 'natural' source, since it was admitted on the naturalist side that time had wrought changes in the 'first' forms of words."[4]

The Stoics, defending a naturalist position, put forward metaphor and the other traditional figures of speech such as metonymy and synecdoche as principles by which a word's range of meaning might be extended in what they alleged to be a natural way from an original to a secondary application.[5]

In this way, metaphor is linked early on with another preoccupation of the Greek grammarians, etymology. Since Homeric times it had been common to provide etymologies, or fanciful etymologies, for proper names, so Aeschylus "describes Helen as '*helenaus, helendros, heleptolis* (destroyer of ships, destroyer of men, destroyer of cities' . . .)".[6] However, with the debate over nature and convention, the task of devising purportedly 'true' or original meanings for words ('etymology' coming from the Greek stem *etymo-* signifying 'true' or 'real') took on new significance—for the extreme naturalist, "to lay bare the origin of a word and thereby its 'true' meaning was to reveal one of the truths of nature"[7]. Thus in the search for 'true' or original meanings behind the borrowed, transferred, and extended uses, the devising of etymologies was like the production of borrowed or metaphorical 'names' in reverse. The ancients were by no means unaware, however, of the danger, against which modern linguists warn us, of seeing current meaning as dependent on real or fanciful metaphorical derivation; Plato has some fun in the *Cratylus* with the etymology of σῶμα, the body, suggesting it might derive from the grave, σῆμα, in which the soul is buried in the present life, or be perhaps the index of the soul since the soul gives indications, σημαίνει, with the body, and so on.[8]

Why should it be that interest in metaphor was so early and closely associated with the first systematic reflections upon language, and with some of the first formal attempts to use words to describe words, and thoughts to study thoughts? One answer is that metaphor is a clear violation of the intuitively appealing theory of language which Wittgenstein, in the first paragraph of the *Philosophical Investigations*, attributes to Augustine:

It is this: the individual words in language name objects—sentences are combinations of such names.—In this picture of language we find the roots of the following idea: Every word has a meaning. This meaning is correlated with the word. It is the object for which the word stands.[9]

Metaphor presents a puzzle for any theory of language which views the basic semantic relation as one of naming (each word naming a thing and that thing being its meaning) for with metaphor, as Dr Johnson has remarked, we get "two ideas for one".[10] Metaphor poses problems at two levels for the commonplace if unsatisfactory theory of language criticized by Wittgenstein; first, if words name objects, how can one word name more than one thing? and second, what place has metaphor in considerations of how language, whether naturally or by convention, mirrors or describes the world? These problems recall those the naturalists sought to resolve.

While we might regard the classical debate over *phýsis* and *nómos* as fruitless and misguided from the point of view of modern linguistics, Jonathan Barnes points out that there were two quite distinct questions involved which often are confused:

The first question concerns the *origins* of language, or of 'names': was language deliberately created and imposed by a 'name-giving' person of divine, heroic, or human status? or did language gradually evolve from brutish grunts and growls, without the intervention of any conscious agent? . . . The second question concerns the relation between language and the world: does language fit the world naturally, like skin on an animal? or is it an artificial matching, like clothes on an Edwardian *belle*? Are names fixed to what they name by a natural adhesive? or is the glue man-made?[11]

The first question may be a misshapen question of linguistics, but the second is decidedly philosophical and one which has recurred in subsequent philosophical speculations about language.

There has been a tendency from late antiquity down to the present day to overlook aspects of the classical accounts that considered the ways in which metaphor might be used to name the unnamed, and to regard the classical interest in metaphor as merely an interest in an ornament of style. It is therefore important to note how closely the phenomenon of metaphor is linked, implicitly perhaps by the Presocratics and Plato, but explicitly by Aristotle and the Stoics with problems concerning the 'imposing' of names, the extending of language, and the relation between language and the world.

1. ARISTOTLE AND QUINTILIAN

There can be no doubt that the account of metaphor given by Aristotle in the *Poetics* and, to a lesser degree that of Quintilian in the *Institutio Oratoria* have influenced, both by intrinsic merit and by historical circumstance, almost all subsequent discussions of metaphor. It is not surprising that we find contemporary analysts returning to them, for the ambiguities to which they give rise and the problems they attempt to resolve largely remain those that the student of metaphor must face. It is because of this as well as the fact that the remarks of Aristotle and Quintilian have so guided—or as some would argue misguided—subsequent studies that we consider them in detail here.

The primary text from Aristotle is Chapter 21 of the *Poetics*. He says this:

A 'metaphorical term' involves the transferred use of a term that properly belongs to something else; the transference can be from genus to species, from species to genus, from species to species, or analogical. By 'from genus to species' I mean, for example, 'Here my ship is still', as lying at anchor is a species of being still. By 'from species to genus', 'Odysseus conferred ten thousand benefits', as 'ten thousand' is a specific example of plurality and he uses this instead of 'many'. By 'species to species', 'drawing the life with the bronze' and 'cutting off [the water] with the unwearying bronze'; in these examples 'drawing' is used for 'cutting off' and 'cutting off' for 'drawing', and both are species of the genus 'removing'. By 'analogical' I mean where the second term is related to the first as the fourth is to the third; for then the poet will use the fourth to mean the second and vice versa. And sometimes they add the term relative to the one replaced: I mean, for example, the cup is related to Dionysus as the shield is to Ares; so the poet will call the cup 'Dionysus' shield' and the shield 'Ares' cup'; again old age is to life what evening is to day, and so he will call evening 'the old age of the day' or use Empedocles' phrase, and call old age 'the evening of life' or 'the sunset of life'. Sometimes one of the four related terms has no word to express it, but it can be expressed through a comparison; for example, scattering seed is called 'sowing', but there is no term for the scattering of light by the sun; but as this is related to the sun as sowing is to the scatterer of seed, we have the expression 'sowing the god-created flame'. There is yet another form of analogical metaphor: this is the use of the transferred term coupled with the denial of one of its implications, for example, calling the shield 'the wineless cup' instead of 'Ares' cup'.[12]

Despite the apparent accessibility of his comments, Aristotle's classifications are not quite the same as ours. For example, Chapter 21, while largely given over to a discussion of metaphor, purports to be a discussion of nouns (ὀνόματα). Aristotle lists metaphor amongst other different types of nouns, one of which he terms the 'ordinary' or 'ruling' noun (ὄνομα κυριον), by which he seems to mean what we call a literal use of a term.[13] There remains some ambiguity, however, because the Greek ὄνομα does not always signify our grammatical category of noun. The term may also signify 'word in general', so some commentators have suggested that ὄνομα as used in Aristotle's description of metaphor signifies any linguistic sign whatever.[14] This is too sweeping, for Aristotle himself in opposing nouns to verbs in the *Rhetoric* (1404b) remarks that he has discussed nouns already in the *Poetics* in a way that makes it reasonable to suppose that he regarded Chapter 21 as dealing with substantives. Others, including both Paul Ricoeur and Eberhard Jüngel, have seen Aristotle as classing metaphor within the grammatical category of noun.[15] This seems more satisfactory, but should bear the gloss that ονομα can sometimes also be rendered 'name'. It might be even better to say that Aristotle puts metaphor amongst the types of 'names' since this emphasizes the close association made in the classical period between words and naming. In any case, whether as noun or name or word in general, Aristotle tends to speak of metaphor as a phenomenon of the individual word rather than of any wider locus of meaning such as the sentence; and this, as we shall see, is an important theoretical limitation.

Aristotle's definition achieves an initial clarity by means of the examples which he provides to illustrate his four classes of metaphor, but these same examples are what prompt one to ask if what Aristotle is describing is what the modern analyst would count as metaphor at all. The first two of Aristotle's types of transfer (from genus to species, and from species to genus) pick out what is now customarily regarded as the separate trope of synecdoche (the substitution of part for whole, or whole for part), and one of Aristotle's examples ('ten thousand' as a species of 'large number') is a clear instance of hyperbole. Rather than distinguishing metaphor from other figures of speech, it seems—as Ricoeur has pointed out—that for Aristotle the term 'metaphor' "applies to every transposition of terms".[16] Of course, this is only to say that Aristotle's 'metaphor' designates a broader category than does 'metaphor' as placed in later taxonomies of the tropes, and this need not be a shortcoming if Aristotle's general account proves adequate.

However, if we look to Aristotle's account for a theoretical explanation of metaphor we are soon perplexed. In the first sentence of the passage we have quoted, Aristotle sets out a description, fertile in itself, but full of ambiguities when regarded as a definition:

μεταφορὰ δέ ἐστιν ὀνόματος ἀλλοτρίου ἐπιφορὰ ἢ ἀπὸ τοῦ γένους ἐπὶ εἶδος ἢ ἀπὸ τοῦ εἴδους ἐπὶ τὸ γένος ἢ ἀπὸ τοῦ εἴδους ἐπὶ εἶδος ἢ κατὰ τὸ ἀνάλογον.[17]

(A 'metaphorical term' involves the transferred use of a term that properly
belongs to something else; the transference can be from genus to species,
from species to genus, from species to species, or analogical.)[18]

Aristotle here follows the derivation of the term 'metaphor' in
saying that *metaphora* (carrying across) is a kind of *epiphora* (carrying over), a comment which is scarcely explanatory. It has thus
been suggested that *epiphora*, which carries the burden of Aristotle's meaning, might be glossed as 'a bringing upon', 'an application', or 'an imposition', but these glosses while avoiding direct
repetition are no more helpful, for they still do not explain the
nature of the 'imposition' or 'bringing upon'.[19]
And what, in any case, is it that is to be imposed or transferred?
Our translation indicates that it is a 'term', hence a word or rather
a word's meaning, which is transferred. So Samuel Ijsseling translates, "metaphor is a transference of a word (i.e. the meaning of a
word) to something else".[20] But while the notion that it is words
which are transferred is difficult to make sense of, the notion that it
is the meanings of words which are transferred, with its suggestion
that meanings are detachable things that words have, is no easier.
We cannot imagine that words 'have' meanings in the same way
that people have boots or bicycles.[21]
One cannot, on the basis of etymology alone, establish that
metaphor involves some sort of transference. Etymology is not a
sure guide to synchronic meaning and nor, as even medieval
philosophers like Thomas Aquinas knew, is it a sure guide to
structure and function; the word 'hydrogen' derives from 'that
which produces water' but we do not now look to this etymology to
tell us about the functioning of that element.[22] The difficulty with
any mention of transference is that it immediately begs the question 'transference of what to what?' Inability to answer this question casts doubt upon the value of speaking in terms of transference at all. In Aristotle's use of the notion there is a further
ambiguity over whether he intends us to regard metaphor as the
process of transference, or as the product of it. He seems to mean
both, yet his account of any process of transference is scarcely filled
out.
The sections of the *Institutio Oratoria* that posterity has fastened
upon as central to Quintilian's views about metaphor contain his
oft-cited adage equating metaphor and simile—"In totum autem

metaphora brevior est similitudo''[23]—and his classification of metaphor into four groups:

Metaphors fall into four classes. In the first we substitute one living thing for another, as in the passage where the poet, speaking of a charioteer, says,

> "The steersman then
> With mighty effort wrenched his charger round."

or when Livy says that Scipio was continually *barked at* by Cato. Secondly, inanimate things may be substituted for inanimate, as in the Virgilian,

> "And gave his fleet the rein,"

or inanimate may be substituted for animate, as in

> "Did the Argive bulwark fall by sword or fate?"

or animate for inanimate, as in the following lines:

> "The shepherd sits unknowing on the height
> Listening the roar from some far mountain
> brow."[25]

These comments are, if anything, less explanatory than those of Aristotle yet none the less, mediated by the rhetorical tradition, they have exercised considerable influence. Evidence of the continuing influence of the classical definitions on accounts of metaphor can be seen in works as recent as Stephen Ullman's *Semantics*, where the author devotes by far the largest part of his discussion of metaphor to an account of what he terms the 'four major groups of metaphor: anthropomorphic, animal, concrete to abstract, and "synaesthetic"'. Although the categories themselves differ, the format is strikingly similar to that of Quintilian and bears witness to the same ancient presupposition that one of the most important things for an analyst of metaphor to do is to provide types of metaphor according to their subject-matter.[25]

What, then, are we to make of the classical accounts of metaphor? It is certain that we shall taste the freshness of their insights only if we free them from the obligation to answer questions that were never theirs to ask. In particular, we should unburden Aristotle and

Quintilian of responsibility for giving an account of the 'mechanism' of metaphor, and in doing so we will see the inadequacy of attributing to them the so called 'substitution view' of metaphor. This requires a word of explanation.

It is by now almost a commonplace that Aristotle is the originator and Quintilian the exponent of the clearly unsatisfactory view that metaphor is simply the substitution of a decorative word or phrase for an ordinary one. So Max Black speaks of "the blind alley taken by those innumerable followers of Aristotle who have supposed metaphors to be replaceable by literal translations"[26] and says that "until recently, one or another form of a substitution view has been accepted by most writers (usually literary critics or writers of books on rhetoric) who have had anything to say about metaphor".[27]

Indeed, if one views transference as Aristotle's proposed 'mechanism' of metaphor, one is led inevitably to the conclusion that Aristotle considers metaphor a case of simple substitution. This interpretation is supported by Chapter 22 of the *Poetics* (1458a) where, in discussing riddles, Aristotle speaks of using metaphors in place of the actual words for things. His suggestion, in the *Rhetoric* 1410b), that metaphor is roughly the same as simile might also be taken as indicating a substitution view, for Black attributes to those who equate metaphor and simile a 'comparison view' of metaphor that is really only a special case of the substitution view, "For it holds that the metaphorical statement might be replaced by an equivalent literal *comparison.*"[28] By this criterion Quintilian too holds a substitution view of metaphor.[29] Quintilian's discussion, perhaps because of his explicit equating of metaphor and simile, has been even more dismissively treated than Aristotle's. Quintilian is at fault, according to Samuel Levin, in focusing on the terms involved in the metaphoric process rather than on the process itself, and, since Quintilian's chief theoretical notion is that of substitution, his account is 'static', for "substitution per se is a quite superficial and unexplanatory concept."[30]

The case for attributing to Aristotle and Quintilian a facile substitution or ornamentalist view of metaphor seems strong, but we suggest that to do so is to underestimate Aristotle and Quintilian and to misrepresent the nature of their accounts. There is evidence, even within the *Poetics*, that Aristotle by no means considered metaphor as simply a substituted name. A metaphor may name that which has no name. In discussing metaphor by analogy, he says:

Sometimes one of the four related terms has no word to express it, but it can be expressed through a comparison; for example, scattering seed is called 'sowing', but there is no term for the scattering of light by the sun; but as this is related to the sun as sowing is to the scatterer of seed, we have the expression 'sowing the god-created flame'.[31]

Here and in other places Aristotle shows his sensitivity towards the capacity of metaphor to name the unnamed, that is to fill what linguists now call lexical gaps; and while he indicates that this capacity provides a useful device for the poet in his riddle-making and perfection of diction, he by no means excludes the more interesting suggestion that metaphor may be active in the extension of our understanding. Another remark in the *Poetics* suggests that Aristotle, despite his reticence, kept in mind this more profound aspect of metaphor. He writes:

It is extremely important to use in the proper place each of the kinds I have mentioned, but by far the most important is to be good at metaphor. For this is the only one that cannot be learnt from anyone else, and it is a sign of natural genius, as to be good at metaphor is to perceive resemblances.[32]

It must be remembered that Aristotle's purpose in the *Poetics* is not to give a rigorous description of linguistic practice but to describe metaphor in order to help the poet to achieve excellence in style. Levin assumes too readily that "in focusing on transference" Aristotle attempts to describe the poet's "conceptual process".[33] It is more likely that, in the *Poetics*, Aristotle was not concerned to give accounts of mechanisms and processes, but simply wished to provide his reader with an identifying description of metaphor. For this purpose his account is satisfactory. In the *Rhetoric* (1405b), Aristotle remarks that the fittingness of a metaphor is to be judged not only by its degree of correspondence to the thing signified, but also by its sound, or by the appeal it makes to the eyes or to some other sense. In considering euphony as well as semantics Aristotle is writing for the poet and not the philosophical analyst of metaphor. Similarly, to impute to Quintilian a static view of metaphor as substitution is to misjudge the nature of Quintilian's account. The *Institutio Oratoria* was intended for the teaching of oratory and the discussion of metaphor in that work takes place in a chapter dealing with the tropes. The purpose of training the speaker is made clear in the lively illustrations he gives to illuminate their use:

hyperbole lies, though without any intention to deceive, [it . . .] is employed even by peasants and uneducated persons, for the good reason that everybody has an innate passion for exaggeration or attenuation of actual facts, and no one is ever contented with the simple truth. [34]

Yet despite his interest in entertainment and in style, Quintilian does not regard the tropes simply as figurative versions of what may be formulated literally. He notes, as did Aristotle, that we may use a trope because there is no other term available for that of which we wish to give account. In a passage which should clear him from any charge of holding a substitution view, Quintilian says:

the changes involved concern not merely individual words, but also our thoughts and the structure of our sentences. In view of these facts I regard those writers as mistaken who have held that *tropes* necessarily involve the substitution of word for word. [35]

Quintilian's account is less explanatory than that of Aristotle, for he is less of a philosopher; both accounts are, by the canons of modern semantic theory, flawed most importantly by their tendency to speak of metaphor as something which happens to the individual word. Yet it is difficult on reading these two classical accounts not to be impressed by their perspicacity and sensitivity concerning the complex relationship of thought to language.

2. THE ORIGINS OF THE SUBSTITUTION VIEW OF METAPHOR

The foregoing is more than mere face-saving for Aristotle and Quintilian, even should one presume to judge that necessary, for it unveils an interesting question: if Aristotle and Quintilian did not view metaphor solely as ornament replaceable by literal translation, then what is the origin of the substitution view which Max Black claims, with some justification, has dominated discussions of metaphor down to the present century? One suggestion is that the substitution view, though not strictly that of Aristotle or Quintilian, was fastened upon by the students of rhetoric who followed them and passed, via classical rhetoric, into accounts of metaphor in subsequent philosophy, linguistics, and literary criticism. [36] This suggestion is partially correct. Metaphor, as chief amongst the tropes, was indeed a principal subject for the rhetoricians; but to suggest that the rhetoricians saw metaphor as a useful but expendable technique is to misrepresent them. We suggest that the crude substitution view of metaphor is not so much that of the rhetoricians as of their empiricist critics, and that suspicion of metaphor is so much linked with suspicion of rhetorical methods as to warrant a brief digression into the history of rhetoric, and its disparagement at the hands of philosophers. [37]

Rhetoric has not, for some time, formed a significant part of what we would call philosophical study. Indeed, to suggest today that an argument uses rhetoric is tantamount to saying that it is not a philosophical argument. One of the first influential criticisms of rhetoric was Plato's. In the *Gorgias*, Socrates attacks the 'technical' rhetoric of the Sophists who are made to appear as teachers of speech-making by rote and persuasion by verbal trickery. In this dialogue, rhetoric is defined as the art of delivering a speech that makes a conviction acceptable to people, and the Sophist Gorgias is forced by Socrates to admit that rhetoric is "the kind of persuasion which produces belief, not knowledge (454e 8)". [38] Rhetoric, says Socrates, is not a *techne* or art in any true sense but rather a *tribe* or knack, "an empirically acquired cleverness at something"; a cleverness, that is, at winning arguments by trickery. [39] As the knack of persuasion, rhetoric was not a medium for true knowledge and could, in fact, run contrary to it. In consequence, the 'art' of rhetoric, unlike Plato's preferred method of dialectic, could have no significant place in the philosophical study of truth.

But critics as early as Cicero objected that one could not so readily separate what one says from how one says it. So Cicero accuses Socrates of separating

the science of wise thinking from that of elegant speaking, though in reality they are closely linked together . . . This is the source from which has sprung the undoubtedly absurd and unprofitable and reprehensible severance between the tongue and the brain, leading to our having one set of professors to teach us to think and another to teach us to speak. [40]

In fact, neither Socrates nor Plato wished to divorce wise thinking from good speaking. In the *Phaedrus*, Socrates is more sympathetic to rhetoric and suggests that it is not the true philosophical rhetoric to which he objects but rather the rhetoric of the handbooks which teaches style without understanding. For the true rhetorician, "there is little logical difference between dialectic, or the discovery of truth, and rhetoric, or the persuasive exposition of truth". [41] These more positive comments provide a background for Aristotle's

Rhetoric, a work in which the similarities between rhetoric and dialectic are emphasised.

Despite these affirmations of the possibilities of 'true' rhetoric, Plato has been regarded as rhetoric's foe, and Aristotle's attempt to provide a more philosophical rhetoric neglected. Rhetoric of the Roman period was for the most part concerned with style (or *elocutio*), and works such as the treatise by Demetrius *On Style* showed an increasing interest in the naming and classifying of the figures and ornaments of speech, so much so that style and the ornaments of style were regarded in later antiquity, the Middle Ages, and the Renaissance as "the heart of rhetoric".[42]

It has thus been suggested that, while the study of rhetoric (incorporated within the 'trivium' of grammar, rhetoric, and dialectic) continued to be of importance throughout the Middle Ages and the Renaissance, preoccupation with style excluded interest in more philosophical issues. However, the notion that an interest in style and ornamentation diminishes or even precludes an interest in sound argument is distinctly modern. The object of rhetoric was to move the will, but to move the will by good reasoning well presented, and not by verbal trickery.[43]

Perhaps the real source of the idea that ornament and style have no place in pure argument is to be found in those philosophers of the seventeenth century who chose as their model the arguments of mathematics and the new sciences. Thomas Hobbes shows himself to be a modern when, anxious for speech that matches the simplicity of mathematices, he declares it to be an absurdity of the philosophers that they use "Metaphors, Tropes, and other Rhetoricall figures" instead of beginning their ratiocination "from the Definitions, or Explications of the names they are to use; which is a method that hath been used onely in Geometry; whose conclusions have thereby been made indisputable".[44]

Nowhere is the rationalist and empiricist critique of rhetoric and of figurative speech more eloquently or influentially stated than in the chapter, 'Of the Abuse of Words', in Locke's *Essay Concerning Human Understanding*. So representative is it of the attack that we quote at length:

Since wit and fancy find easier entertainment in the world than dry truth and real knowledge, figurative speeches and allusion in language will hardly be admitted as an imperfection or abuse of it. I confess, in discourses where we seek rather pleasure and delights than information and improvement, such ornaments as are borrowed from them can scarce pass for faults. But yet if we would speak of things as they are, we must allow that all the art of rhetoric, besides order and clearness; all the artificial and figurative application of words eloquence hath invented, are for nothing else but to insinuate wrong ideas, move the passions, and thereby mislead the judgment; and so indeed are perfect cheats: and therefore, however laudable or allowable oratory may render them in harangues and popular addresses, they are certainly, in all discourses that pretend to inform or instruct, wholly to be avoided; and where truth and knowledge are concerned, cannot but be thought a great fault, either of the language or person that makes use of them. What and how various they are, will be superfluous here to take notice; the books of rhetoric which abound in the world, will instruct those who want to be informed: only I cannot but observe how little the preservation and improvement of truth and know-ledge is the care and concern of mankind; since the arts of fallacy are endowed and preferred. It is evident how much men love to deceive and be deceived, since rhetoric, that powerful instrument of error and deceit, has its established professors, is publicly taught, and has always been had in great reputation: and I doubt not but it will be thought great boldness, if not brutality, in me to have said thus much against it. Eloquence, like the fair sex, has too prevailing beauties in it to suffer itself ever to be spoken against. And it is in vain to find fault with those arts of deceiving, wherein men find pleasure to be deceived.[45]

Despite the disclaimer that his attack will no doubt be thought "great boldness, if not brutality", Locke seems in little doubt that clear thinking men will agree with it.

It is in such passages that we find the ancestor of the common-place that metaphor is a decorative but strictly expendable sub-stitute for what can (and should when doing philosophy) be plainly stated. It is tempting to see behind Locke's own rhetorically masterful attack an intuition of the real difficulties that metaphor poses for empiricist views about language and the challenge meta-phor presents to those who "would speak of things as they are". We shall return to these points later on.

The problems that have arisen from examination of the classical accounts are ones which recur in the study of metaphor. What is to count as a satisfactory definition of metaphor? Is metaphor a product or a process? Is metaphor a deviance in word meaning? Are metaphors figurative substitutes for literal expression? Are classifi-cations of different types of metaphor useful or even possible? How can metaphor be distinguished from other tropes, particularly from simile? And especially, is metaphor actually involved in the creation of new meaning? The first problem to be addressed is that of definition.

II

PROBLEMS OF DEFINITION

ANYONE who has grappled with the problem of defining metaphor will appreciate the pragmatism of those who proceed to discuss
it without giving any definition of it at all. One scholar claims to
have found 125 different definitions, surely only a small fraction of
those which have been put forward,[1] for not only is the subject-
matter elusive, but a definition of metaphor useful to one discipline
often proves unsatisfactory to another. The interests which bring the
poet or literary critic to a study of metaphor differ from those which
arouse the curiosity of the psychologist or physicist and it is consequently not surprising, nor necessarily to be deplored, that definitions on the literary critical side should tend to terms like 'vision',
'imagination', and 'fusion', whereas those from the philosophy of
science tend to terms like 'paradigm', 'analogy', and 'model'.
Perhaps it is not necessary or possible to devise a substantial
definition of metaphor satisfactory to all, yet it is useful to have a
minimal definition adequate across disciplines, which can be
elaborated in ways suited to the purposes of theology and philosophy of religion as our study continues. As a working definition of
metaphor, we shall say that *metaphor is that figure of speech
whereby we speak about one thing in terms which are seen to be
suggestive of another*. The virtues of this skeleton definition will
become apparent as our study continues. We can here briefly clarify
some of our terms; 'speaking' is intended to mark that metaphor is
a phenomenon of language use (and not that it is oral). Similarly,
'thing' signifies any object or state of affairs, and not necessarily a
physical object; the moral life, the temperament of the Russian
people, and the growth of the soul are all equally 'things' in this
sense. Finally, 'seen to be suggestive' means seen so by a competent
speaker of the language.

This definition is extremely simple and avowedly broad. Its merit
is that it allows us to note things about metaphor so rudimentary
that they are often overlooked, the most important of which is that
metaphor, as a figure of speech, is a form of language use.

1. METAPHORS ARE NOT MENTAL EVENTS

All sorts of confusion can arise from neglect of the simple point that metaphor is a form of language use. Consider this definition of metaphor given by Sir Herbert Read: [metaphor] ''is the synthesis of several units of observation into one commanding image; it is the expression of a complex idea, not by analysis, nor by abstract statement, but by a sudden perception of an objective relation''. [2]

Literary critical accounts of metaphor are peppered with definitions that claim that metaphor is a process of imagination, a kind of perception or an emotive response, and these, as we have indicated, may be perfectly satisfactory remarks within the context of literary theory. It is less helpful when philosophers speak of metaphor, as they sometimes do, as the 'act' of employing symbolic relations or a ''fusion of sense and sensa'', or more dryly, when they say that metaphor is by common definition a transfer of meaning. However suggestive these remarks may be, as definitional comments they are misleading. While it may be that the successful employment of metaphor involves non-linguistic observations, perceptions, and responses, it should not be thought that metaphor is primarily a process or a mental act, and only secondarily its manifestation in language. Metaphor is by definition a figure of speech and not an 'act', 'fusion', or 'perception'. Were this not the case we should not know where to look for metaphor at all.

The introduction of misleading psychological terminology into definitions of metaphor arises from a failure to distinguish two tasks: that of providing a nominal definition that allows us to identify metaphor, and that of providing a functional account that tells us how metaphor works. The working definition we have given deliberately avoids terms like 'transfer', 'substitution', 'comparison', 'interaction', or 'process' and indeed does not specify any other means by which the speaking about one thing in terms suggestive of another is effected. This is intentional, for there is no need for a definition to contain a full functional account; such definitions will either be cumbersome definitions or misleading accounts. The second difficulty is that, by including in a definition a discussion of function involving, as that must, psychological terminology, one suggests that metaphor really is a process or event in the mind, and this obscures the more fundamental point that metaphor is a mode of language use and that the study of metaphor should begin in a linguistic setting. [3]

2. PHYSICAL OBJECTS ARE NOT METAPHORS

Related to the point that metaphors are not mental events is the one that physical objects and states of affairs are not in themselves metaphors. He who points to the daffodils in the garden and says that they are metaphors for rebirth speaks carelessly and indeed metaphorically. Daffodils are not in themselves and could not be metaphors, for they are not linguistic at all. We shall argue later that one can reasonably say that the daffodil is a symbol of rebirth or that it provides an analogy for rebirth, since neither the category of symbol nor that of analogy is strictly linguistic.[4] However, although we can construct a metaphor in which we speak of daffodils in order to describe rebirth, the daffodils themselves are not metaphors.

Our purpose here is not to criticize the Sunday preacher who says his daffodils are metaphors, or the poet who says that a metaphor is a kind of 'vision'; these are loose but perfectly satisfactory ways of speaking in those contexts. If, however, the context is that of a critical study of metaphor and the object is to map distinctions between metaphor and other forms with which it is associated and often confused, such as symbol, image, model, myth, and analogy, clarity at the outset on the linguistic nature of metaphor is essential.

Colin Turbayne is confused, then, when he says that "Some cases of metaphor may not be expressed in words" and suggests that Michaelangelo's 'Night' is a metaphor. And Nelson Goodman is misleading when he says that "Non-verbal as well as verbal labels may, of course, be applied metaphorically, say in a cartoon of a politician as a parrot, or of a despot as a dragon. And a blue painting of a trombone player involves complex, if unsubtle, transfer".[5] This is to say that any form of conceptual transfer or comparison is metaphorical. The term used so broadly precludes the possibility of making the kinds of distinctions between metaphor and its associates which are, for a critical analysis, most interesting. So, then, whatever else it may be, metaphor is a figure of speech.

Despite this admonition, the tendency to speak of metaphor as though it were a special kind of mental act is by no means without significance for our study. It is an important feature of metaphor that, if the metaphor is a good one, in appreciating it one goes well beyond the bare formulation of the utterance. In appreciating a poetic metaphor such as Emily Dickinson's

A Narrow Wind complains all Day
How some one treated him

we go beyond the given that the wind 'complains' into consideration of the wind as animate, personal, wilful, and churlish.[6]
Perhaps it is for this reason that some philosophers speak of metaphor as a special fusion of "sense" and "sensa" which produces a
mixture of thought and experience unavailable from more prosaic
expression.[7] This is to respond to the dynamism of a good metaphor; because appreciation of the metaphor involves more than the
simple given, it is conjectured that the metaphor goes beyond the
linguistic into the realm of the psychological and perceptual. It is
here that the temptation arises to regard metaphor as a mental event
which might sometimes have a linguistic manifestation and
sometimes a physical one, as when one says that the physical
daffodil is a metaphor. But our reason for denying that metaphor is
a non-linguistic mental event is not that we cannot make sense of
such a notion (since clearly we have non-linguistic thoughts), but
simply that, as a figure of speech, metaphor is linguistic.

We are not, then, rejecting psychological terminology completely, but rejecting the suggestion that metaphor is fundamentally a sort of mental event. A metaphor may prompt us into
non-linguistic recognitions and comparisons, but of equal if not
greater importance are the linguistic associations to which it gives
rise. When in appreciating a metaphor one goes beyond the bare
utterance into a network of implications, it is not so much that one
goes beyond words, but that one goes beyond the words one is
given. We go beyond the given that "A Narrow Wind complains all
Day/How some one treated him" to the further, but still language-
linked, reflections that the wind is mean and bad-tempered. We
can summarize this point by saying that while the implications of a
metaphor may go beyond the utterance, they are not necessarily
extra-linguistic.

3. METAPHOR DOES NOT TAKE A PARTICULAR SYNTACTIC
FORM

To say that metaphor is a kind of language use is to say that
metaphor should not be classed amongst such grammatical categories as noun, verb, or adjective. Nor should one think that
metaphor always displays a particular syntactic form. Consider:
'The smoke danced from the chimney.'
'The trees bowed in the dance of the seasons.'

'Dancing waters surrounded the canoe.'
The lexical item that provides what has been called the metaphorical "focus" in each of these phrases is in one instance a verb,
in another a noun, and in the third a participle.[8] Similarly,
metaphor is not confined to any one sort of sentence mood; in
particular, metaphorical utterances are not always assertions as can
be readily shown:
'God is our heavenly father.'
'Is God our heavenly father?'
'Heavenly father, come to our aid!'
This emphasizes the difficulty of treating metaphor as a particular
kind of speech act akin, say, to stating or commanding, and one
should note here L. Jonathan Cohen's important point that metaphor cannot be explained as such a speech act because the "metaphor is not overridden by the passage from oratio recta to oratio
obliqua". The element of "metaphorical meaning" remains constant, suggests Cohen, when one moves from "The boy next door is
a ball of fire," to "Tom said that the boy next door is a ball of
fire".[9]
These points seem obvious, even trivial, yet a good deal of
unclarity arises from discussions of metaphor that fail to make clear
when it is that they are speaking of syntactic form, and when of
logical form or, worse still, that fail to see such a distinction should
be made. One is told, for example, that metaphor is an assertion of
similarity without being told that metaphor need not be, grammatically, an assertion. Above all there is an unhelpful tendency for
philosophers discussing metaphor to confine their examples to
metaphors of the form 'x is a y' ('Man is a wolf', 'Time is a thief',
'Money is a curse') which suggests not only that, grammatically,
metaphors are assertions but also that the metaphorical focus is
always in the grammatical predicate. Neither of these is necessarily
the case; consider, for instance, 'Is that wolf here again?' It is
misleading to say that metaphor is an assertion of similarity without
making clear that this does not mean that every metaphor is a
grammatical assertion, and it is equally misleading to discuss metaphor as predication without making clear that this is, if anything, a
logical predication and not necessarily a syntactical one. Metaphor
displays no one syntactic form because the criteria by which it is
distinguished are not merely syntactic, but semantic and pragmatic
as well.

4. THE STRUCTURE OF METAPHOR

This being the case, one would think that very little could be said about the structure of a metaphor, if by this one means an external, grammatical structure. Yet it is a most pervasive opinion that there is such an external structure to metaphor and that it is one which involves two terms which are contrasted and compared.

"The basic structure of metaphor is very simple" says Stephen Ullmann, "There are always two terms present: the thing we are talking about and that to which we are comparing it." Max Black, in a very influential article, denies that comparison takes place, but retains the idea of two present terms when he says that "A metaphorical statement has two distinct subjects, to be identified as the 'primary' subject and the 'secondary' one",[10] backing up his claim by examples such as "Man is a wolf" and "Richard is a lion". If restricted to examples like these (and Black nowhere indicates why we should be so restricted), the contention that each metaphor has two distinct subjects has an initial plausibility, but this plausibility is soon diminished when one considers metaphors with other syntactic forms. Equally metaphorical is 'The pages were covered with a writhing script': where, here, are the two terms or two distinct subjects? 'Script' could presumably be one, but 'writhing' could not be the other. Perhaps, then, we should say that we compare the script not to a 'writhing' but to an unknown x which is capable of writhing? But this 'unknown x' fails to meet Ullmann's stipulation that there be two *present* terms, and Black's that there are two distinct subjects; an unknown x is neither a present term nor a distinct subject. Perhaps one might argue then that phrases like 'writhing script', 'darker purposes', and 'rosy-fingered dawn' which lack two subjects are not metaphors at all but misplaced epithets. But one could then cite other examples which lack two terms: 'The children flew to the window' or 'He went about in a nimbus of despair'. To eliminate instances like these because they lack two explicit subjects would be to eliminate most of what we take to be metaphor. In any case, both Max Black and Stephen Ullmann cite similar examples as metaphors; Ullmann lists among his metaphors 'bitter disappointment' and 'sweet voices' without saying how these are to be reconciled with his contention that there are always two terms present in the basic structure of metaphor— "the thing we are talking about and that to which we are comparing it".[11]

5. SCOPE

Metaphors like 'writhing script' and 'darker purposes' raise the question of the textual scope of metaphor. In common parlance we say of the sentence 'Life is a parade' that 'parade' is here a metaphor of life. In doing so we suggest that we think of metaphor as a word which has an odd or deviant meaning. But since the criteria for identifying metaphor are semantic, the unit in which a metaphor consists must be greater than the word. Even were metaphor the consequence of deviant word meaning we should not be able to recognize a particular meaning of the word as deviant apart from its context. We only say 'parade' is used metaphorically because it is describing life. [12] Nor, in many cases, would we be able to construe unambiguously the meaning of a metaphor apart from some wider context. Dorothy Mack cites the example 'blossoms of smoke' and makes the point that, apart from context and reference, it is unclear whether this describes gray blossoms, or billowing smoke, or feelings of emptiness, or all or none of these. [13]

These criticisms highlight how unsatisfactory is the precedence accorded to the word as the primary unit of meaning in the traditional discussions of metaphor, a precedence which has been criticised by I. A. Richards and others following him. In this context, Paul Ricoeur speaks of the "tyranny of the word" as a consequence of "the excessive and damaging emphasis" that traditional rhetoric placed on the word, "or, more specifically, on the noun or name, and on naming, in the theory of meaning; whereas a properly semantic treatment of metaphor proceeds from the recognition of the sentence as the primary unity of meaning." [14] The primacy of the sentence is a constant theme of Ricoeur's *The Rule of Metaphor* and it is at the heart of his condemnation of traditional tropology which had as its focus word meaning. We need not, however, replace the hegemony of the word with an hegemony of the sentence. We can detect and construe metaphorical usage in clauses like 'and standing, faced the rosy-fingered dawn' before knowing its place in a complete sentence. It is a curious fact that it may take more than one sentence to establish a metaphor. For example, consider the sentence 'That is a cold coal to blow at.' As an isolated sentence, it does not embody a metaphor, but if the wider context is a dialogue in which one character says, "I hope the king will forgive the rebels" and another responds "That's a cold coal to blow at", we know the sentence to be metaphorical, since clearly our speaker is not speaking of a coal but about the slim chances of a royal pardon. Here the metaphorical usage only becomes apparent in a wider context than that of the sentence, and this example highlights the importance to metaphor of context and shared beliefs. [15]

We can make a distinction between establishing a metaphor and extending it. A metaphor is established, we shall say, as soon as the reader is able to detect that one thing is being spoken of in terms suggestive of another. This may be as little as a phrase or may require several phrases or sentences conjointly, as in this passage from Denham on the Thames:

> O could I flow like thee, and make thy stream
> My great exemplar as it is my theme!
> Though deep, yet clear; though gentle, yet not dull;
> Strong without rage; without o'erflowing, full. [16]

This notion of 'establishing' a metaphor encompasses the semantic criteria felt to be desirable without artificially imposing the sentence as the unit of metaphor.

Once a metaphor has been established it may be extended as long as suits the writer, but an extremely lengthy spelling out of a metaphor runs the risk of becoming a conceit. Brevity is for the most part a virtue of metaphor and it is rare that one escapes the confines of a few sentences. This can happen, though, as it does at one point in *Tristram Shandy* where several pages are taken up with the narrator's elaboration of the rather moribund metaphor of 'hobby-horse':

Be it known to you, that I keep a couple of pads [hobby horses] myself, upon which, in their turns, . . . I frequently ride out and take the air;—though sometimes . . . I take somewhat longer journeys than what a wise man would think altogether right . . . Nor does it much disturb my rest, when I see . . . great Lords and tall Personages . . . all of a row, mounted upon their several horses, some with large stirrups, getting on in a more grave and sober place;—others on the contrary, tucked up to their very chins, with whips across their mouths, scouring and scampering it away like so many little party-coloured devils astride a mortgage. . . . [17]

It might well have been Sterne's idiosyncratic objective here to confuse the reader, and confuse the reader he does. When a metaphor is so much extended, it runs the risk of allowing the reader to forget what is being talked about. Usually, extensions are left to the reader's surmise and it is an indication of a good metaphor if it is unnecessary to spell out its implications for the reader.

We conclude, then, that the minimal unit in which a metaphor is established is semantic rather than syntactic; a metaphor is established as soon as it is clear that one thing is being spoken of in terms that are suggestive of another and can be extended until this is no longer the case. It can be extended, that is, until the length of our speaking 'of one thing in terms suggestive of another' makes us forget the 'thing' of which we speak.

The points we have made so far, that metaphor is not a mental event, that things are not in themselves metaphors, that metaphor does not take a particular syntactic form and is not confined to a particular syntactic unit, have all been negative ones, for it has become apparent that very little positive can be said of metaphor without semantic considerations. We now turn to these.

III

THEORIES OF METAPHOR

THE various theories of metaphor discussed in the philosophical literature involve assumptions of what it is that metaphor does and attempt explanations of how metaphor does it.[1] The theories can be divided, according to their visions of the metaphorical achievement, roughly into three groups: those that see metaphor as a decorative way of saying what could be said literally; those that see metaphor as original not in what it says but in the affective impact it has; and those that see metaphor as a unique cognitive vehicle enabling one to say things that can be said in no other way. Although some accounts fall in between, for the most part a division into what can be called the Substitution, Emotive, and Incremental theories is useful.

1. SUBSTITUTION THEORIES

The basic Substitution theory, the one which we have already mentioned was accredited to Aristotle and Quintilian, holds that metaphor is another way of saying what can be said literally. I. A. Richards summarizes:

> Throughout the history of Rhetoric, metaphor has been treated as a sort of happy extra trick with words, an opportunity to exploit the accidents of their versatility, something in place occasionally but requiring unusual skill and caution. In brief, a grace or ornament or *added* power of language, not its constitutive form.[2]

The latent explanatory notion for the Substitution theory is one of deviant word meaning; metaphor is regarded as an improper word which substitutes for the proper one but which is, presumably, replaceable by it at any time; so one says 'He is a fox' but could equally say 'He is cunning'. Metaphor has the virtue of clothing tired literal expression in attractive new garb, of alleviating boredom, and, as Aquinas says, of being accessible to the uneducated, "who are not ready to take intellectual things neat with nothing else".[3] What metaphor lacks, according to this ornamentalist theory, is a cognitive content not provided equally by the literal term for which the metaphor is the figurative replacement.

We have already spoken of the limitations of the Substitution theory in Chapter One. It reduces metaphor to the status of a riddle or word game and the appreciation of metaphor to the unravelling of that riddle. Were the Substitution theory correct, the only use of figurative substitution for the literal, apart from that of literary embellishment, would be didactic, as the quotation from Aquinas suggests. Even then, the use of the metaphorical substitute for plain talk might be just as likely, as Locke says, to confuse as to enlighten. The assumed ready availability of a literal substitute makes the value of metaphor, especially for the purposes of philosophical and scientific reasoning, negligible.

One important criticism of the Substitution theory is that its suggestion that the poet, scientist, or theologian, in using a metaphor, is doing no more than translating from a prior and literal understanding into an evocative formulation, runs counter to the experience of the maker of metaphor: the latter realizes that the particularity of a metaphorical description is not that it translates literal thought, but that the very thinking is undertaken in terms of the metaphor. What interests us in metaphor is precisely that we find in it an increment to understanding.

It is, in fact, impossible to make sense of a Substitution theory which says that no difference to significance at all is made by the metaphor. Even a wearisome metaphor like 'He is a fox' must signify something more to us than 'He is cunning'; otherwise we would regard 'fox' (as used metaphorically) and 'cunning' as synonyms, and have as our only reason for choosing between them that 'fox' in some cases actually sounded better than 'cunning'. But clearly one says 'He is a fox' not because it is more pleasing to the ear but because it suggests something other than 'He is cunning'. Although we might say that an ornamental metaphor like 'bedizened grasses' is a florid way of speaking about lawns covered with dew, we would not say that the phrases 'bedizened grasses' and 'dewy grasses' were synonymous. Even where metaphor does function as an ornament, it does so by virtue of making some addition to significance, be that ever so slight.

We conclude that, while someone might say unreflectively that metaphor is simply an ornamental substitute for a literal expression, as a theory such a view is untenable; and that, though often attributed to Aristotle and to Quintilian, the basic Substitution theory is in all probability a 'nobody's theory' of metaphorical meaning.

A slightly more sophisticated version of the Substitution theory is the Comparison theory. On this account, there is more to metaphor than the mere substitution of term for term, but it is still regarded as an essentially ornamental usage in which two 'like' things are compared, as in 'This house is (like) a beehive'. The Comparison theory has been criticized on the grounds that, while making the metaphorical attribution intelligible, it fails to explain what is interesting about it.[4] Max Black maintains that ''a 'comparison view' is a special case of a 'substitution view.' For it holds that the metaphorical statement might be replaced by an equivalent literal *comparison.*''[5] This fails to mark the fact that the good metaphor does not merely compare two antecedently similar entities, but enables one to see similarities in what previously had been regarded as dissimilars.

2. EMOTIVE THEORIES

The basic Emotive theory of metaphor not only denies to it a special cognitive content but denies it a cognitive content at all. Instead, it is argued, the impact of metaphor is affective. This non-cognitivist view of metaphor is sometimes associated with certain dicta concerning meaning put forward by the logical positivists. Monroe Beardsley (although not himself supporting the Emotive theory) makes this summary:

according to the Emotive Theory, a word has meaning only if there is some way of confirming its applicability to a given situation—roughly, only if it has a clear designation. For example, the sharpness of a knife can be tested by various means, so that the phrase 'sharp knife' is meaningful. We may also suppose that 'sharp' has some negative emotive import, deriving from our experience with sharp things. Now, when we speak of a 'sharp razor' or a 'sharp drill', the emotive import is not active, because these phrases are meaningful. But when we speak of a 'sharp wind', 'a sharp dealer,' or 'a sharp tongue,' the tests for sharpness cannot be applied, and therefore, though the individual words are meaningful, the combinations of them are not. In this way the emotive import of the adjective is released and intensified.[6]

What the Emotive theory thus stated shares with the basic Substitution theory is the assumption that metaphor is a consequence of deviancy in word usage and that a given metaphor could be suppressed with no detriment to the cognitive content of the text in which it was found. Indeed, its suppression might clarify the meaning of the text.

On the other hand, it is suggested by the Emotive theory that, while the deviant usage loses any genuine cognitive content, at the same time it gains an unspecified emotional one. It is, however, difficult to make sense of this notion of extra emotive content. In Beardsley's summary above we read that the terms of metaphor surrender their claim to be genuinely meaningful but thereby gain an emotive 'import'. But what is this extra 'import' to be if not meaning of some sort? The Emotivist theory of metaphor has many parallels with the well-known emotive theory of religious statements and the even better known emotive theory of ethics. In much the same fashion, these emotive theories denied to religious or ethical claims assertive or cognitive significance but claimed that, through this default, they gained a powerful emotional meaning.[7] Notoriously, it has been difficult to formulate a convincing theory of 'emotive meaning' bereft of cognitive content. There must be some guiding cognitive features which the emotive response is the response to. We cannot conceive of emotive 'import' apart from a cognitive content which elicits it.

Furthermore, as Beardsley has pointed out, the Emotive theory of metaphor is unable to account for the fact that non-standard uses of the same term can have opposing emotive import, e.g. why it is that in the deviant usage of 'sharp' in 'a sharp wind' we recognize a 'negative emotive import', and in 'a sharp wit' a positive one. Without further explanation of this the Emotive theory must fail to account for metaphorical construal.

Donald Davidson has put forward a theory of metaphor which is both imaginative and difficult to categorize. In some respects, it is similar to the Substitution and to the Emotive theories; like the former, it insists that a metaphor does not 'say' what could not be 'said' literally and like the latter, it is non-cognitivist. Yet Davidson intends no diminution of metaphor. He does not think that metaphor is ''confusing, merely emotive, unsuited to serious, scientific, or philosophic discourse''. He insists that ''Metaphor is a legitimate device not only in literature but in science, philosophy, and the law;

it is effective in praise and abuse, prayer and promotion, description and prescription."[8] When he says that metaphors have no distinctive meaning and denies that they 'say' anything not 'said' literally, 'say' and 'said' are being used in ways specific to his kind of analysis. Davidson's comments on metaphor must accordingly be assessed in the context of some of his more general theories.

Contrary to the idea that a metaphor uniquely presents a certain meaning, Davidson's thesis is that "metaphors mean what the words, in their most literal interpretations, mean, and nothing more".[9] His solution then to the problem of how metaphors mean is to deny that they have any distinctive 'meaning' at all. Davidson's thesis depends crucially on his distinction between what words mean and what they are used to do, and on his insistence that metaphor belongs exclusively to the domain of use. This, then, is a form of a speech act theory in which metaphor is a phenomenon of the speech situation, and not a matter of word or even sentence 'meaning'.

"What distinguishes metaphor is not meaning but use—in this it is like assertion, hinting, lying, promising, or criticizing. And the special use to which we put language in metaphor is not—cannot be—to 'say something' special, no matter how indirectly. For a metaphor *says* only what shows on its face—usually a patent falsehood or an absurd truth."[10] The difficulty, then, which one has in trying to paraphrase metaphor is not the consequence of the richness of some distinctive metaphorical meaning which resists formulation in plain prose, but rather arises "because there is nothing there to paraphrase. Paraphrase, whether possible or not, is appropriate to what is *said*" and metaphor, according to Davidson, says only what the words that compose it say.[11]

However, we must not fail to distinguish, he goes on, between what a metaphor means or says and what a metaphor "draws our attention to" or "nudges us into noting".[12] At the level of meaning, Goneril's comment in *King Lear* that "old fools are babes again", is a patent falsehood, but at the level of use, this metaphor "nudges" us into seeing a special relationship between confused old age and infancy.[13] On this theory, metaphor is significant not for what it says, but for what it does (hence Davidson's linkage of metaphor to speech acts like hinting, promising, lying, etc.); he is able to agree with other modern theorists in saying that metaphor accomplishes a great deal, but also to deny that this accomplishment is in any way an increment to meaning. Davidson is prompted to so radical a thesis concerning metaphor by other features of his general theory of meaning which we will not discuss here, for it is possible to criticize his position without discussing them. [14]

Part of the attractiveness of Davidson's theory is the insistence, surely correct, that metaphor cannot be simply a play with word meaning but is necessarily a matter of use. The shortcoming of his approach is that by so emphasizing use, semantic considerations seem banished entirely with some odd consequences.

Davidson's insistence that the particular achievement of metaphor is that it nudges us into noting similarities betrays the assumption that metaphor is essentially a kind of comparison, an assumption reinforced by his tendency to illustrate the theory with metaphors of the 'A is a B' form ("Metaphor is the dreamwork of language", "Old fools are babes again", Tolstoy is "a great moralizing infant"), all of which imply that the task of metaphor is that of comparison. [15]

And like the Emotivist theory, Davidson's rests on the notion that metaphor is a consequence of the failure of literal reading. His argument is that because a metaphor defaults at a literal reading, either by being patently false ('Man is a wolf') or trivially true ('No man is an island') we are somehow jolted into seeing similarities between men and wolves, and men and islands. He insists that this comparison or seeing of similarities should not be regarded as part of the special 'meaning' of the metaphor. Rather than carrying a special cognitive content metaphor "can, like a picture or a bump on the head, make us appreciate some fact—but not by standing for, or expressing, the fact." [16]

The idea that metaphor is more closely akin to a bump on the head than to an expression of a proposition is a difficult one to make sense of—metaphor, hypnosis, and bumps on the head may all three make us see similarities, but metaphor is importantly different from the other two, for it does so as a form of language use and as such must involve some inference from the speaker's utterances.

Typically, we do not regard "Old fools are babes" as a patent falsehood which jolts us into vision, but take the implications of the metaphor (that old fools are helpless, weak, petulant, fractious, etc.) as part of the construal. If a speaker is asked what he means by such a metaphor, typically he will expand upon it in such a way. As Max Black has pointed out, it seems arbitrary "to restrict a metaphor's content to what is *explicitly* expressed by it . . ." [we] "take the metaphor's author to be committed to its implications".[17]

To be consistent, Davidson must reply to this that he, too, regards the metaphor's author as committed to its implications, but that these implications are not part of what the metaphor 'means'. At this stage, his argument reduces to a stipulation about the way one should use the term 'meaning' and Davidson's use, though far from arbitrary, and valuable within his wider theory, is excessively narrow for a discussion of metaphor. We could imagine the following conversation:

Davidson: He is a jackal.
Interlocutor: You mean that he is a coward and a scrounger?
Davidson: No, although I am committed to regarding him as a coward and a scrounger and although I intended by my utterance to make you see him thus, I only said and I only meant 'he is a jackal'.

Davidson's position would be stronger here if he made a distinction between what a sentence says, and what someone means or says in uttering that sentence, but he denies himself this option by saying "a metaphor doesn't say anything beyond its literal meaning (nor does its maker say anything, in using the metaphor, beyond the literal)".[18] As it stands, his distinction between what a metaphor 'says' and what it jolts us into noting is counter-intuitive.

Furthermore, Davidson's theory lacks explanatory force. How is it that, when faced with some patent falsehoods, we are brought to notice similarities (thus deciding the utterance to be metaphor) and, with others, to decide the utterance to be a nonsense? How is it that the metaphor calls our attention to similarities? In what way does it 'nudge' us? The same criticism applies to Davidson's theory as to the Emotivist theory; if a metaphor does something, it must be because it says something. It may be, as he suggests, that we are 'nudged' by a metaphor, but we are nudged in a certain direction. The metaphor 'life is a circus' nudges us into noting similarities between life and circuses, and not between life and theatrical productions or life and race courses. Davidson's notion of nudging is not explanatory. Unless he can explain why the failure of a literal reading should issue in a recognition of a *particular* similarity, his theory cannot supplant one in which the implications are regarded as being, in some sense, part of the meaning of the metaphor. It is to such theories that we now turn.

3. INCREMENTAL THEORIES

Substitution theories argue that the content or meaning of metaphor could equally well be expressed in non-metaphorical terms, and emotive theories that there is affective impact but no increment to meaning. The Incremental theorists disagree with both. Basic to their position is the view that what is said by the metaphor can be expressed adequately in no other way, that the combination of parts in a metaphor can produce new and unique agents of meaning. There is, however, a variety of opinion as to how metaphor achieves its unique cognitive task.

One of the less satisfactory theories, but one that deserves attention because of the frequency with which it occurs as an implicit background to discussions of metaphor, is the Intuitionist theory of metaphor. According to its exponents, metaphor involves a complete transformation, a destruction of the standard senses of the terms. The unique significance of metaphor is the product of an intuitive act which follows on this destruction of literal meanings.

The Intuitionist theory makes a strong claim about the uniqueness and irreplaceability of metaphor, and one that has affinities with the Emotivist theory. In both the accounts, metaphorical construal follows on the destruction of any literal sense; but whereas in the Emotive theory this yields an emotive impact, in the Intuitionist theory it leads, through some inexplicable act of intuition, to a new but fully cognitive meaning.

The shortcoming of the Intuitionist theory is, of course, precisely that it is non-explanatory. As Israel Scheffler has pointed out, "describing the process of understanding metaphorical expressions as an act of intuition does nothing more than put a name to the mystery".[19] What is it that prompts and directs this intuition? It is clear that although the meaning of a metaphor may not be a crude function of the literal senses of its terms, these literal senses must in some way direct the metaphorical construal. Were this not the case, the complete destruction of the familiar senses of the terms would leave an utterance at the mercy of any number of entirely different readings, which is clearly absurd.

Other incrementalists have tried accordingly to account for metaphorical construal on the basis of the senses of the terms which compose it. Some writers, like Samuel Levin, suggest that, given an adequate linguistic theory, metaphorical construal can be explained with little or no reference to non-linguistic factors of context, intention, reference, and presupposition.[20] We shall call theories that suppose that metaphor can be explained in this way formal theories.

(A) Beardsley's 'Controversion' theory

Monroe Beardsley puts forward in his *Aesthetics* a theory of metaphor that is formal in this way and which he calls the "Controversion theory"; in subsequent articles, he develops it as the "Verbal-opposition theory". Beardsley wishes to explain both how one recognizes a metaphor and how one determines its significance, and to do so in such a way as to make these dependent only on the meanings of the terms used in the metaphor. We shall discuss Beardsley's theory at some length both to show the strengths and weaknesses of a formal approach, and as a means of refining our own requirements for a satisfactory theory of metaphor.

In *Aesthetics*, his discussion of the Controversion theory is prefaced with a discussion of "self-controverting discourse". The essential principle is that

the speaker or writer utters a statement explicitly but in such a way as to show that he does not believe what he states, or is not primarily interested in what he states, and thereby calls to attention something else that he has not explicitly stated—'If he wins, I'll eat my hat'. It is discourse that says more than it states, by cancelling out the primary meaning to make room for secondary meaning.[21]

He then argues that the case of metaphor is similar, but that in metaphor there is an instance of self-contradictory attribution. In the metaphor there is a modifier which is "logically" incompatible with the subject it modifies; for example, in the attribution "metaphysical streets" there is a conflict between the modifier 'metaphysical' and the subject 'streets', which are by definition physical and not metaphysical.[22]

But metaphors, though self-contradictory, are not devoid of meaning. To account for this metaphorical meaning Beardsley makes a distinction between designation, denotation, and connotation; the term 'wolf' ''designates certain characteristics that define a class of animals; it also *denotes* the animals that have those defining characteristics in common'' and it connotes characteristics that wolves have, or are believed to have, such as fierceness, persistence, and predatory clannishness. [23] In a metaphor one confronts a falsehood or logical absurdity that makes reading at the level of the designation of the terms impossible. One consequently falls back onto the connotations of the terms, and it is explication at the level of connotation that we call metaphor. If ''metaphysical streets'' is meaningful at all, Beardsley says, ''it is because some of the connotations of 'metaphysical' apply to streets; the latter may 'with Prufrock's streets—wander like a metaphysical argument . . .' '' thus proposes

that whenever an attribution is indirectly self-contradictory, and the modifier has connotations that could be attributed to the subject, the attribution is a *metaphorical attribution*, or metaphor. [24]

As long as there are some such connotations, we have a metaphor and if there are none, we have nonsense. However, Beardsley points out, it is not easy to find any clear cut instances of nonsense; ''even if we put all English adjectives in one hat, and all nouns in the other, and drew them out at random, we would find that the strangest combinations yield possible meanings upon reflection . . .''. As regards this last point, Beardsley sees it as a particular merit of the Controversion theory that it can thus account for

one of the most puzzling and important features of metaphor, its capacity to create new contextual meaning . . . The reason is that the connotations of words are never fully known, or knowable, beforehand, and very often we discover new connotations of the words when we see how they behave as modifiers in metaphorical attributions. The metaphor does not create the connotations, but it brings them to life. [25]

His idea is that, because terms possess connotations independent of our knowing them, new and utterly random combinations like ''rubber hopes'' and ''rubber melody'' may ''yield a strange new meaning because the subject 'hopes' or 'melody' singles out for attention a hitherto unnoticed connotation of the modifier''. [26]

Beardsley's notion of 'connotations', as discussed in *Aesthetics*, is extremely vague and has been criticized at length elsewhere. [27] In

particular, he seems to make no distinction between the connotations of a term and the properties of the object designated by that
term; for example, when talking of the connotations of the term
'wolf', he seems to mean not only all the associations wolves are
likely to have for the speaker (their ferociousness, their clannishness, their territorial zeal), but also the actual properties of wolves
(their blood or bone types, their actual feeding habits, and so on).
This inclusion of actual properties into the set of connotations of the
term accounts for Beardsley's curious idea that the connotations of
words are never fully known or knowable beforehand. In later
versions of his theory, he drops this point and stresses that the
important properties for metaphor ''are not the actual properties of
things denoted by the metaphorical term, but believed properties''
or what he calls ''credence-properties''. [28]

The 'Verbal-opposition' theory of metaphor discussed in ''The
Metaphorical Twist'' is a restatement of the earlier Controversion
theory. The central idea remains that the metaphoricalness of
metaphor stems from a conflict of meaning in the terms themselves;
as Beardsley says, ''The opposition that renders an expression
metaphorical is, then, within the meaning structure itself''. [29] The
main refinement is to make metaphor dependent upon the existence of

two sets of properties in the intension, or signification, of a general term:
first, those properties that . . . are taken to be necessary conditions for
applying the term correctly in a particular sense (these are the defining, or
designated, properties, or the central meaning of the term in that sort of
context); second, those properties that belong to the marginal meaning of
the term or (in the literary critic's sense of the word) its connotation. . . .

The mechanism of metaphor is such that,

when a term is combined with others in such a way that there would be a
logical opposition between its central meaning and that of the other terms,
there occurs that shift from central to marginal meaning which shows us the
word is to be taken in a metaphorical way. [30]

Metaphor is thus,

a special feat of language, or verbal play, involving two levels of meaning in
the modifier itself. When a predicate is metaphorically adjoined to a
subject, the predicate loses its ordinary extension, because it acquires a new
intension—perhaps one that it has in no other context. And this twist of

meaning is forced by inherent tensions, or oppositions, within the metaphor itself.[31]

It will be noted that Beardsley is using the term 'intension' in an
unusual way, for normally the intension is the set of defining or
necessary properties and never the wider connotations. But even if
we allow him this usage, the argument is question-begging. What
can it mean to say that it is "the shift from central to marginal
meaning which shows us the word is to be taken in a metaphorical
way"? This is to put the cart before the horse, for it is the fact that
we impose a metaphorical construal which focuses our attention on
the marginal meanings of the terms. Although the introduction of
the notion of two sets of properties within the 'intension' of the
term goes part of the way to resolving the earlier ambiguity between
properties of objects and connotations of terms, the Verbal-
opposition theory relies on the same two basic notions as did the
Controversion theory: that in metaphor there is a conflict of word
meaning, and that this conflict is resolved by moving down a
hierarchy of readings. The same general principles are at work
in Beardsley's article, "Metaphorical Senses", where he says that
each general term has by virtue of its connotations both a literal
sense and a metaphorical sense, and that we shift from the former to
the latter when faced with absurdity or incompatibility in the
utterance.

It is important to note that Beardsley's account is essentially a
formalist one, in so far as it attempts to account for metaphor as a
phenomenon of word meaning without bringing in to any significant extent factors like context and speaker's intention. In his later
attempts to tidy up the original Controversion theory, Beardsley
inevitably falls into formalist terminology, for example, speaking of
metaphor as a violation of "selection restrictions", or saying that
the combination of a metaphorical segment with a non-
metaphorical remainder of a sequence is "barred by a rule".[32]
Although Beardsley himself suggests that his theory will displease
those who approach metaphor from the standpoint of formal
semantics, the objection they might have would be in regard of the
untidiness of his account, and not of his general diagnosis of
metaphor or suggestions for its construal. His basic assumption that
"the opposition that renders an expression metaphorical is within
the meaning structure itself" is a formalist one, and our reason for

discussing his theory in such detail is to point out the obstacles facing any theory that seeks to account for metaphor as a calculus of word meanings.

A significant limitation of any theory which relies on the notion that there is in metaphor a logical opposition between the meaning of its terms is that it cannot account for metaphors where there is no such logical conflict. As Max Black has pointed out, "In context, 'Man is not a wolf' is as metaphorical as its opposite, yet it clearly fails the controversion test".[33] Nor can the Verbal-opposition theory, or any formal theory that pays no attention to the non-linguistic setting, account for metaphors such as our earlier example "Those are cold coals to blow on", precisely because the metaphor here does not arise from a clash of word meaning but a linguistic phenomenon relating to context, the speaker's intention, and other extra-utterance factors. This shortcoming, while not decisive, limits the applicability of the theory.

However, there are other difficulties. It is not clear that Beardsley's theory, even in its revised form, can account, as he wishes it to do, for how we recognize metaphor and how we distinguish metaphorical attributions from nonsense. Beardsley says that, given a conflict of central meanings, as long as there are some marginal meanings or connotations of the modifier which are appropriate to the subject, we have a metaphor. For example, in 'metaphysical streets', as long as there are some connotations of 'metaphysical' appropriate to 'streets' we have metaphor and not nonsense. But this is to eliminate the possibility of nonsense altogether. Given a notion of connotation as broad as Beardsley's, any two syntactically compatible terms will have shared connotations; 'Man is a stone' (both men and stones are physical objects); 'Mirrors are trees' (both mirrors and trees are inanimate), and so on. Indeed, when Beardsley, far from acknowledging that he has eliminated nonsense altogether, claims that it is a particular merit of his theory that it explains the fact that any two terms randomly paired are a metaphor he gives the lie to his whole concept. Metaphors are not strings of terms which a computer programmed with all English nouns and adjectives could generate, and then, by eliminating the logically contradictory readings, construe. A metaphor is only a metaphor because someone, speaker or hearer and ideally both, regards it as such; the intentional component is essential. Beardsley is misled by the fact that, given a random combination of terms like 'rubber cliffs', the ingenious speaker of English could devise a context in which it is a metaphor (and not nonsense), into thinking that what makes the metaphor a metaphor is a conflict inherent in the terms themselves entirely independent of context or intention. Thus he says that the "opposition that renders an expression metaphorical is . . . within the meaning-structure itself".[34]

This clearly cannot be so. Although we might regard a combination like 'rubber cliffs' as unusual and might devise various contexts in which it would make sense, apart from some such context we would have no means of explicating it at all. We would not know if the phrase referred to cliffs that looked as if they were made of rubber, or rubber that was stacked up into piles like cliffs, or was simply nonsense. Thus, in so far as it is a theory based on verbal-opposition attempts to provide a "logic of explication", Beardsley's theory is bound to fail.

We now have two reasons for rejecting formal theories of metaphorical construal based on verbal opposition; the first is that they cannot account for metaphor where no such opposition occurs, and the second is that they cannot explain, independently of pragmatic factors, how it is that the native speaker determines the meaning of phrases like "rubber cliffs" which might conceivably involve such opposition. A third serious difficulty concerns the dependence of such a theory on a move from central to marginal meanings, and can be illustrated again with reference to Beardsley.

As we have noted, in 'The Metaphorical Twist' Beardsley tightens up the earlier Controversion theory by suggesting that within the 'intension' of a general term there are two sets of properties—defining or necessary properties (which he equates with the central meaning), and connoted or accidental properties (which he equates with the marginal meaning). This restatement, while seeking to clarify the previously unsatisfactory notion of 'connotations', in fact only weakens Beardsley's position; properties here must be properties of things, and by introducing the notion of properties Beardsley unavoidably returns to some variant of the comparison theory which he has spurned.[35] But even disregarding this inconsistency, there remains the enormous problem of determining which properties are to count as the necessary properties of an object and which as the accidental, and consequently of determining what is to count as the intension of a term and what as its associated characteristics.

Beardsley, in telling us that the central meaning is drawn from the defining or necessary properties of the object, seems to have in mind such a metaphor as our old friend 'Man is a wolf', where being an animal and being a carnivore count as defining properties that give rise to the central meaning of the term 'wolf', and being clannish and being cruel as accidental properties that give rise to the marginal meaning of the term. But while this scheme has a limited applicability for 'wolf', it will prove much more difficult to establish such a hierarchy of central and marginal meanings based on necessary and accidental properties for terms like 'giddy' in 'giddy brink', or 'metaphysical' in 'metaphysical streets'. What sense can be given to the notion of the necessary properties of 'giddy' or 'metaphysical'? Beardsley's difficulty here is that he illustrates his 'defining properties/marginal properties' distinction with natural kind terms like 'wolf' for which, on some philosophical accounts, such defining properties can be given. But this thesis falls down when faced with predicates such as 'metaphysical' which are not natural kind terms. It seems that Beardsley has made the mistake, pointed out so well by Hilary Putnam, of making arguments appropriate, at best, to a few hundred words applicable to hundreds of thousands.[36] It is not surprising that Putnam makes this point in an article entitled 'Is Semantics Possible?' for, although we apply it here only to Beardsley's account, the difficulty of establishing hierarchical readings for the terms of a metaphor undercuts the validity of any formalist theory of metaphorical construal which focuses upon the notion of conflict of meaning at a primary level and reconciliation at a secondary one.

In conclusion, we can say that all our objections to Beardsley's theories are objections to his central thesis that metaphor is a matter of conflict of word meaning arising within the 'meaning-structure' of language itself independent of factors of context and intention. We take this to be an objection to all theories of metaphor which exclude pragmatic factors such as context, speaker's intention and, as we shall discuss, reference.

(B) Black's 'Interactive' theory

In many ways the most satisfactory contemporary philosophical account of metaphor, and certainly the most often cited, is that of Max Black. His discussion, "Metaphor" in *Models and Metaphor*, was the first to approach the neglected topic from the point of view of modern analytic philosophy. Black's concern in this article is with the "logical grammar" of metaphor; with questions such as 'How do we recognize a case of metaphor?', 'Can metaphors be translated into literal expressions?', 'What are the relations between metaphor and simile?' and 'In what sense, if any, is a metaphor "creative"?'[37] In response to these questions, he makes a welter of suggestions, and assesses the traditional substitution and comparison view of metaphor which he finds lacking for reasons we have already discussed. He then, with acknowledged indebtedness to the work of I. A. Richards, puts forward what he calls the "interactive" view of metaphor.

In *The Philosophy of Rhetoric*, I. A. Richards had said, by way of an abbreviated account of "the principle of metaphor", that "when we use a metaphor we have two thoughts of different things active together and supported by a single word, or phrase, whose meaning is a resultant of their interaction".[38] These two thoughts he called the "tenor" of the metaphor (its underlying subject) and the "vehicle" (the mode in which it is expressed). Black, while dismissing Richards's suggestion that in the metaphor two thoughts are active together as an "inconvenient fiction", retains what he takes to be Richards's basic theory of interaction. According to Black, in understanding a metaphor like "The poor are the negroes of Europe", our 'thoughts' about the European poor and American Negroes interact to produce a new meaning. Black says,

I think this must mean that in the given context the focal word 'negroes' obtains a new meaning, which is not quite its meaning in literal uses, nor quite the meaning which any literal substitute would have. The new context (the 'frame' of the metaphor, in my terminology) imposes extension of meaning upon the focal word. And I take Richards to be saying that for the metaphor to work the reader must remain aware of the extension of meaning—must attend to both the old and the new meanings together.[39]

We shall argue later in this chapter that Black has significantly misunderstood Richards's account.

Black makes the assumption in "Metaphor" that a metaphor is an "expression in which *some* words are used metaphorically while the remainder are used nonmetaphorically."[40] In the same article Black argues that words 'used metaphorically' (such as 'negroes' in the above example) form the metaphorical "focus" in a literal "frame" provided by the rest of the sentence, and because of this new context the focal word obtains a new meaning. The problem, then, is to explain how this extension or change of meaning is brought about and it is to account for this that he puts forward his "interaction view".

We can say at the outset that what looks to be a damaging criticism of his account—that it falls into the old, unsatisfactory habit of describing metaphor as a change in word meaning—is in fact not as serious as it seems at first. Black can easily, and does in a later article, abandon talk of shift of word meaning and say that it is, of course, "shift in *speaker's* meaning—and the corresponding *hearer's* meaning" which interest him. He can also say that his interaction theory concerns the way metaphorical statements work, rather than, as was earlier suggested, how some words come to be used metaphorically.[41] Thus he can dismiss his earlier, unhappy formulation of what metaphor achieves and yet retain his interactive theory of how metaphor achieves it.

The basic notion of the early interactive view is that a metaphor has two distinct subjects, a principal and a subsidiary one, and that the distinctive cognitive content of the metaphor is the consequence of an interaction between these two subjects, or, more properly, between the two systems of implication to which these subjects give rise. In the statement "Man is a wolf" the principal subject, man (or men), is illumined by being seen in terms of the subsidiary subject, wolf (or wolves): "The wolf-metaphor suppresses some details, emphasizes others—in short, *organizes* our view of man".[42]

Black proposes that we regard this activity as a kind of 'filtering' or 'screening' and compares the metaphorical activity with that of looking at the night sky "through a piece of heavily smoked glass on which certain lines have been left clear".[43] As the glass filters and organizes our view of the stars, highlighting some things and suppressing others, so, too, in the metaphor the subsidiary subject (wolves) organizes our thoughts about men in a new way. This operation is distinctive of metaphor and makes metaphor insusceptible of reduction to literal terms. Metaphor is thus neither a kind of substitution of terms nor a matter of simple one-for-one comparison, which is the province, Black suggests, of the simile. In some cases, "It would be more illuminating . . . to say that the metaphor creates the similarity than to say that it formulates some similarity antecedently existing."[44]

In the interactive metaphor, both principal and subsidiary subjects bring with them their own "systems" of "associated commonplaces"; for example, the construal of 'Man is a wolf' relies on both
speaker and hearer having a body of shared knowledge or assumption about the nature of men and the nature of wolves, for example
that the latter are clannish, cruel, and so on. One important
contribution of Black's theory is to make explicit that the efficacy of
the metaphor does not depend on the factual accuracy of these
commonplaces, but simply on the fact that roughly the same set of
associations are made by speaker and hearer. When Black says that in
a metaphor the two subjects interact, he means that their two
systems of associated commonplaces interact in such a way as to
produce a new, informative, and irreplaceable unit of meaning.

It is indeed the cognitively irreplaceable status of such metaphors
that Black is at pains to stress and that constitutes, for him, their
difference from mere comparison. He says, "This use of a 'subsidiary subject' to foster insight into a 'principal subject' is a
distinctive intellectual operation . . . demanding simultaneous
awareness of both subjects but not reducible to any comparison
between the two." Furthermore, he points out that in this interaction considerations about *both* subjects of the metaphor are altered;
for "If to call a man a wolf is to put him in a special light, we must
not forget that metaphor makes the wolf seem more human than he
otherwise would."[45]

Black's account, by introducing concepts like associated commonplaces and by bringing in speaker's and hearer's meanings, goes a
good deal beyond a theory such as Beardsley's. But while the
interaction view of metaphor has met with considerable general
acceptance, and "Metaphor" has indeed come to be regarded as a
seminal article, the terminology that Black uses there to describe
metaphor has attracted criticism. The notion of 'interaction' is after
all itself metaphorical and requires some explication, as does talk of
the metaphorical 'focus' and 'frame', and also the notion that
metaphor, like a "piece of heavily smoked glass on which certain
lines have been left clear" acts as a 'filter' or 'screen'.

The notion of filtering has particularly come under attack, for
while we may use 'filtering' to explain how a metaphor works, we are
then left to explain how the filtering works. What takes place and
what constraints are exercised upon it? Why are some commonplaces
selected and not others? How does the screening of interpretation in

a metaphor differ from that which presumably takes place in understanding non-metaphorical utterances such as 'I love strawberries' (as opposed to 'I love my mother')?

Another and more serious criticism of 'filtering' is that this term is inconsistent with Black's claim that metaphors do not merely pick out antecendently existing similarities but in some cases actually create them; a filter, at best, brings out what was already there. And, finally, the explanatory notion of 'filtering' is in conflict with the explanatory notion of 'interaction', and particularly with Black's contention that both subjects of the metaphor are illumined by their interaction, for this double effect is difficult to reconcile with the one-directional connotations of 'filtering'. It is hard to see how a smoked glass filter is in any way affected by its interaction with the night sky.

By way of reply, Black has written "More about Metaphor", an article in which he largely adheres to his previous position while attempting to clarify and defend his earlier choice of terms. The major change is his recognition of a closer bond than he had previously admitted between models and metaphor, and between metaphor and analogy. This provides his reply to the difficulties of filtering. Black suggests that between primary and secondary subjects (or more precisely between their two implication complexes), there exists an isomorphism of structure: "Hence, every metaphor may be said to mediate an analogy or structural correspondence."[46] But with this comment more serious inconsistencies in the interactive view become apparent, for while the notion of isomorphism of structure provides some answer as to how the filtering may be controlled, it sounds surprisingly close to the comparison view of metaphor which Black had earlier rejected ("If a writer holds that a metaphor consists in the *presentation* of the underlying analogy or similarity, he will be taking what I shall call a *comparison view* of metaphor.").[47] Although Black insists in that later article that he is not suggesting that metaphor differs in form only from simile and comparison, his talk of analogy, isomorphism, and structural correspondence belies this claim.[48]

Black's theory of interaction is weakened by his new contention in "More about Metaphor" that it is *only* the secondary subject (for example, 'wolf') which is to be regarded as bringing with it a system of associated commonplaces, and not both the primary and secondary subjects. 'Interaction' now seems a much less appropriate term for what is going on. He also modifies his earlier suggestion that metaphor, rather than formulating antecedently existing similarities, creates similarities. In the later article, he says that rather than actually creating similarities "some metaphors are what might be called 'cognitive instruments,' indispensable for perceiving connections that, once perceived, are *then* truly present . . ."[49] But this is to make metaphors into the heuristic aides that Black once so boldly claimed they were not. It seems, then, that Black's defence of the terminology of his first essay has resulted in the withdrawal of most of what made his original interactive theory both interesting and interactive. We should say, however, that whatever the shortcomings of Black's interactive theory, we can acknowledge the validity of his objectives. His contention that metaphor is not a matter of comparison, however poorly his theory supports it, is meant to demonstrate that metaphor is not a mundane pairing of similars but the fuller activity of bringing out similarities in what might previously have seemed dissimilars. In those metaphors which he calls 'strong' ones, a special cognitive role is performed precisely because the analogy was not previously attended to. And, furthermore, whatever the shortcomings of his notions of 'filtering' and 'screening', it is not fair to ask Black exactly how this filtering takes place unless one makes clear what kind of an answer is expected. If one expects a description of a mechanism by which the mind understands language, whether figurative or not, then Black is justified in maintaining silence, for this is not a question which philosophy can answer.[50]

Interaction is an attractive explanatory notion, but why does Max Black's interactive view fail? Our suggestion is that both the potshots taken at Black's terminology and his attempts to answer them miss the mark. The real failure of his theory is not due to the looseness of terms like 'filtering' and 'screening', but is a consequence of Black's continued insistence that each metaphor has two distinct subjects. As well as being applicable, as he expounds it, only to metaphor of the form 'A is a B' ('Man is a wolf'), the 'two subjects' position invariably lapses into a comparison theory and ceases to merit the title 'interactive'.

(C) An 'Interanimation' theory of metaphor

The criticisms we have made of the various theories of metaphor indicate the lines on which our own preferred theory of metaphor should be drawn. It should regard metaphor neither as a simple substitution for literal speech nor as strictly emotive. Metaphor should be treated as fully cognitive and capable of saying that which may be said in no other way. It should explain how metaphor gives us "two ideas for one", yet do so without lapsing into a comparison theory. These are basics. Ideally, a theory of metaphor should go even further and discuss not only the speaker's intention in using metaphor but also the hearer's reception of it, how the hearer decides that the speaker is speaking metaphorically rather than nonsensically, and so on. This would involve consideration not only of what is said but of the context in which it is said, the beliefs held mutually by both hearer and speaker, and the patterns of inference the hearer employs in determining the speaker's meaning. Not all of these matters can be dealt with in this chapter; some will be dealt with in later chapters and others left for the linguists to explain within a theory of speech acts more comprehensive than it is practicable to attempt here.[51] What follows here is not a theory of metaphor in any exhaustive sense—it is the object of the whole book to give an account of metaphor, and even then it will not be exhaustive—but an attempt to illumine the issues that the theories under discussion have isolated. In particular, we wish to show how metaphors can be cognitively unique, that is, how without being mere comparison they can give us "two ideas for one".

It is our suggestion that I. A. Richards has come nearest to providing a satisfactory account, for while his discussion lacks the terminological refinements of later debates and suffers from certain obvious inconsistencies, he was possessed of great insight into metaphor. We shall call our account, employing a term used by Richards, an 'interanimative' theory of metaphor.

In *The Philosophy of Rhetoric*, Richards discusses metaphor only after lengthy consideration of what he terms "the interanimation of words". The discussion is intended to counter the misleading 'Usage Doctrine' espoused by literary critics and rhetoricians from the mid-eighteenth century onwards. This 'Doctrine' holds that elegant prose is a matter of proper word usage and, more significantly, it "takes the senses of an author's words to be things we know before we read him, fixed factors with which he has to build up the meaning of his sentences as a mosaic is put together of discrete independent tesserae."[52] Instead of this, Richards argues that the senses of the author's words "are resultants which we arrive at only through the interplay of the interpretive possibilities of the whole utterance'', that is, from the complete interanimation of words.[53] From the outset, then, Richards establishes that in his opinion meanings are things determined by complete utterances and surrounding contexts, and not by the individual words in isolation. When he turns to metaphor he therefore does not talk of 'some words being used metaphorically', as Black suggests he does, but of metaphor as the consequence of the interanimation of words in the complete utterance.

This stress on the whole utterance forms an important background for Richards's contention that:

when we use a metaphor we have two thoughts of different things active together and supported by a single word or phrase, whose meaning is a resultant of their interaction.[54]

Max Black, perhaps recalling the ideational theory of meaning associated with I. A. Richards in *The Meaning of Meaning*, dismisses the above notion that two 'ideas' work upon one another as psychological language and an 'inconvenient fiction', but there is no reason why this terminology is any more inconvenient than Black's own suggestion of two present subjects.[55] Indeed, if we allow by a principle of historical charity that these 'thoughts' can be extra-utterance without being extra-linguistic, the inconvenience of the ideational theory is overcome and the merits of Richards' argument become apparent.

Richards intends to emphasize that metaphor is an intercourse of thoughts, as opposed to a mere shifting of words or a substitution of term for term as was suggested by the ornamentalist view and, no doubt, by the adherents of the 'Usage Doctrine'. To explain this 'interanimation' he makes his distinction between the tenor, or underlying subject of the metaphor, and the vehicle that presents it. So, in the following quotation,

A stubborn and unconquerable flame
Creeps in his veins and drinks the streams of life.[56]

the 'tenor' is the idea of the fever from which the man is suffering, and the 'vehicle' for it is the description of the flame. Note that in this passage the *fever is never explicitly mentioned*, hence Richards's suggestion that it is thoughts and not words which are active together, although the thoughts are of course bound up with the words.

The advantage of Richards's formulation is that it allows us to distinguish between the tenor and the vehicle of the metaphor without suggesting that the metaphor has two subjects. The one subject-matter of the metaphor above is the fever from which the man suffers. A further advantage is that Richards's distinction leaves room for the phenomenon of what he calls 'subsidiary vehicles'; the primary vehicle in the example is that of the flame, but the flame modifier is itself modified by language descriptive of a beast of prey when the author says that the flame "creeps in his veins and drinks the streams of life".

A good part of Max Black's dissatisfaction with Richards's notion that in metaphor one's ideas or thoughts are active together arises because he does not seem to have grasped Richards's distinction between tenor and vehicle. Black takes these to be confused equivalents of his own 'principal' and 'subsidiary subjects', so that in his example, "Man is a wolf", 'man' is the tenor and 'wolf' the vehicle. This completely misses Richards's more subtle point that the tenor and the vehicle are not necessarily two *terms* of the utterance at all. A better example to illustrate Richards's point would be 'That wolf is here again'.

Black is not the only one to misunderstand Richards's distinction. Paul Ricoeur takes tenor and vehicle to be less precise equivalents of Black's 'metaphorical focus' and 'literal frame'.[57] But while Black's 'focus' might have some rough equivalence to Richards's 'vehicle', his 'frame' (the non-metaphorical remainder of the sentence) is in no way to be equated with the 'tenor' which, for Richards, denotes the true subject-matter of the metaphor. If anything, it is Black's terms which are imprecise. When he speaks of the 'focus' of a metaphor as the "words used metaphorically", he displays the tendency, criticized by Richards, of regarding only certain words in an utterance as metaphorical rather than seeing that the metaphor is the product of the whole.

It is this misreading of the distinction between tenor and vehicle that prompts Max Black to insist, even in the later article, that in each metaphor "two distinct subjects" are present, a claim that is clearly untrue. It is untrue even if by 'present' one means 'present in the mind'; for while the primary subject of 'fever' may be present in the mind in the metaphor we have been discussing, it is by no means the case that a distinctive secondary subject is present in the mind in a metaphor such as 'the giddy brink'. Black's account in terms of two subjects cannot, in fact, deal with metaphors like 'giddy brink', 'writhing script', and 'angry wind' although Black clearly regards these as instances of metaphor.

The stipulation that each metaphor has two distinct subjects is responsible for most of the serious inconsistencies of Black's interactive theory. It lies behind his claim in "Metaphor" that both subjects are modified in the interaction, a puzzling notion which had to be abandoned in the later article and which was inconsistent with the one-directional notion of filtering. Stripped of this kind of interaction, but hampered still by the notion of two distinct subjects, Black's analysis in "More about Metaphor" drifts ineluctably towards the comparison view which he had earlier criticized.

It can now be seen that Richards's account is not so limited as Black's. The advantage with Richards is that he concentrates on words and the 'interanimation' of words, whereas Black moves too quickly away from words to things, to the interaction of two subjects. Richards has no need for two explicit subjects. He can say of 'giddy brink' that the tenor is the brink and the vehicle giddiness, and the associations one has with giddiness. Of 'writhing script', he can say that the script is the tenor and the vehicle is writhing, and the associations we have with writhing. It may be that at some stage the reader will think of writhing in terms of a thing, or things, that writhe, such as a snake, or a man in pain, or a piece of paper on the fire, or possibly all of these, but none would be either an explicit or a necessary second subject of the metaphor.

It is only by seeing that a metaphor has one true subject which tenor and vehicle conjointly depict and illumine that a full, interactive, or interanimative, theory is possible. An example shows this best. Consider the interaction of tenor and vehicle in Virginia Woolf's metaphorical description of Mrs Ramsay in *To the Lighthouse*:

Never did anybody look so sad. Bitter and black, half-way down, in the darkness, in the shaft which ran from the sunlight to the depths, perhaps a tear formed; a tear fell; the waters swayed this way and that, received it, and were at rest. Never did anybody look so sad. [58]

What is being spoken of is not both a private grief *and* a shaft of some kind but simply some private, sickening grief. Yet to identify the subject as a private grief is to fall short of the genuine descriptive content of the metaphor. The content, the full meaning of the metaphor, results from the complete unit of tenor and vehicle. The vehicle of the shaft is not by itself the 'metaphor' for the grief. Nor is the tenor of grief by itself the 'meaning' of the metaphor. The metaphor and its meaning (it is artificial to separate them) are the unique product of the whole and the excellence of a metaphor such as this one is not that it is a new description of a previously discerned human condition but that *this* subject, this particular mental state, is accessible only through the metaphor. What is identified and described is identified and described uniquely by this metaphor. It is in this way that a metaphor is genuinely creative and says something that can be said adequately in no other way, not as an ornament to what we already know but as an embodiment of a new insight.

The real inadequacy of the substitution theory and the crude comparison theory is very much akin to that of

the 18th Century assumptions that figures are a mere embellishment or added beauty and that the plain meaning, the tenor, is what alone really matters and is something that, 'regardless of the figures', might be gathered by the patient reader.[59]

for, 'regardless of the figures', one does not have the same meaning at all. Seeing this, we can also see how deeply misguided is the common query, 'But what is X a metaphor for?', if by 'for' the enquirer wants a tenor stripped of its cumbersome vehicle. Tenor and vehicle are inseparable and without the sense of the particular metaphor one may not have the same sense at all. As Richards says,

the vehicle is not normally a mere embellishment of a tenor which is otherwise unchanged by it, but that the vehicle and tenor in cooperation give a meaning of more varied powers than can be ascribed to either.[60]

We can also see now what is unsatisfactory about defining metaphor, as does Owen Barfield amongst others, as 'speaking about one thing and meaning another'. Our dissatisfaction with this is not that, *pace* Donald Davidson, we think it makes no sense to talk of speaking about one thing and meaning another. On the contrary, this seems quite a good description of what goes on in satire and some types of allegory. But for metaphor the distinction is not appropriate; when W. H. Auden says in '1st September 1939' that

> The unmentionable odour of death
> Offends the September night

he is not speaking about a smell at all, much less speaking about smell and meaning something else. He is speaking about the forebodings of war in terms which are appropriate to odour. Rather than speaking about one thing and meaning another he is '*speaking about one thing in terms which are seen to be suggestive of another.*' The rather cumbrous locution which we used to define metaphor has come into its own at last.

It is now possible to flesh out our earlier definition of metaphor, that metaphor is a speaking of one thing in terms which are seen as suggestive of another. We have said that metaphor cannot be understood, as Beardsley suggested, as simply a matter of conflict of word meaning; nor can it be understood, as Black says, as an interaction of two subjects. Yet by defining metaphor as a speaking about one thing in terms suggestive of another we retain aspects of both these theories; like Beardsley, we maintain that metaphor is properly a linguistic phenomenon—an interanimation of terms—and like Black, we hold that a metaphor has, if not two subjects, then at least the twinned elements of tenor and vehicle. The view which we wish to develop is that metaphor is a form of language use with a unity of subject-matter and which yet draws upon two (or more) sets of associations, and does so, characteristically, by involving the consideration of a model or models.

It is, in fact, difficult to know what to make of Black's continued insistence on 'two subjects' since he does not clarify what he means precisely by a 'subject' and especially since, as we have mentioned, he draws his conclusions on the strength of one kind of metaphor (A is a B) without explaining why he thinks all others would behave in a similar way. Although his logical grammar is not fully explained, it is reasonable to conclude that his talk of two subjects reflects a conviction that each metaphor in some way refers to two things, at least in the early "Metaphor" where he contends that both these subjects are illumined by their interaction.

While we deny that metaphors have two subjects, we agree that each metaphor involves at least two different networks of associations. In the metaphorical statement 'Man is a wolf', these associations are with 'man' and 'wolf'. But to make the interanimative theory work for the broader set of metaphors it is important to say that these networks of associations are not necessarily generated by two distinct *subjects* of a metaphor (say, men and wolves) but can also be networks surrounding particular *terms* of a metaphor. For example, in a metaphorical use of the phrase 'metaphysical streets', these associations would be with the terms 'metaphysical' and 'streets'. This is more than a quibble, for if we think of this initial interanimation as not between subjects but between terms, we can make the theory applicable not only to metaphors like Black's "Marriage is a zero-sum game" but also to metaphors like "He examined his tattered scruples". In the latter we do not have two distinct subjects but we can still say that there is interanimation between the associations of 'tattered' and those of 'scruples'.

But one cannot stop here. The tension in this initial interanimation of terms is not enough to explain metaphorical construal, nor even to distinguish metaphor from other anomalous combinations of terms. We suggest, therefore, that at a secondary level metaphorical construal is characterized by its reliance on an underlying model, or even on a number of such models, and that metaphor and model are indeed, as Black has suggested, closely linked. Of course, the model, or models, will not always be explicit. It is sometimes a merit in metaphor that they are not. There is latitude in our account for the fact that in construing a metaphor like 'writhing script', one might associate with 'writhing' not only actions similar to writhing such as twisting and squirming, but also entities which are known to writhe, such as snakes or persons in pain. These models form part of what we shall call the associative network of the term 'writhing'.

We might consider the associative network of a term as its placement in a semantic field where the 'value' of the term is fixed not simply by the terms for which it might be exchanged (such as 'twisting' and 'squirming') but also by the entities of which the term would customarily be predicated (such as snakes and persons in pain). We associate with 'writhing', in this context, entities which do writhe. In this way, even adjectival metaphors like 'writhing script,' 'giddy brink', and 'tattered scruples' give rise to latent models, for they are suggestive of things which are writhing, giddy, and tattered.

Our suggestion is that model and metaphor are closely linked; when we use a model, we regard one thing or state of affairs in terms of another, and when we use a metaphor, we speak of one thing or state of affairs in language suggestive of another. This close association of model and metaphor is important not only for explaining how metaphors work but for explaining why metaphors can be so useful, a topic that we shall discuss at length later.

Theories of metaphor which see metaphor as the consequence simply of verbal tension (an oddity of predication) fail to see that, while the reader may be alerted to the fact that a metaphorical construal is required by an odd conjunction of terms (say, 'giddy brink'), his construal of this oddity as metaphor depends upon his ability to see it as suggesting a model or models which enable him to go on extending the significance of what he has read or heard. This close relationship to model explains how one can have metaphor where there is no oddity of predication: it is not odd to say of a poet's work that it flows, or runs smoothly, or is full, or steady, or deep, but we can prompt a metaphorical construal by saying all of these things in succession and thereby alerting the reader to the fact that the poetic work is being spoken of in terms suggestive of a river. It is the capacity of the lively metaphor to suggest models that enable us to 'go on' which gives the clue to the richness of metaphorical description.

It must be stressed that in committing oneself to a duality, or indeed plurality, of associative networks for each metaphor, one is not thereby committed to the idea that each metaphor has two or more points of reference. While duality of associative networks is integral to metaphor, a duality of reference would undercut the whole of what makes metaphor interesting. We shall deal with the important topic of reference in the chapters that follow, but we should now make initial clarifications on our use of terms.

4. SENSE, REFERENCE, AND METAPHOR: SOME DISTINCTIONS

The distinction between 'sense' and 'reference' has been made in a variety of ways and a certain amount of terminological confusion has arisen between the various sets of paired terms which have been used to mark Frege's original distinction. So it is that the pairs 'sense' and 'reference', 'connotation' and 'denotation', 'meaning' and 'reference', and 'intension' and 'extension' have been used in different accounts to map roughly the same distinction.[61] At least part of the considerable confusion which affects accounts of meta-phorical reference arises from this terminological confusion, and particularly from a failure to see that there is a distinction between the reference of the metaphor and the so-called reference of terms used in the metaphor. Our account of reference and our terminology follows that of John Lyons in *Semantics*, and is guided by recent work on reference by Keith Donnellan.

In the usage of Donnellan and Lyons, 'reference' is something that a speaker makes on a particular occasion of making an utterance, and not something made by individual vocabulary terms (lexemes) in isolation. As Lyons puts it, reference is "an utterance-dependent notion". He says:

When a sentence like 'Napoleon is a Corsican' is uttered to make a statement, we will say that the speaker refers to a certain individual (Napoleon) by means of the referring expression. If the reference is successful, the referring expression will correctly identify for the hearer the individual in question: the referent. It should be noted that, according to this conception of the relation of reference, it is the speaker who refers (by using some appropriate expression): he invests the expression with reference by the act of referring. [62]

Keith Donnellan's contribution has been to point out that there is a difference between a successful reference, and one which uses a factually accurate definite description. A reference can be successful even if the description in the referring expression does not actually fit the referent; for example, in context, the utterance "The man drinking the gin and tonic" can successfully refer even though the man referred to may in fact be drinking soda water. This is another way of highlighting the point that reference is something effected by speakers making an utterance in a context, and not something which inheres in definite descriptions or lexemes *per se*. [63]

We will use the term 'meaning', too, as an utterance-bound notion and speak of meanings as, properly speaking, the meanings of utterances and not of individual lexemes. Referring utterances, then, have meaning and make a reference.

Lexemes, on the other hand, can be said to have a sense and a denotation. By 'sense' here we intend the dictionary definition of a lexeme, and not some set of necessary properties of that which the lexeme denotes. By 'denotation' we mean the relation between the lexeme and the persons, things, states of affairs, etc. (if any) which it designates in the world; so the lexeme 'dog' denotes the class of dogs. [64]

We have now distinguished, on the one hand, between the meaning and reference of an utterance, and on the other, between the sense and denotation of a term. One must keep these distinctions clear if one is to make sense of an interactive theory of metaphor.

Following Richards's notion of the 'interanimation' of words, we suggest that the meaning of the metaphor should *not* be thought of as the meaning of some words that in an utterance are 'used metaphorically' or have peculiar 'metaphorical meanings', but rather as the meaning of the complete utterance as construed in its context of uttering. Similarly we argue that the reference which the metaphor makes is not, as some suggest, a split reference determined by the individual terms used in a metaphor (like 'man' and 'wolf'); it is rather the reference effected by the speaker's employment of the whole utterance in its context. In some cases, the speaker may fix the reference by ostension or by some means independent of the terms of the utterance, as Churchill did when he described Mussolini as 'That utensil'. In other cases, the description effected by a metaphor may succeed in uniquely picking out a referent, as in Virginia Woolf's metaphorical description of Mrs Ramsay. In this way, a particular meaning, and in some instances a particular fixing of references of the metaphor, is not reducible to the 'sense' and 'denotation' of the terms which it contains. The metaphor is cognitively unique.

To return to Richards's terminology: we conclude that the metaphorical vehicle is not used to pick out a second subject, or another referent, but to describe the referent picked out by the whole of the utterance or, more accurately, by the speaker in making the utterance. When Churchill described Mussolini as 'That utensil', the *reference* of the metaphor was fixed by Churchill, but the significance of the metaphor was given in considering Mussolini in the terms of the associative network of 'utensil'. It is in this way that we get Dr Johnson's "two ideas for one", a unity of subject-matter and a plurality of associative networks, and this is what we intended to mark by defining metaphor as a speaking about one thing or state of affairs in terms which are suggestive of another.

IV

METAPHOR AMONGST TROPES

NOTABLY absent from the contemporary philosophical accounts of metaphor is any discussion of metaphor as placed amongst the other figures of speech, the tropes. This silence may, on the part of the English-language writers, indicate either suspicion or ignorance of the distinctions made by traditional rhetoric, yet even writers more familiar with the rhetorical tradition, like Paul Ricoeur, have suggested that it is wise to avoid the discussion and classification of tropes, the tropology of traditional rhetoric. Certainly the science of rhetoric has had, like all sciences, its good and bad practitioners and no one would want to bring back the armies of distinctions which were at one time the fashion in the discussion of tropes; nevertheless, it is interesting that almost none of the modern commentators, including Ricoeur, can refrain when discussing metaphor from mentioning other figures of speech.[1] The energy which philosophers like Max Black have put into distinguishing metaphor from simile, for example, seems a *de facto* indication that distinctions between tropes, or at least between some tropes, are both possible and interesting; and if, as we shall argue, some distinctions between tropes have to do with cognitive function, it is wise not to disregard or to abandon tropology, but to reconsider it in the light of current theory. All this is lifted from the level of the theoretical to that of the applied if one's focus of interest is religious language, for here as perhaps nowhere else figures of speech are the vessels of insight and the vehicles of cognition. Let us see, then, what distinctions we can make by regarding metaphor amongst the tropes.

1. METAPHOR AND MORE DISTANT RELATIONS

We defined metaphor as that trope, or figure of speech, in which we speak of one thing in terms of suggestive of another; so when we speak of God as a farmer, and say of him that he plants his seeds, nurtures the young shoots, separates the wheat and the tares, we are speaking metaphorically. From the outset, the identification of metaphor as a figure of speech enables us to distinguish metaphor from a number of categories with which it is often confused. The

most important of these for our purposes is 'model', especially since
it seems the universal practice in the theological literature to use
the terms 'model' and 'metaphor' synonymously. Models can be
distinguished from and related to metaphor in this way; an object or
state of affairs is said to be a *model* when it is viewed in terms of
some other object or state of affairs. A model need not be a
metaphor, for a model need not be linguistic at all, as with a model
train. Thus we say, if we use the mechanism of the computer to
explain the supposed action of the brain, that the computer is
functioning as a model for the brain. If, however, we then go on to
speak about the neural 'programming', we are using metaphorical
language based on the computer model, for, strictly speaking,
'programming' has not the same sense when used in terms of brains
as it does with computers. In theology, if we use the concept of
fatherhood as a frame on which to develop our understanding of
God, then 'fatherhood' is the model. But if we go on to speak of
God's loving concern for his children, we are speaking metaphorically on the basis of the fatherhood model. Talk based on
models will be metaphorical, so model and metaphor, though
different categories and not to be—as frequently they are by
theologians—equated, are closely linked; the latter is what we have
when we speak on the basis of the former.

Symbol can similarly be distinguished from metaphor as a category which includes the non-linguistic; the cross is a symbol for
Christianity, Rosa Luxemburg is a symbol for the revolutionary
movement. 'Analogy', too, is a term commonly used to describe a
form of argument, or a type of relation; hence one says that there
exists analogy of structure between a model aeroplane and the
full-scale one. Model, symbol, and analogy of this sort include the
non-linguistic, as does 'image' which, along with being a generic
term for figures of speech, is used to designate mental events and
visual representations.

On the other hand, categories such as allegory and satire are fully
linguistic but differ from metaphor in both scope and intention.
First, they differ in scope—because in many cases allegory and satire
extend beyond use in the sentence or discrete utterance; their locus
being more properly the text, they are not truly tropic. Secondly,
they differ in intention from metaphor—for both speak of one
thing in the guise of another. This guise is chosen for its ability to
render the statement oblique, especially in the case of satire,

whereas metaphor intends only to speak about its primary subject
and to do so in a direct way with no dissembling. Metaphors may
be found in allegories and satires, and this may be why the former
especially is sometimes regarded as being extended metaphor. But
the two are not properly figures of speech, they are forms of
prose. [2]

Finally, if briefly, myth is all too often not distinguished in
theological discussion from metaphor. Like allegory and satire,
myth has its locus in textual or narrative analysis, and not in
discussion of figures of speech.

These distinctions are made here only briefly, for many of them
demand a study in their own right. However, even this brief
outline can alert us to instances where terms are used incautiously.
For example, as we have already pointed out, no matter what one's
historical opinion, it is strictly incorrect to say that "John F.
Kennedy is a metaphor for the 1960s"; whatever else Kennedy
may have been, he was a person and not a figure of speech. Or, to
give a theological example, one hears it said that "Jesus was the
ultimate 'parable' or 'metaphor' for God". Such a statement may
be appropriate from a pulpit, but out of place in a work whose
object is to clarify the function of metaphor and parable within a
text. In such a context, to say that Jesus was a metaphor or a
parable is either to have an odd Christology or, more likely, poorly
conceived definitions of metaphor and parable. [3]

2. METAPHOR AMONGST TROPES

Thus far we have been speaking of things which, while associated,
are not classifiable with metaphor; they are distant relations. The
near relations of metaphor are its fellow tropes and even here some
are clearly less closely related than others. Amongst these are
hyperbole, or exaggeration ('He never stops talking'), oxymoron,
which is the combining of incompatibles ('He's a delightful bore',
She's a horrible charmer'), and litotes, assertion by denying the
contrary ('That's no joke!'). All of these are less interesting than
metaphor in that their use is more tightly circumscribed. More
interesting are metonymy, synecdoche, and simile, tropes which
together with metaphor are generally recognized as being at "the
center of the figural space". [4]

3. SYNECDOCHE AND METONYMY

Synecdoche is the trope in which one uses a species term to stand in for a genus, or a genus term for a species, or a more comprehensive term for a less and vice versa; so one says 'the ships opened fire' when one means the guns opened fire, or 'that creature is here again' when one means that person is here again. Metonymy is similar, except that here one uses an adjunct to stand for the whole; so we say 'the White House said yesterday' when we mean that 'the presidential authority of the United States made public yesterday'. A distinction between these two and metaphor may be made like this: metonymy and synecdoche seem superficially similar to metaphor, but they are functionally (that is, semantically) different. In metonymy and synecdoche, one word or phrase stands in for a more straightforward reference and this 'standing in' is of a different nature from that which characterises metaphor. The plugging in of an adjunct for the whole, or a more comprehensive term for a less, is essentially an oblique and less prosaic way of making a direct reference. Instances of metonymy and synecdoche point one directly to the absent term; it would be a failure in comprehension if, on hearing the phrase 'the White House said today', one wondered if shutters and doors opened like mouths; or of, on hearing that 'twenty sails entered the harbour', one wondered how the sails got there without the ships. Metonymy and synecdoche function as oblique reference and as such they, if any of the tropes, fit the bill for being primarily ornamental ways of naming.

But metaphor goes beyond the role of ornament. A metaphor should if it is a good one, suggest just that cluster of ideas which a good metonymy ought not to, so that when the poet says of his mysterious love

> nobody, not even the rain, has such small hands
> (e.e.cummings: Somewhere I Have Never Travelled)

the power of the metaphor rests in its casting up in the reader's mind thoughts of what kind of hands rain might have, suggestions of fragility, delicacy, transcience, ability to reach the smallest places. The purpose of this metaphor is both to cast up and organize a network of associations. A good metaphor may not simply be an oblique reference to a predetermined subject but a new vision, the birth of a new understanding, a new referential access. A strong metaphor compels new possibilities of vision.

Thus metonymy and synecdoche, while superficially similar to metaphor, differ in function, for they are both largely ornamental. Put another way, with both metonymy and synecdoche, meaning is largely subsumed by the reference it makes. With metaphor, this is far from always the case.

4. SIMILE

The greatest rival of metaphor, simile, in its most powerful instances does compel possibilities. Simile is usually regarded as the trope of comparison and identifiable within speech by the presence of a 'like', or an 'as', or the occasional 'not unlike'; "the porter is like a great pigeon, roosting at his post, fluffing his feathers and pecking the glass at passing offenders".

Following Max Black, a number of writers have argued that metaphor must not be regarded as just simile without the 'like'. Reasons given for this are twofold: first, that simile lacks the impact of metaphor, and, secondly, that simile as simple comparison, or 'saying the same', cannot rival the richer interactive meaning of metaphor.[5] But both these points stand only if one takes as examples uninspiring similes such as 'the sun is like a golden ball' or 'these biscuits are like cement', where the comparison is narrow and insipid. These similes are prosaic not because they are similes but because the insights they embody are prosaic. Metaphors with the same content would be no better; viz. 'these biscuits are made of cement', 'the sun is a golden ball'. In this quotation from Lord Byron, loathsome to generations of schoolchildren,

> The Assyrian came down like a wolf on the fold,
> And his cohorts were gleaming in purple and gold;
> And the sheen of their spears was like stars on the sea,
> When the blue wave rolls nightly on deep Galilee.
>
> The Destruction of Sennacherib

we regard the similes as flat not because they are similes but because the parallels drawn seem trite.

Consider this more striking simile from Flaubert's *Madame Bovary*: "Human language is like a cracked kettle on which we beat out tunes for bears to dance to, when all the time we are longing to move the stars to pity.''[6] The comparison in this simile is in no way obvious or boring, nor would its impact be altered by deleting the 'like' to make it a metaphor. Our contention here is that the presence of a 'like' in the figure above is an aspect of superficial grammar, and in no real way impedes meaning. In such cases, metaphor and simile, while textually different, are functionally the same.

Max Black's dissatisfaction at the equation of simile with metaphor arises from his eagerness to point out that metaphor does far more than just effect simple comparisons. His point is a good one, but his mistake lies in suggesting that similes are all point-by-point comparisons as is the case in crude similes such as 'these biscuits are like cement'. But to regard simile as necessarily mere 'same-saying' of the trivial sort is greatly to misrepresent that trope. Simile may be the means of making comparisons of two kinds, the comparison of similars and of dissimilars, and in the latter case, simile shares much of the imaginative life and cognitive function of its metaphorical counterparts. For this reason, we can say that metaphor and simile share the same function and differ primarily in their grammatical form.[7]

There is, in fact, a range amongst similes with some discharging more fully a metaphoric role than others. A useful distinction can be made in terms of function, between what might be called 'illustrative' similes and 'modelling' similes. The difference is shown in these two horticultural examples, both taken from a novel by Henry James:

A dissatisfied mind, whatever else it may miss, is rarely in want of reasons; they bloom as thick as buttercups in June.

and

Her mind was to be his—attached to his own like a small garden-plot to a deer park. He would rake the soil gently and water the flowers; he would weed the beds and gather an occasional nose-gay. It would be a pretty piece of property for a proprietor already far-reaching.[8]

The first of these similes, reasons for discontent blossoming as thick as buttercups in June, is largely illustrative, and serves to emphasize the numerousness of reasons for being dissatisfied. But the second simile provides a model susceptible of considerable development, such as James has undertaken here. The first sort of simile is the least like metaphor, or like any interesting sort of metaphor, as its implications are restricted (cf. He works like a horse, she's pretty as an angel). The modelling simile, on the other hand, is close in function to the metaphor; one could, in fact, delete the 'like' and make it into a metaphor.

To conclude: as regards simile, we say that if any opposition in terms of cognitive function is to be made, it should be made not between simile and metaphor but between illustrative simile, and modelling simile or metaphor. The rationale for this distinction lies partly in a question of epistemic distance, for in the illustrative simile one compares, point for point, two known entities. If I compare the sun to a golden ball, I have sufficient knowledge of the sun and of a golden ball to compare the two; the efficacy of an illustrative simile depends on that. But in the modelling simile or metaphor, we may use a subject that is reasonably well known to us to explain or provide schematization for a state of affairs which is beyond our full grasp; this happens when one says that God is our father, or that light is waves, or that the human community is governed by natural law. One has a good notion of law, waves, and fatherhood and uses these notions to give form to the more amorphous concepts of society, light, and deity.

One should not assume that the modelling simile or metaphor is therefore superior to the illustrative; nor should one waste time in controversy over whether metaphor is superior to simile by virtue of its richer web of implication, or simile to metaphor because of its greater precision, or whether both are superior to metonymy and the other tropes. No such generalizations can possibly be made, for in each instance the author's intention, and sometimes his epistemological limitations, determine what form is best. An illustrative simile may be required if a certain precision is desirable, a modelling simile or metaphor if one wishes to produce an exploratory schema. There is no virtue in metaphor for its own sake, no point in saying 'she is a duck' if one means 'she walks like a duck'. Inferior and superior are judgements that can be made only with regard to the adequacy of a figure in conveying the speaker's intentions in a particular situation.

In the light of similarities between metaphor and simile, should we not dispense with the distinction between the two and, for instance, call them both metaphor if the difference is only one of superficial grammar? Apart from a natural reluctance to abandon a distinction commonly made in our speech, there is a good reason why the distinction should be kept; it is that while metaphor and simile differ primarily in grammatical form, there is one important role which, by virtue of grammatical form, metaphor performs and simile cannot. We shall follow the rhetorical tradition in calling this catachresis.

5. CATACHRESIS

Catachresis is the supplying of a term where one is lacking in the vocabulary; it took place when the lower part of a mountain came to be called its 'foot', or the bounding line of an angle its 'leg', or the narrow base of a wine glass its 'stem', because no straightforward term was extant in our vocabulary (or lexicon) for this purpose. In the language of the linguists, catachresis is the activity of filling lexical gaps.

Simile cannot, for reasons of syntactic form, be used in catachresis. A gap in the lexicon is filled by a term, such as 'leaf' of a book, or by a phrase such as 'dead end', but not by an 'is like' clause. One can say of the voluble guide, 'He's just like Cicero' but the catachretical form will be 'he's a cicerone'.

It should not, however, be thought that metaphor is the only means by which language is extended, although it is perhaps the most interesting. Three other distinct forms of extension are extension by parallel syntax, extension by synecdoche (or metonymy), and extension by neologism. In extension by parallel syntax, a parallel grammatic formation is applied to produce, for example, a verb from an adjective or from a noun. Thus Gerard Manley Hopkins, master of misuse, does in "Spring and Fall"

> Márgarét are you gríeving
> Over Goldengrove unleaving?

where 'unleaving' is devised by parallel syntax to describe the process by which trees lose their leaves. Extension by metonymy takes place where an adjunct gives a name to the object under discussion, as when sherry took the name of the Spanish city that produced it, Xeres, or when the name of a scientist becomes the name of a component of his theory as with 'amp(ere)', 'volt', and 'ohm'. Finally, language may be extended by pure invention of words, although this is a far less common occurrence than one might imagine; so 'nylon' was created to parallel 'cotton' and 'rayon'.[9]

But all these forms of extension, whether by syntax, synecdoche, metonymy or neologism, are intrinsically less interesting than is extension via metaphor: *for, while all the above may fill lexical gaps, metaphor may also create them.* To call a particular unit of electrical energy an amp (the current that one volt can send through one ohm) is merely an act of naming, straightforwardly referential, whereas to describe electrical energy as having a 'current' suggests that it flows and can be dammed; it rests, in fact, on a hydraulic theory of electricity. One names a wine 'sherry' and stops at that, but in speaking of fate as a 'mistress' one can go on to consider her whims, her favours, and her favourites; or, in the scientific example used earlier, speaking of the brain as a computer is for the neurologist more than a *façon de parler* because it constitutes a model which structures the further observations he is able to make and which prompts him to consider whether the brain gives 'feedback', is 'programmed', and has 'data banks'.[10] The strong metaphor does not prompt the routine renaming of aspects otherwise identifiable, but suggests new categories of interpretation and hypothesizes new entities, states of affairs, and causal relations.

The insights we derive from these literary observations go beyond literary analysis. We have argued that the tropes may be distinguished from each other by form, and some more importantly by cognitive function. Some tropes are used only for ornamental reasons, but others, especially simile and metaphor, present one with a significantly new interpretative web which may affect further analyses. Of simile and metaphor, metaphor has the added capacity to expand our lexicon, and in so doing, it expands the conceptual apparatus with which we work.

The implications of this may be far-reaching. Metaphors become not only part of our language but also part of the way in which we interpret our world, and the implications of one metaphor are very different from those of another. One who sees the political unit as a 'body politic' may have a different procedure than one who regards it as 'the ship of state', for if the nation is a body and the monarch its head, if one cuts off the head the body will die, whereas on a ship of state mutiny against an incompetent captain is not only possible but obligatory.[11] So, too, as the work of Karl Rahner and Joseph Ratzinger suggests, the Church as the body of Christ is no longer a neutral or even helpful image if 'body' has come to be associated in the Christian West with 'body politic' and the organization of a monarchical state; better, then, to speak of 'the pilgrim people of God'.[12] These reflections enable one to see that metaphor is not a neutral or ornamental aspect of speech. Rather, in almost all areas of abstract thought (mathematics might be an exception but even that seems doubtful), the very frames within which we work are given by metaphors which function in structuring not only what sort of answers we get, but what kind of questions we ask. Given the dependence of religious language in almost all traditions upon metaphorical talk, it is a great over-simplification to ask of a given statement whether it is an assertive or an emotive utterance, whether it is the language of fact or of poetry. The language of fact may be of an extremely complex nature, no less so in the theoretical sciences than in religion, and no philosophical account of religious language will be either complete or sufficient if it fails to take account of the ways forms of figurative discourse, like metaphor, function in the task of saying that which cannot be said in other ways.

To dissuade us from probing the Divine mysteries, Francis Bacon says:

there is no proceeding in invention of knowledge but by similitude: and God is only self-like, having nothing in common with any creature, otherwise than as in shadow and trope.[13]

It is now becoming apparent that, to speak somewhat paradoxically, the task of saying the unsayable is aligned to that of knowing the unknowable. This has been judged to be particularly, and some say exclusively, so in religious matters and yet there has been an equally common assumption that figures and tropes and, in particular, metaphors somehow give us a means of speaking of God. In the chapters which follow, we defend this assumption, but before discussing why metaphor is particularly suited to the theologian's task we must consider the question, 'is all religious language metaphorical?'

The answer depends on what we take religious language to be. If one takes the Bible as a body of religious language, it is clear that by no means all, or even the greater part, of religious language is metaphorical; along with nearly every other trope, the Bible includes language of narrative, chronology, and description which is not figurative at all. But people who ask whether all religious language is metaphorical usually mean something more specific by 'religious language' and something rather broad by 'metaphor'. By 'religious language' they mean language which is specifically about God, and by 'metaphorical'—pictorial language like those metaphors which we have described as spinning out the implications of a model, such as God as father. From now on, we shall take 'religious language' in the narrow sense, as talk about God, unless we specify otherwise. Even so, we consider that not all talk about God is metaphorical and to show why, we must examine analogy.

6. ANALOGY

The term analogy, as we have said, can signify several things: it can designate a type of relationship, so that we speak of analogy of structure between a model aeroplane and a real one, or it can designate the kind of argument based on putative analogy of structure. There is also what we shall call linguistic analogy and it is this we mean to explain.

Analogy as a linguistic device deals with language that has been stretched to fit new applications, yet fits the new situation without generating for the native speaker any imaginative strain. This can best be shown by example: suppose that one encountered intelligent life on another planet (in philosophers' examples this is always Mars), life that communicated by means of the arrangement of fibres on its body. If we were able to interpret this new mode of communication, even though it involved no sounds at all, we should quite naturally say that the Martian 'told' us such and such, or made this or that 'comment'. We would probably not regard this as speaking metaphorically; more likely we would regard it as justified extensions of what 'told' and 'comment' really mean. This would be not a metaphorical but a 'stretched' or analogical use of language. Analogy is, to redirect a phrase of Nelson Goodman's, more properly than metaphor "a matter of teaching an old word new tricks—of applying an old label in a new way".[14]

It is surprising that none of the philosophical accounts of metaphor with which we are acquainted make use of this category. It is useful not only in historical linguistics to classify instances where a word, while perhaps retaining a central core of meaning, comes to have a wider domain of application (thus 'riding', once appropriate to horses, is now appropriate to bicycles as well), but also synchronically to provide a category between straightforward language and metaphorical. [15]

Since the writing of the *Summa Theologica*, analogy has, however, been much discussed by theologians with regard to religious language. These discussions often link Aquinas's linguistic theory of analogy inextricably with the ontological or epistemological variants of the theory descending from Cajetan. But it can be argued that Aquinas's theory was logico-linguistic, as well as metaphysical in intention, and more concerned with determining how we can *speak* of God than with devising crude ontological linkings between finite creatures and infinite Deity.

Aquinas introduced his theory of analogy to provide a middle way between terms used in only one straightforward sense, univocally, and terms used in more than one sense which bear no relation to one another, equivocally. The phrases 'river bank' and 'merchant bank' use 'bank' equivocally, but to say 'Tom is happy' and 'this song is happy' is to use the common term analogously, for these uses, though not exactly equivalent, are none the less related.

Yet it would be misleading to suggest that Aquinas was concerned with strictly linguistic relations. Because of the particular theory of meaning with which he worked these linguistic relations were also ontological ones. Analogical relations all refer to the same thing, they all have the same *res significata* but they refer to it in different ways—Tom has happiness, the song is a cause of happiness. We will leave aside Aquinas' account of analogy to keep to a more strictly linguistic point of view. One should say in passing, however, that Aquinas does not claim that everything we say of God is said analogically. For example, we do not say analogically of God that he is heavy or sweet or happy (although we might say these things metaphorically of Him). Because of the ontological relation involved in 'naming' things analogically, only a select group of the perfection terms can be so applied to God. We say analogically of God that he is one, wise, good, and so on. [16]

Analogical usage can be distinguished from a metaphorical usage by the fact that from its inception it seems appropriate. We feel no jolt or strain saying 'my dog is happy', 'my dog is eager to go', or 'the Martians discussed their policy'. We regard such analogy as a legitimate extension of a word's domain of application, and this accounts for our intuitive reluctance to say that 'riding a bicycle' is or ever was metaphorical. Furthermore, the intelligibility and use of such an analogy does not depend on the recognition of a latent model, but simply on the recognition that the term employed is of sufficient generality to be appropriate in this new context. Rather than giving us a new picture, analogy, like some of the other catachretical forms discussed above, fits into standard speech without imaginative strain. Linguistic analogy concerns stretched usages, not figurative ones.

To say that metaphor is not to be identified with the ''middle way'' of analogy does not mean that metaphor is either equivocation or univocation. Equivocation, univocation, and analogy are all types of literal speech and nowhere concerned with expanding descriptive powers, whereas metaphor, as we have seen, is not to do with straightforward speech but with a figurative 'speaking about' that generates new perspectives. The categories of univocal, equivocal, and analogical are different in kind from that of metaphor.

Thus, when we speak of God as infinite, perfect, or transcendent we speak analogically of God (for example, 'infinite' here is a related but not an identical use to the infinite we speak of in mathematics) but not, as some have suggested, in a flagrantly pictorial or metaphorical way.

There are still a good many problems with analogical predication in our talk of God. Here our purpose has been only to separate this kind of discourse from figurative usages; to stretch human terms is not the same as to speak metaphorically on the basis of a model. We must conclude, however, that while not all our talk of God is metaphorical or even figurative, even the most dusty, philosophical things one can say of God, such as that He is infinite or perfect, may have a qualified, analogical status. So Aquinas replies with seeming resignation to the objection that since, etymologically, 'perfect' means 'thoroughly made', we cannot say God is perfect by saying ''What is not made cannot properly be called perfect, but, as Gregory says, *stammering, we echo the heights of God as best we can.*'' (*S.T.*, Ia.4,1)

V

METAPHOR AND 'WORDS PROPER'

M A N alone amongst creatures is subject to Absurdity, says Thomas Hobbes,

And of men, those are of all most subject to it, that professe Philosophy. For it is most true that *Cicero* sayth of them somewhere; that there can be nothing so absurd, but may be found in the books of Philosophers.

For this absurdity Hobbes gives seven reasons, the sixth of which is: "The use of Metaphors, Tropes, and other Rhetoricall figures, in stead of words proper."[1]

Hobbes is by no means alone in critically opposing metaphor to 'words proper'. This distinction and ones similar to it are so common in both our philosophical tradition and our habit of speech that any attempt to rehabilitate metaphor for critical purposes must battle against the categorizations unwittingly reinforced by linguistic custom. One often hears, and not just from the philosophers, talk of 'mere metaphor' or of something being 'only metaphorical' or 'only metaphorically true', or in contradistinction, 'literally true'.

The low regard in which Hobbes and early empiricists such as Locke held metaphor within the texts of philosophy was scarcely reversed by early-twentieth-century accounts of meaning. The tendency of those influenced by logical positivism to speak of empirically testable statements as those possessing 'literal meaning' (as opposed to figurative or emotive meaning) reinforced the tendency to view figurative speech as the very junior partner to 'words proper'. Even since the discrediting of logical positivist treatments of meaning, we find in the writings of linguistic philosophers such as J. L. Austin a distinction between 'serious' or 'normal' use of language, and 'parasitic uses', with the suggestion that metaphor, like jokes, falls into the latter category.[2] The same judgement is implicit in recent studies which treat metaphors as instances of 'semantic deviance'.

'Literal' and 'metaphorical' becomes a distinction of special pertinence to our study when it is further held to imply a distinction between kinds of significance or kinds of truth. The student of religion soon runs across the distinction between literal (empirically respectable) language and metaphorical (emotive and decorative) language, a distinction used for the most part uncritically by the foes and friends of theism alike; so A. J. Ayer says that,

> to say that 'God exists' is to make a metaphysical utterance which cannot be either true or false. And by the same criterion, no sentence which purports to describe the nature of a transcendent god can possess any literal significance. [3]

On the other side we find in the writings of the friends of religion talk of the ''metaphorical truth of the ascension'', or of the Beatific Vision being ''more than a metaphor'' or of the language of transcendence as losing its original mythic value and becoming ''mere metaphor''. [4] Clearly there is a good deal about the relationship of metaphor to 'words proper' which should be sorted out.

Amongst the common assumptions grouped around the distinction between literal and metaphorical which we shall consider are the following: that there is a sort of 'metaphorical meaning'; that there is a kind of 'metaphorical truth' which is distinguishable from and inferior to 'literal truth'; that language deceives us by means of dead metaphors which covertly suggest to us pre-scientific modes of thought; that metaphor has its origins in myth and that it is a mode peculiar to primitive peoples who are unable to distinguish the literal from the metaphorical; that each metaphor has two meanings, a literal meaning and a metaphorical one, and that correspondingly every metaphor is simultaneously both metaphorically true and literally false, and, finally, that a metaphor, if it is to be credited with cognitive significance, should always be reducible without loss to a literal statement. To facilitate discussion of this rather loosely linked body of assumptions it will be convenient to discuss the literal/metaphorical distinction from two perspectives, the historical or diachronic, and the synchronic. But first we should make some remarks on two phrases that recur throughout the chapter, namely, 'metaphorical meaning' and 'metaphorical truth'.

Literal senses of words can be given apart from instances of use—this is what makes the dictionary possible. But we have already shown that the locus of metaphor is not the word but the complete speech act. There could be no dictionary of metaphorical senses for words because words do not have metaphorical senses in themselves and only participate in the production of meaning at the level of complete utterance. Although we tend to oppose 'metaphorical' to 'literal', a better opposite to 'literal speech' is 'non-literal speech', a category encompassing a wide range of speech phenomena including the use of most tropes and many prose forms such as irony, satire, and allegory. So Bach and Harnish point out that 'Mac is a fine friend' uttered with intended insincerity is a non-literal utterance; the speaker intends it that way and the hearer understands it that way. Similarly, in the right context and with the right intonation a statement like 'I will return' can be used non-literally as a threat. Performative verbs, too, can be used non-literally—'I promise to pay you back'.[5] None of these are metaphorical usages, but all are non-literal. Metaphors can for the most part be regarded as non-literal speech, although, as we shall see, there may be some ambiguity over dead metaphors such as 'running water' and 'vicious circle' which, while having literal applications are discernibly metaphorical in origin.

We should note here that literal and non-literal are not determined at the level of word-meaning but at the level of complete utterance. There are many ways in which a speaker can provoke a non-literal construal from his hearer, for example, by means of intonation, by the incongruity of his remark if construed literally, or by oddity of predication. We will not develop these points any further here as they regard all non-literal speech and take us far from what particularly concerns metaphor. As a shorthand, we shall say that literal speech is accustomed speech and proceed on the basis of that. We also speak, for brevity's sake, of 'metaphors' or 'metaphorical utterances' where the reader should understand that we mean these utterances as they occur in complete contexts of speech.

In a great many but not all metaphorical utterances, metaphorical construal is precipitated by oddities of predication; but it is unhelpful, as William Alston has pointed out, to think in terms of literal and metaphorical as types of meaning. "The confusion thickens", he says, "when it is supposed that 'literal meaning' is respectable meaning, as opposed to what is indifferently labelled 'emotive meaning', or 'metaphorical meaning'."[6] Even if we were to limit meaningfulness to statements that were referential, it could not be doubted that 'he knit his brow' is, in context, as effective referentially as 'he caused wrinkles to appear on his brow'. To say, then, that an utterance is a metaphor is to make a comment on its form and is not to say that it has a particular and questionable 'metaphorical meaning'. This is most important, as is a related point about 'metaphorical truth'. A given truth may be expressed by a metaphor, may perhaps only be expressed by using the metaphor, but this is not to say that it exemplifies a sort of 'metaphorical truth' distinguishable from and inferior to 'literal truth'. We may warn someone, 'Watch out! That's a live wire', but even if we think wires are not literally 'live' we do not add 'but of course that is only metaphorically true'. It is true and it is expressed with the use of a metaphor.

The phrase 'metaphorically true' should be used with qualification, if at all. Consider this statement from David Stacey's *Interpreting the Bible*: "No orthodox Christian of today would surrender the *metaphorical truth* of the ascension, but the mythology that holds the metaphor cannot now command respect."[7] (my emphasis.) I believe that Stacey here is trying to caution his readers about the special kind of *language* of ascension, but it sounds as though he is cautioning them about its special kind of *truth*. Here lies the opportunity for confusion, and for the critic to say that such 'metaphorical truth' seems like 'no truth at all'; so Paul Edwards says in criticism of Tillich:

The concession by an author that he is using a certain word metaphorically is tantamount to admitting that, in a very important sense and a sense relevant to the questions at issue between metaphysicians and their critics, he does not mean what he says.[8]

But again, to say that a statement is metaphorical is a comment on its manner of expression and not necessarily on the truth of that which is expressed. To say 'He is suffering from a gnawing pain' is to speak metaphorically, but if it were true, it would be perverse to say that it expressed a 'metaphorical truth'.

Is the distinction between literal and metaphorical then spurious? It cannot be, if the same phrase can be used at one time literally and at another metaphorically (e.g. 'He is down in the dumps.') It is important to see, however, that it is particular *usages* that are literal or metaphorical, and not particular facts. To say an utterance is literal is to say that its terms are being used in an accustomed fashion. We do not imagine that there are two kinds of states of affairs, literal and metaphorical, but we do acknowledge that there may be two (or more) ways of expressing the same state of affairs, e.g. 'He rutted his brow' and 'He wrinkled his brow'. Our idiomatic use of the phrase 'only metaphorically true' does not indicate a special category of metaphorical truths but is a means by which we alert the listener to a possible ambiguity of our utterance. It is similar to saying 'I'm joking' or 'I exaggerate'. Where there is no risk at the time of utterance of being misunderstood (as with Churchill's designation, 'That utensil'), we feel no need to qualify in this way.

1. THE DIACHRONIC PERSPECTIVE: DEAD METAPHOR

Discussion of the literal/metaphorical distinction from the dia-chronic perspective centres on the important topic of dead meta-phor. If we define literal usage as accustomed usage, we see that it is possible to have what initially seems a contradiction: metaphorical usages which are literal speech. Both ordinary and technical lan-guage is littered with usages which we take to have been originally metaphorical, like 'stem of the glass', 'leaf of the book', 'flow of electricity', but which now have no figurative connections for the native speaker. These are commonly called dead metaphors. We have already mentioned (in Chapter One) that such 'transferred' words and phrases were of interest to grammarians in the classical period, some of whom were prompted by the phenomena of dead metaphor to search for, or to contrive, the etymological or 'true' meanings of the words. The extension of language by the incorpor-ation of metaphor which becomes accustomed usage has been a subject of continuing interest to grammarians and linguists; for it is most interesting that, when considering vocabulary and word meaning, language which, when viewed synchronically, seems to be stable, viewed historically, gives evidence of a constant flux. Even the most commonplace words have the most unlikely histories; so the *OED* tells us that the Old French 'nice' meant silly (from the Latin *nescius*, ignorant) and that within English usage the same word has variously meant foolish, stupid, wanton, strange, coy, reluctant, and precise.

Considerations like these led Ferdinand de Saussure to speak of "the arbitrary nature of the sign". This meant, in part, that no innate relationship exists between a given stream of phonemes and what it signifies, but had the wider implication that language *in toto*, by virtue of being conventional, is arbitrary. "In fact,"

Saussure says, "every means of expression in society is based, in principle, on collective behaviour or—what amounts to the same thing—on convention."[9]

The radical mutability of language which Saussure suggested has been called into question by more recent studies of the systematic traits of natural languages. The capacity of native speakers to produce an indefinite number of original yet intelligible sentences has encouraged some linguists, notably Noam Chomsky, to think that language may rest on innate patterns and thus, in an ultimate sense, be systematic. But it remains undeniably the case that the most random and improbable factors influence natural languages, particularly as regards the introduction of new terms. The English 'zany' originated in the *Commedia dell'Arte* where 'Zani' was the dialect diminutive of 'Giovanni', the traditional name of the servant-bufoon, and the unfortunate Captain Boycott has added his name in verb form not only to the English but also to the German and Italian languages (to boycott, *boykottieren, boycottare*).

This is catachresis, an activity in which, as we have already noted, metaphor plays an important part. When an originally metaphorical usage like 'leg of the table' comes to be regarded by speakers of English as a standard usage (becomes 'lexicalized'), it broadens out the accepted, dictionary definition of the term. At this stage, the originally metaphorical usage is a literal and polysemic one.

The transition from life to death can be gradual, and at any time some usages will seem to the native speaker to be more clearly metaphorical than others; so 'running water' and 'vein of minerals' seem further from any original vivacity than 'the heart of the matter' and 'hearing through the grape-vine'. Indeed, the precise point at which a metaphorical usage becomes an accustomed or literal usage cannot easily be established.

The question arises, ought one to regard dead metaphor as metaphor at all? On this, there is some variance of opinion. I. A. Richards treats 'leg of the table' and 'wooden leg' as though both were actively metaphorical. Max Black, on the other hand, says that dead metaphor is not metaphor at all. The distinction between living and dead metaphor, Black says "is no more helpful, than, say, treating a corpse as a special case of a person: a so-called dead metaphor is not a metaphor at all, but merely an expression that no longer has a pregnant metaphorical use".[10]

Neither of these positions is satisfactory: Richards fails to mark the fact that usages become lexicalized, while Black (as well as having questionable views about the status of dead bodies!) gives no regard to the fact that native speakers can, on reflection, detect dead metaphor in their speech. Because they can do so, it is useful to retain the category 'dead metaphor', particularly since it is useful theoretically in other areas.

Three rough guidelines can be given for distinguishing living from dead metaphors. The first is that one recognizes a dissonance or tension in a living metaphor whereby the terms of the utterance used seem not strictly appropriate to the topic at hand: do winds really howl, do poplars sigh? Is Peter really in a stranglehold? This tension varies with the strength of the metaphor. A hackneyed or dead metaphor generates no tension because we are accustomed to its juxtaposition of terms, although it may still be a non-standard juxtaposition. This is illustrated by the occurrence of mixed metaphors like "Jesus was an oasis of calm in a torrent of angry faces" and "All our black sheep have come home to roost". Such usages are so commonplace that we understand the speaker's intention directly; hence mixed metaphor is a sin against eloquence rather than a sin against meaning. A second guideline is the relative ease of paraphrase. The more dead a metaphor the more readily it lends itself to direct and full paraphrase; 'the heart of the matter' is easily redescribed as 'the centre of the issue', but I. A. Richards gives this summary of the more lively metaphor, 'giddy brink':

As the man totters in vertigo, the world spins too and the brink becomes not merely giddy-making but actually vertiginous, seems itself to stagger with a dizziness and to whirl with a bewildering rapidity.[11]

Finally, the most important means by which one distinguishes dead from living metaphor, and both from non-metaphorical speech, concerns the relationship of metaphor to model. An originally vital metaphor calls to mind, directly or indirectly, a model or models so that when one says 'the wind howled about the eaves' there is a suggestion that the wind, like a dog or a madman, howls. As the metaphor becomes commonplace, its initial web of implications becomes, if not entirely lost, then difficult to recall.

The fact that some metaphors pass gradually from being alive to being dead does not preclude the possibility that others are from their inception dead or at least short-lived. This is particularly the case with metaphors devised to fill lexical gaps, such as 'head of the hammer' and 'teeth of the saw'. These short-lived metaphors are closely related to what we called analogy, but in the case of short-lived metaphor the usage is seen to be derived from another domain of application; an analogical usage, on the other hand, is deemed to be consistent with others in the original domain of application. Analogy, as we are using the term, is not model-related.

The link, however vestigial, of a dead metaphor to a model is a further good reason for regarding dead metaphor as being in some sense still metaphor. It is precisely the relationship of dead metaphors to models that is most interesting about them. When we reflect that to describe a social or political situation as one in which 'pressure is mounting', or 'there is a need to let off steam', is to rely on language suggestive of the steam-boiler, it seems to us that this model has been latent in our consideration of the matters at hand. So, too, might Michael Walzer's Puritan saints have been influenced by the talk of 'ship of State' into their radical interpretation of the individual's duties to the state. It may sometimes seem to us that dead metaphor has brought into our language, and into our habits of thought, a structuring of experience of which we are for the most part unaware. The phenomenon of dead metaphors 'coming to life' and surprising us by their implications corroborates our claim that metaphor and model are closely linked. It is the hidden or unacknowledged models they suggest which sometimes disturb us over dead metaphor, whereas 'dead' metonymies like 'shoe horn' (from the days when these were made of horn) or dead synecdoches like 'the kettle is boiling' (instead of 'the water in the kettle is boiling') may interest us, but disturb us not at all.

The idea that our thought is moulded by language and particularly by the dead metaphors within it gives rise to a perennially compelling thesis about the relationship of metaphor to thought which, inasmuch as it may be strangely attractive to the theologian, we shall discuss. This can be called the 'strong metaphor' theory; it has had proponents as diverse as Giambattista Vico, Bruno Snell, Owen Barfield, and Jacques Derrida. Those who put forward the strong metaphor thesis characteristically are struck by the ubiquity of dead metaphor and derive from this certain conclusions about the nature of thought, or about the history and nature of human consciousness itself. Some make the more radical claim that the human world is one constructed by and perceived through a language which is a tissue of dead and misleading images.

Strong metaphor theorists are impressed, as were the Greek grammarians, with etymologies and see in these not merely histories of words but a history of human consciousness. One of the most impressive and substantial studies in this vein is Bruno Snell's *The Discovery of the Mind*. Here he suggests that

the rise of thinking among the Greeks was nothing less than a revolution. They did not, by means of a mental equipment already at their disposal, merely map out new subjects for discussion . . . They discovered the human mind.[12]

He goes on to argue that this discovery was inseparable from the devising of metaphorical terms to denominate the life of the mind, for one cannot speak of the intellectual or the spiritual without falling back on metaphor. So in the Greek language

At first the mind is understood by analogy with the physical organs and their functions; the *psyche* is the breath . . . the *thymos* is the organ of internal (e)motion, and the *nous* is the mind in its capacity as an absorber of images. Knowledge (*eidenai*) is the state of having seen; recognition (*gignoskein*) is associated with sight, understanding (*synienai*) with hearing, know-how (*epistasthai*) with practical ability.[13]

Once these distinctions were made, they were readily passed down into the modern European languages in the forms we know today. In a very real way, then, the history of consciousness is bound up with metaphor.

The thesis that a certain historical primacy must be accorded to metaphorical speech is by no means new. A view (first credited to Vico) is that, despite the common assumption that metaphorical speech is an ornamental accretion on an original literal underlay, in fact, the metaphorical is chronologically prior and only gradually gave place to what we call 'literal' description. The metaphors and figures which primitive men used are not, for Vico, mere embellishments on a literal description of rocks, trees, and battles which otherwise resembles our own, but are indicators of a wholly different way of seeing the world; a world in which blood is actually boiled, winds whistled and waves murmured.[14] Owen Barfield has argued along similar lines against a thesis (which he attributes to Herbert Spencer and Max Müller) that primitive man saw things much as we do, named the objects about him, applied these names for physical things figuratively to describe his inner life, then fell into myth by mistakenly taking his own metaphors literally. Against this, Barfield suggests that what we know of the origins of language gives us little reason to suppose that language was ever pre-metaphorical. Primitive man, rather than having general notions like 'to shine' which could then be applied figuratively to spring-time or to hymns of praise, would, in fact, lack the non-figurative, established senses of terms which make a distinction between literal and metaphorical possible. [15]

What is of indisputable value in these arguments, particularly those of Snell and Vico, is the recognition that the intellectual world we inhabit is, to a great extent, of our own construction and that our medium of that construction is language. Isaiah Berlin summarizes Vico's intuition in this way.

Much of his genetic etymology and philology is clearly faulty or naïve or fantastic. But it is equally clear that he was, so far as I know, the first to grasp the seminal and revolutionary truth that linguistic forms are one of the keys to the minds of those who use words, and indeed to the entire mental, social and cultural life of societies. He saw much more clearly than anyone before him . . . that a particular type of locution, the use and structure of a language, has a necessary, 'organic' connection with par-ticular types of political and social structure, of religion, of law, of economic life, of morality, of theology, of military organization, and so on. [16]

Described in this way, Vico's approach would seem to be the forerunner not only of modern analytic philosophy of language but also of modern phenomenological accounts of language. As James Edie puts it, Vico was the first to recognize that minds are formed by language and not language by minds. [17]

More difficult to corroborate and of less certain value is the related thesis that the primitive inhabits a world of images and figures where distinction between the literal and the figurative in language is neither useful nor possible. This thesis is particularly questionable when applied, as it has been by Frederick Ferré, to the figurative religious language of the Old Testament. "The explicit recognition of metaphor as metaphor . . ." Ferré writes, "logically presupposes some structured beliefs or theory about what may and

may not be considered 'literally appropriate' modes of representation when applied to religious subject matter.''[18] This distinction,
he maintains, was first reached explicitly by the Greeks. By contrast:

The Bible, as Western civilisation's principal religious book, illustrates the
pervasiveness of unselfconcious imagery—only later to be distinguished as
metaphor—in primary or non-theoretical religious discourse. There can be
no fixed boundaries delineating what is 'image' from what is not . . .[19]

Ferré gives us as examples of 'unselfconscious imagery' in the Old
Testament Amos's personification of Israel as a young woman,
Hosea's depiction of God as a compassionate herdsman and of Israel
as an adulterous wife, Jeremiah's description of God as a fountain of
living water, a husband, a father, a planter of good seed and so on.
In apocalyptic literature such as the Book of Daniel, we find,
according to Ferré, the end of unselfconscious religious imagery and
the emergence of a conscious distinction between literal and metaphorical which gives evidence of a Hellenized Palestine.[20]
    This last illustration is used by Ferré to support his thesis that the
ability to distinguish between literal and metaphorical religious
language arose with the advent of the critical consciousness of the
Greeks, for, ''Only when there is a theory about what is 'literally so'
can there be explicit recognition of oblique, allegorical, symbolic—
in a word, metaphorical—alternative uses of significant forms.''
(p. 203) Ferré's suggestion that Old Testament imagery through to the
apocalyptic literature is unselfconscious in this way would be more
convincing had he not taken among his examples figurative descriptions of God ('compassionate herdsman', 'planter of good seed'
and so on). It is difficult to believe that the prophets, although
perhaps lacking a developed set of grammatical distinctions which
enabled them to designate metaphors as metaphors, were unaware
that in speaking of God as a herdsman or planter they were using
language not strictly appropriate to him. Long before Heleniz-
ation, the God of Israel was known as a Deity beyond human
conceiving. The proliferation of imagery used by Prophets and
Psalmists to denote the God of Israel is evidence, surely, not of a
failure to discriminate between language literally appropriate or
inappropriate to God, but of the realization that no image could be
adequate to 'I AM WHO I AM'. (Exodus 3:14). To suggest that the
Hebrews were unconscious of figuration in their religious writings

prior to Hellenization is to imply a cultural psychologism for which we have insufficient evidence.

It is a short step from recognition of the place of metaphor in the history of thought to the idea that metaphors represent concealed myths in everyday speech. Perhaps no thesis concerning metaphor has received such dramatic treatment as this one, and nowhere is there more need for moderation than in one's estimation of it. The thesis is most strikingly stated by Nietzsche:

What therefore is truth? A mobile army of metaphors, metonymies, anthropomorphisms: in short a sum of human relations which became poetically and rhetorically intensified, metamorphosed, adorned, and after long usage seem to a nation fixed, canonic and binding: truths are illusions of which one has forgotten that they *are* illusions; worn-out metaphors which have become powerless to affect the senses; coins which have their obverse effaced and now are no longer of account as coins but merely as metal. [21]

For Nietzsche, it is not metaphors which are the villains of the piece, but the human tendency to view one's own manner of categorizing as "fixed, canonic and binding", as the one true account of truth.

While Nietzsche revels in this power of language to undercut our pretensions to certainty, others have warned us against being misled by dead metaphor in our speech. Some writers on metaphor have regarded Wittgenstein's *Philosophical Investigations* as a source for admonitions of this kind, particularly the passages where he speaks of the ways in which we can be misled when doing philosophy by our grammar, by pictures which lie in language and hold us captive by continually repeating themselves to us. This kind of argument is particularly successful when applied to our grammar concerning inner states; so when the philosopher says,

'I can only *believe* that someone else is in pain, but I *know* it if I am' . . . What looks like an explanation here, or like a statement about a mental process, is in truth an exchange of one expression for another which, while we are doing philosophy, seems the more appropriate one. [22]

And in *The Concept of Mind*, Gilbert Ryle cautions us in terms reminiscent of Wittgenstein's that:

The phrase 'in the mind' can and should always be dispensed with. Its use habituates its employers to the view that minds are queer 'places', the occupants of which are special-status phantasms. [23]

Our language gives us certain pictures of how things are which, when we are doing philosophy, suggests 'this must be so'.

It must be stressed that it was not Wittgenstein's object to criticize metaphor. Metaphor, as a common feature of ordinary language, is unobjectionable. It was aspects of our ordinary grammar (for instance, the grammar of the first person singular) which interested him, and his criticism fell on those philosophers (e.g. Cartesians) who were bewitched by our grammar into improbable claims about the nature of the 'I'. Yet Wittgenstein's comments have been represented as criticisms specifically of metaphor; one of Ryle's disciples, Colin Turbayne, has devoted a book, *The Myth of Metaphor*, to the task of warning us of the dangers of dead and hidden metaphor. He treats these as a species of Ryle's 'category-mistake'; an allocating of concepts "to logical types to which they do not belong".[24] According to Turbayne, "The use of metaphor involves the pretence that something is the case when it is not" and, although it is not objectionable to "cross sort" in this way, it is objectionable to be unaware that one is doing so.[25] "There is", he says, "a difference between using a metaphor and being used by it, between using a model and mistaking the model for the thing modeled".[26] We are being used by a model when we say that sounds *are* vibrations and that the body *is* a machine.

The victim of metaphor accepts one way of sorting or bundling or allocating the facts as the only way to sort, bundle, or allocate them . . . He is thus, unknowingly, a metaphysician.[27]

Turbayne's thesis is already over-strong in regarding metaphors as category mistakes, and in its latent assumption that our 'literal' categories are rigidly fixed by the empirical facts (Paul Ricoeur rightly remarks on the "ultimately neo-empiricist character" of Turbayne's thesis).[28] But his position is taken a step further into absurdity by Marc Belth. Belth says that:

Not to recognise metaphors, but to speak or write them is to be used by those metaphors and to be entangled in them. To recognise them is to use them, consciously alert to the influence and consequences of their use . . . Indeed, a dead metaphor, a metaphor transferred into a literal statement is clearly mythic.[29]

This is the admonitory thesis at its extreme, where behind each dead metaphor ('tongue' of the shoe, 'flow' of conversation, 'corner' of the world) lurks a deceptive myth. To be "consciously alert" to all dead metaphor would more likely be a sign of madness than of intellectual rigour.

At this stage, the admonitory thesis of the metaphor-as-myth comes closely to resemble the anarchic view of Nietzsche and of modern writers influenced by him. It is important to remember, however, that Nietsche does not so much caution against being deceived by the occasional dead metaphor in otherwise represent-ational speech as proclaim the more radical thesis that all language, and indeed all 'truth', is but a tissue of dead and faded images. Man only deceives himself when he regards his own linguistic constructs as embodying some trans-anthropological truth. Escape to a purer, strictly representational language is not even possible; at most, one can revel in the fact that man, like the spider, spins out of himself the world which he inhabits.

Nietzsche's theme is picked up by Jacques Derrida in 'The White Mythology' where, in discussing metaphor in the 'text' of philoso-phy, Derrida argues that there is a sensible figure behind each metaphysical use. After their introduction, the original displace-ment of metaphorical terms in philosophy is forgotten and the new meaning is taken as the proper one; they become Nietzsche's effaced coins. In this context, Derrida quotes the progressive etymologizing by Anatole France of the metaphysical claim that

The spirit possesses God in proportion as it participates in the absolute.

This becomes progressively

The breath is seated on the shining one in the bushel of the part it takes in what is altogether loosed (or *subtle*)

and finally, until it "has acquired quite the ring of some fragment of a Vedic hymn",

He whose breath is a sign of life, man, that is, will find a place . . . in the divine fire, source and home of life, and this place will be meted out to him according to the virtue that has been given him . . . of sending abroad this warm breath, this little invisible soul, across the free expanse . . .[30]

The metaphysicians, France concludes, live in a world of allegory, "they produce white mythology".

We cannot here individually assess these various theses about metaphor-as-myth, coming as they do from different philosophical traditions and tending to different ends, but we can provide some general guide to their assessment. One of the most interesting things about the metaphor-as-myth thesis is that, despite its actual antiquity, it is invariably presented as a new and startling theory concerning the victimization of thought by language. One of the most recent books to present it in this way is George Lakoff's and Mark Johnson's *Metaphors We Live By*, which argues that metaphor forms the implicit and unrecognized structure of most ·human life. [31] It is tempting to think that a thesis which remains perpetually youthful in this way is probably one which, for good reasons, has not been more widely taken up; but there are things to be said both for and against it. Carried to an extreme, it is in danger of falling into the fallacy, criticized by James Barr in *The Semantics of Biblical Language*, of confusing word derivation with word meaning. Word meaning, modern linguistics stresses, is properly understood synchronically; few present-day speakers of English know that 'ancillary' derives from the Latin term for a serving maiden, yet they may none the less understand perfectly the current meaning of the term. Similarly, it is absurd to think that one misunderstands the 'true' meaning of 'dandelion' if one does not know of its origins in '*dent-de-lion*', or of 'malaria' because one fails to associate it with '*mal aria*', bad air. Etymologizing such as that of Anatole France is spurious if it puts itself forward as the 'true' meaning of the terms, for, as Barr has pointed out, "the etymology of a word is not a statement about its meaning but about its history". [32] Of course, advocates of the metaphor-as-myth thesis do not usually exemplify their claim with etymologies of terms like 'dandelion' and 'malaria' but with terms like 'ingenious' and 'intellect', the assumption presumably being that, while the designation of 'dandelion' can be specified ostensively, with abstractions one is at the mercy of the original metaphor. But there is little reason to suppose that the current meaning of abstract terms like 'intellect' or 'consciousness' is any less rooted in synchronic practice than that of concrete ones. 'Matrimony' may derive etymologically from 'the making of mothers', but this historical fact is of limited value in determining the current significance of the term. [33]

There is need for balance. The histories of words and their figurative origins provide interesting information about the form-ation and growth of abstract concepts, but the thesis goes too far when all dead metaphors are represented as mythic structures or, alternatively, when it is suggested that each man's world is determined by the metaphors his language forces upon him. What the Germans call 'laden bread' (*belegtes Brot*) the Americans call 'open-faced sandwiches'; does this display a difference of ontology whereby what the one culture sees as bread with something extra, the other sees as a sandwich with something missing?

A final criticism of the extreme metaphor-as-myth thesis is this: if it is the case that our thought is directed by our language (and in some sense this must be so), this is no less true of so-called literal language than it is of metaphorical. For example, talk of the sun 'rising' is not dead metaphor but superseded literal description, as is our mention of 'high spirits', 'low spirits' and 'depression', all of which derive from the Vital Spirits theory about the blood. To single out metaphor as the particular culprit in this bewitchment of our intelligence by means of language is to miss Wittgenstein's more subtle suggestion that, when we are doing philosophy, we are easily misled by the pictures which all our language presents to us, not just our figurative language, but also literal usages of terms like 'know', 'believe', 'intend', and 'pain'. Wittgenstein is not criticizing ordinary language but the tendency of philosophers to generate philosophical conundrums out of what are unproblematic forms of language use.

Labelling is certainly not always value-neutral, but again this is not the problem of dead metaphor alone but of all descriptive language; to 'reform' the alcoholic from his vice is different from 'curing' him of an illness; to 'modernize the old town' is different from 'destroying' it; we may accept the bombing of 'strategic hamlets' or 'nests of terrorists', and express our distress at the bombing of 'peasant villages' and 'refugee camps'. Even when we restrict ourselves to literal speech, we are by no means out of the danger of being misled by our categories.

If it is the case that we are to fear metaphors, then the metaphors we should fear are not the dead but the living; for these, in virtue of their close relation to models, can influence the way we sort and categorize states of affairs. As George Eliot says:

It is astonishing what a different result one gets by changing the metaphor! Once call the brain an intellectual stomach, and one's ingenious conception of the classics and geometry as ploughs and harrows seems to settle nothing. But then, it is open to someone else to follow great authorities and call the mind a sheet of white paper or a mirror, in which case one's knowledge of the digestive process becomes quite irrelevant. [34]

To summarize: in our discussion of 'literal' and 'metaphorical' from the diachronic perspective, we have argued that what we call 'literal' usage is accustomed usage and that metaphorical usages which begin their careers outside the standard lexicon may gradually become lexicalized. These are 'dead metaphors', and in cases where one can detect metaphorical origin, it is still useful to speak of these as being in some sense still metaphors. The association of dead metaphors with superseded models has given rise to a number of theses concerning the place of metaphor in the history of consciousness. Such theories, while not without merit, must not overlook the fact that word meaning is a different matter from word derivation, and one should take care not to attribute to metaphor alone qualities which characterize all descriptive language.

2. THE SYNCHRONIC PERSPECTIVE

(A) Do words have metaphorical meanings?

Literal senses for words can be given apart from contexts of use, but what of metaphorical meanings? We have said that it is misguided to regard metaphor as an expression in which some words are used metaphorically and, in our discussion of 'literal' and 'metaphorical', we have tried to treat the latter as an aspect of word use and the complete utterance in which, of course, the senses of its composite terms are amongst the most important factors. This is to avoid any suggestion that words for which we can specify the literal senses may, in addition, 'possess' a set of metaphorical senses.

Even the determination of the literal senses of words is not as straightforward as at first it might seem, for the same word can have a number of literal senses. We are not speaking here of homonymy, instances of several words which have the same shape (for example, the 'mail' which is armour and the 'mail' which is post), but of polysemy, cases where the same word has a number of related yet different senses. F. R. Palmer lists the following polysemic and literal senses of 'flight': 'passing through the air', 'power of flying', 'air journey', 'Unit of the Air Force', 'volley', 'digression', and 'series of steps'. [35] At a given time, it may be difficult to determine whether a particular usage is properly regarded as embodying one of the lexicalized and literal senses of the term in question or whether it is a figurative usage. For example, according to the *OED*, one of the standard readings for 'language' is the set of symbols and rules which are devised for programming a computer; this shows that, in the view of their lexicographers at least, 'computer language' is now a literal usage in English. Of course, this flexibility does not mean that we cannot specify literal senses for words, but only that these change over time. The mutability of literal senses does pose a problem for some accounts of metaphor, for if one assumes that literal senses and literal truth conditions can readily be assigned to words and sentences independent of contexts of use, then inability to specify precise literal senses of terms will block any exhaustive description of a natural language. The flexibility of a natural language will be at odds with the demands of formal theory.

But, to return to 'metaphorical meanings', even when one can specify literal senses of terms it is of doubtful value to treat metaphor as aberrant word sense. Consider the use of 'charged' in 'She *charged* the servants to bring his head on a platter', and 'The north wind *charged* the trees to drop their leaves'. The second would presumably be the kind of case in which 'charged' had a metaphorical sense, but if one could speak in terms of word sense alone, 'charged' has much the same sense in both these statements; in both it could be replaced with the synonyms 'commanded' or 'ordered that'. The difference seems to lie not so much in the sense of the isolated term 'charged', but in the oddity of its being predicated of the wind. While it is possible to specify literal senses for terms, metaphorical meaning pertains not to the individual terms but to the complete utterance.

(B) Does each metaphor have two meanings?

At the level of utterance, where we should properly consider the meaning of a metaphor, we find yet another thesis about literal and metaphorical, namely that every metaphor has at the same time a literal meaning and a metaphorical one. Sometimes it is suggested that the tension that characterizes metaphor is the tension between these two readings. This 'dual meanings' thesis arises at the intuitive level because many metaphors, particularly those of the much favoured 'A is B' kind, are ambiguous out of context, and this prompts the thought that certain uses of a sentence like 'Her ears were seashells' contains two meanings—one literal (and false), the other metaphorical (and true). To show how unhelpful this 'two meanings' thesis is we need only notice that with many metaphors, indeed many of the most interesting ones, the alternative to understanding them as metaphors is not to understand them literally but to fail to make sense of them at all. Consider the passage already cited from Virginia Woolf's *The the Lighthouse*:

Never did anyone look so sad. Bitter and black, halfway down, in the darkness, in the shaft which ran from the sunlight to the depths perhaps a tear formed; a tear fell; the waters swayed this way and that, received it, and were at rest. Never did anybody look so sad.

There are not two meanings here, one literal and one metaphorical, but one meaning; the alternative is nonsense. Either we understand this passage as a metaphor or we do not understand it.

The thesis that each metaphor has two meanings rests on a confusion between what the speaker says (the words and sentences he or she uses) and what the speaker intends by uttering them within a particular context. Usually, a speaker has one intended meaning for an utterance—otherwise speech would be impossibly ambiguous. So, given the presumed context in which the remark is appropriate, a speaker who says 'Her ears were seashells' intends a remark about his loved one's ears, and intends that this should be evident to the hearer from the context of utterance. By the time the hearer has recognized an utterance as metaphorical, he has normally grasped the speaker's intention and his (single) meaning.

It is true that a particular sentence ('Her eyes are sapphires') may bear two construals, a literal one and a metaphorical one. But this only points to the ambiguity of the sentence prior to full consideration of its context. Many sentences have two or more literal construals; consider 'The chicken is ready to eat'. In a metaphor, as in a non-metaphorical ambiguity, the hearer must infer from the wider context what the speaker intends, that is, what the speaker means in making this utterance. The meaning is under-determined at the level of sentence alone. We do not say in the case of non-metaphorical ambiguity that the speaker has two meanings in mind, one that a particular chicken is hungry and wants feeding, and another that a chicken is in the oven and is now ready to be consumed. Characteristically, the speaker means one or the other and the context of utterance makes this clear. The same is true for metaphor.

All this has a bearing on the claim that metaphorical statements are simultaneously true and false, what we might call the thesis of 'dual truth'. Nelson Goodman says this:

The oddity is that metaphorical truth is compatible with literal falsity; a sentence false when taken literally may be true when taken metaphorically, as in the case of 'The joint is jumping' or 'The lake is a sapphire'.[36]

This does not indicate an oddity about metaphor but rather the oddity of considering sentences apart from any context of utterance, and Goodman's comment trades on the fact that he provides no context for his two examples.

It is confusing to speak about truth and falsity here. Any number of claims might be made with regard to the sentence 'The lake is a sapphire'. Apart from the context, we do not even know if the speaker might be speaking of an actual lake or of a mosaic composed of precious stones in which the depicted lake is a piece of sapphire. The truth and falsity of the particular claim made (whether literal or metaphorical) can only be assessed at the level of complete utterance, taking context into consideration. Once we understand the claim to be metaphorical, we can make a judgement as to its accuracy. Our construal of 'She's an old battleship' as metaphor is prior to our decision as to whether the intended claim is true or false, and the considerations we use to assess its truth will be roughly of the same sort as those we use for assessing a literal statement. In an important sense, then, the truth or falsity of the metaphorical claim can be assessed only at the level of intended meaning. Thus Aquinas has reason when he says that the literal sense (*sensus litteralis*) of Scripture is its intended sense: "When Scripture speaks of the arm of God, the literal sense is not that he has a physical limb, but that he has what it signifies, namely the power of doing and making."[37] By this means Aquinas was able to argue that, despite its figurative nature, Scripture is 'literally' true since, in his terms, "the metaphorical sense of a metaphor is then its literal sense, so also the parabolic sense of a story".[38] In this sense, the literal truth of Scripture would not preclude but necessitate critical exegesis and hermeneutical analysis.

In *The Rule of Metaphor*, Paul Ricoeur comes perilously close to committing himself to both a 'dual sense' and a 'dual truth' thesis such as the ones that we have just argued against. Since Ricoeur's work has been so influential, his thesis deserves comment at some length here, although some readers may wish to pass on to the next section. His discussion comes in the chapter 'Metaphor and Reference' where, in an ambitious thesis directed primarily to considerations of sense, truth, and reference in the literary work, and derivatively from that to metaphor, he suggests that metaphor is characterized by a duality of reference. His working hypothesis is that the Fregean distinction between sense and reference, applied by Frege most strictly to proper names, should hold in principle for all discourse (p. 217). So he moves from the sense and the reference of proper names, to sense and reference of propositions ("The sense is what the proposition states; the reference or denotation is that *about which* the sense is stated."), (p. 217), to discourse in general where "what is intended by discourse (*l'intente*) points to an extra-linguistic reality which is its referent". (p. 216.)

Having established this very broad use of the terms "sense" and "reference", Ricoeur proposes what he takes to be the Fregean tenet that "the question of reference is always opened by that of sense". (p. 217.) But he wishes to go further than Frege, for whereas Frege suggests that fictional terms have sense without having reference, Ricoeur wishes to formulate for the literary work a second postulate of reference whereby "every sense calls for reference or denotation" (p. 221). His theory is that in the work of fiction primary reference is suspended but, through this suspension, the work achieves a secondary reference. Hence, his second formulation of the postulate of reference is that

the literary work through structure proper to it displays a world only under condition that the reference of descriptive discourse is suspended. Or, to put it another way, discourse in the literary work sets out its denotation as a second-level denotation by means of the suspension of the first-level denotation of discourse.[39]

It is in terms of this suspension of reference that metaphor is introduced for

Just as the metaphorical statement captures its sense amidst the ruins of the literal sense, it also achieves its reference upon the ruins of what might be called (in symmetrical fashion) its literal reference. If it is true that literal sense and metaphorical sense are distinguished and articulated within an interpretation, so too it is within an interpretation that a second-level reference, which is properly the metaphorical reference, is set free by means of the suspension of the first-level reference.[40]

Ricoeur goes on to develop, on the basis of his notion of split reference, a 'tensional' conception of metaphorical truth. Metaphor is an expression that says both 'it is' and 'it is not':

Let us keep the notion of *split reference* in mind, as well as the wonderful 'It was and it was not', which contains *in nuce* all that can be said about metaphorical truth.[41]

The paradox of a metaphorical concept of truth, he says,

consists in the fact that there is no other way to do justice to the notion of a metaphorical truth than to include the critical incision of the (literal) 'is not' within the ontological vehemence of the (metaphorical) 'is'.[42]

Ricoeur has now built up a considerable edifice of dualities pertaining to the one metaphorical statement; literal and metaphorical sense give rise to literal and metaphorical reference, and these are paralleled by literal and metaphorical truth. But this edifice collapses if, as we have suggested in Chapter 3, plurality at the level of significance (a plurality of associative networks) is compatible with a unity of referential intent. To say that the question of reference is opened by that of sense does not mean that it is necessarily determined by sense. At the level of utterance, it is the speakers who, by means of the words they use, and any number of conversational ploys (pointing, for instance) determine reference. At this level, and this is the level of metaphorical interpretation, 'Her ears are seashells' has one reference, namely the ears spoken of as seashells.

Whatever the merit of Ricoeur's schema of split reference with regard to the literary work, it is a puzzling doctrine when applied to metaphor. It is in a sense true that a metaphorical interpretation is the consequence of the inability or reluctance of the hearer to construe an utterance literally, but this does not entail, except in a trivial sense, the existence for each metaphor of a literal, but unsuccessful, meaning. Ricoeur seems aware of this when he speaks of the literal sense as 'shattered' or 'impossible', but then, by some sleight of hand, he introduces an 'impossible literal reference' to correspond to the hypostatized impossible literal sense. It must be said, however, that just as the alternative to the metaphorical meaning is not the stand-by literal meaning, but absurdity, so the alternative to the reference made by metaphor is not its (shattered) literal reference but no reference at all. The metaphor 'The lake is a sapphire' does not refer to some lake and some sapphire too, but simply to the lake which is described as a sapphire.

Ricoeur's suggestion that the tension of metaphor is ontological is somewhat ambiguous. It is motivated in part by his desire to emphasize the redescriptive powers of metaphor, hence the "critical incision of the (literal) 'is not' within the ontological vehemence of the (metaphorical) 'is'" (p. 255). The most obvious reading of these remarks about redescription and ontological tension is as a restatement of the unsatisfactory (A is a B) 'two-subjects' view that we have criticized in Max Black, thus 'Man is a wolf' and 'Man is not a wolf', 'The lake is a sapphire' and 'The lake is not a sapphire'. Whether or not Ricoeur intends his remarks this way, his discussion of the metaphorical 'is' and 'is not' has been so understood by some writers like Sallie McFague who have been influenced by him. [43] But this approach comes dangerously near to making metaphor a matter of comparison and Ricoeur's use of the term 'redescription' is revealing. The trouble with Black's theory is that, in assuming a two-subjects perspective in which the primary subject (man) is modified by the secondary subject (wolf), he is unable to explain convincingly how metaphors can say something genuinely new. Similarly Ricoeur's language of redescription inevitably suggests comparison because, even when accompanied by talk of an ontological tension, it implies that there is some definite, pre-existing thing (the principal subject of the metaphor in Max Black's terms) that the metaphor is *about* and simply redescribes.

This point deserves emphasis—redescription, however radical, is always *re*-description. The interesting thing about metaphor, or at least about some metaphors, is that they are used not to redescribe but to disclose for the first time. The metaphor has to be used because something new is being talked about. This is Aristotle's 'naming that which has no name' and unless we see it, we shall never get away from a comparison theory of metaphor. Furthermore, we shall never be able to explain what is so radical and new about religious metaphors such as 'Jesus is the lamb of God.' Now Christians do not doubt that the phrase is metaphorical—Jesus was not a young sheep—but this is not to say that the phrase is intended by Christians as only an evocative way of describing an ordinary man. Similarly, for the Christian to say 'Jesus is the son of God' is not merely to say that the man Jesus (principal subject) can

usefully be thought of as a 'son of God' (secondary subject). Rather
we are here stumbling to describe something new and unique—the
divinity of Jesus. The phrases are not redescribing but describing for
the first time.

Consider an even more contentious example, Jesus' phrase 'this
bread is my body'. Is this metaphorical or not? The question is
frequently asked as though one's answer will settle an enormous
theological controversy . . . as though, could we but acknowledge
that phrases such as this one were metaphorical, we would be freed
from the metaphysical difficulties which have troubled centuries of
theological debate. But to think in this way is to fall back into the
ornamentalist theories of metaphor against which we have been
arguing from the beginning of the book. Even a conservative,
catholic Christian could acknowledge that Jesus' phrase 'this is my
body' is, or was, metaphorical but in doing so he would make a
linguistic and not an ontological point. It would be analogous to
acknowledging that the phrase 'there is a strong electrical current
flowing through the wire' is, or was, metaphorical. The point at
issue is not really whether we have metaphor here, but what the
metaphor is doing: is it simply an ornamental redescription, so that
Jesus has redescribed bread in an evocative way? or is the metaphor
genuinely catachretical, not a redescribing but a naming or dis-
closing for the first time? It is one's metaphysics, not metaphor,
which is at issue. To put it another way, the question is not simply
whether we have a metaphor here or not, but what, if anything, the
metaphor refers to or signifies.

We address this most important question of reference in Chapters
Seven and Eight. For the moment we can conclude that the 'is and is
not' thesis discussed above is not only inadequate to explain the
workings of metaphor, but also eliminates the possibility that a
metaphor may be genuinely, even ontologically, novel.

(C) Are all metaphors false?

We have suggested that the idea that each metaphor is simultaneously literally false and metaphorically true lacks plausibility. A
more plausible claim, if considered within the right theoretical
context, is that of Donald Davidson and John Searle that most
metaphors are false.[44] This seems at first to fly in the face of our
insistence that metaphorical format is neutral between the truth
and falsity of the claim made, but the conflict can be seen to be

more apparent than real if we view Davidson's claim in the context of his general views on the theory of meaning.

Davidson maintains that a theory of meaning for sentences should proceed from a theory of truth. In 'Truth and Meaning', Davidson speaks of what he holds to be the

obvious connection between a definition of truth of the kind Tarski has shown how to construct, and the concept of meaning. It is this: the definition works by giving necessary and sufficient conditions for the truth of every sentence, and to give truth conditions is a way of giving the meaning of a sentence.[45]

This desire to ground a theory of meaning in a definition of truth has a number of consequences for Davidson's appraisal of metaphor. In 'What Metaphors Mean', he says that

Literal meaning and literal truth conditions can be assigned to words and sentences apart from particular contexts of use.

and that

as much of metaphor as can be explained in terms of meaning may, and indeed must, be explained by appeal to the literal meanings of words. A consequence is that the sentences in which metaphors occur are true or false in a normal, literal way, for if the words in them don't have special meanings, sentences don't have special truth.[46]

If meanings and truth conditions are established for words and sentences apart from contexts of use, then the only meaning which a metaphorical sentence has, in the strict Davidsonian sense of 'meaning', is its literal meaning. And this means for Davidson that most metaphors (except fatuously true ones like 'no man is an island') are false. Davidson gets around the problem of how it is that these falsehoods 'say' something to us, as we have noted, by arguing that a metaphor does not *say* or *mean* anything apart from its literal meaning: rather it nudges us into noting things.

John Searle, too, in linking meaning to truth conditions is obliged to regard most metaphors as, at the level of sentence meaning, false. Searle, unlike Davidson, freely speaks of the *meaning* of metaphor, but does so by using 'meaning' in two ways: "what the sentence means literally" and what "the speaker means metaphorically".[47] It is important to note that both Searle and Davidson would say that what the *sentence* means is what it means literally, and so would disagree with the suggestion that the same sentence has both a literal and a metaphorical meaning. This insistence by Searle and Davidson on the falsehood of most metaphorical sentences when used metaphorically arises from their desire to preserve a certain truth-conditional theory of meaning for sentences and thus presupposes a different perspective from the one we have taken with regard to the truth of metaphorical utterances.

It is not our task to criticize the truth-conditional theory of meaning here, but we will point out that it yields some odd results when faced with the issue of metaphor and parallel similes (e.g. 'She is like an angel' and 'She is an angel'). For a truth-conditional theory, adding 'like' to a metaphorical sentence makes a crucial difference, for it alters the truth conditions. So Davidson says: ''The most obvious semantic difference between simile and metaphor is that all similes are true and most metaphors are false.''[48] All similes are true, according to Davidson, because every thing is like every other thing, if only trivially. Now the consequence of this position is that, when faced with a metaphor like:

(i) ''Human language is a cracked kettle on which we beat out tunes for bears to dance to, when all the time we are longing to move the stars to pity'',

and Flaubert's actual simile,

(ii) ''Human language is like a cracked kettle on which we beat out tunes for bears to dance to, when all the time we are longing to move the stars to pity'',

Davidson and Searle must say that the first statement is clearly false and the second clearly true. And since the truth conditions for the two statements differ, their meanings do, too. Searle says this explicitly:

the truth conditions, and hence the meaning of the metaphorical statement and the similarity statement are not, in general, the same.[49]

He uses this difference in truth conditions as a ground for rejecting the suggestion that metaphor is elliptical simile:

metaphorical statements cannot be equivalent in meaning to literal statements of similarity because the truth conditions of the two sorts of statements are frequently different.[50]

To others this might seem a better reason for abandoning the truth-conditional theory of meaning itself.

For most native speakers and some distinguished linguists, the semantic purism which prompts theorists to say that most metaphors are false and all similes true is not plausible. [51] For most native speakers of English the difference of meaning between (i) and (ii) above would surely be so slight as to be imperceptible; it is very unlikely that the same (non-philosophical) speaker would say that the difference between them is that (i) is false and (ii) is true. Intuitively we hold that what makes the metaphor 'He's an ogre' true or false is the same as what makes the simile 'He's like an ogre' true or false, and that is, what the man is really like. This does not in itself refute the thesis of Searle and Davidson, for they can reply that they are dealing with the truth and falsity of sentences and with what the sentences mean, and not with what speakers mean or do when using sentences; but in doing so, they would run the risk of seeming somewhat remote from the everyday language whose workings they hope to describe. [52]

3. IRREDUCIBILITY

The last topic we wish to consider under the heading of 'Metaphor and Words Proper' is irreducibility, in particular what have been called 'irreducible religious metaphors'. What has gone before in this chapter gives a hint as to how what is apparently the problem with these metaphors may be resolved.

It is sometimes asserted and more frequently assumed that a metaphor, to be genuinely meaningful, must be reducible without loss to a literal statement. Any metaphor which cannot be so reduced, it is argued, lacks cognitive (referential, assertive) meaning. So Paul Edwards says that

When a sentence contains an irreducible metaphor, it follows at once that the sentence is devoid of cognitive meaning, that it is unintelligible, that it fails to make a genuine assertion. [53]

This quality of irreducibility is judged particularly to inhere in religious metaphor and to constitute part of what is often called the 'logical oddness' of religious language. The complaint usually made is that, as one writer puts it, "religious metaphors should be reducible, but they are not". [54] Edwards's criticism is couched in the

terms of a positivist theory of meaning and in order to assess it we
need to be clear what is meant by 'irreducible metaphor'. Three
notions can be distinguished: the first is that irreducible metaphors
are incorrigibles which are susceptible of no elaboration or explanation whatsoever; the second is that they can only be redescribed in
terms of other metaphors; and the third is that they are metaphors
which purport to be referential, but for which no ostensively
identifiable referent is independently available.

If irreducible metaphors are susceptible of no elaboration whatsoever, Edwards's criticism is valid, but empty. If a passage in a text
resists all attempts to elucidate its meaning, if we can expand on it
or clarify it in no way at all, we should be justified in saying it lacked
significance. But if it were so radically inexplicable, what grounds
would one have for identifying it as metaphor at all? It is characteristic of metaphor to be extendable: to speak of electrical 'current'
suggests that electricity 'flows', is directional, can be stored, etc., or
to say that Jesus is the true vine suggests that life and growth are
possible in union with him, that new branches can be grafted on,
and so on. If no such expansion were possible, we should not
identify the passage as being metaphor. 'Irreducible' metaphors,
then, must be those which can only be redescribed by other
metaphors and/or those which lack independently identifiable
referents. Yet neither of these two traits is restricted to religious
metaphor, for religious phenomena are not the only ones whose
description involves a metaphorical circle. William Alston, for
example, has pointed out the same circularity in language concerning inner states; any redescription of 'stabbing pain' or 'gnawing
pain' is likely to be equally metaphorical, and it is with difficulty
that one searches for a strictly literal paraphrase of 'I see what you
mean' ('I *get* your point', 'I *follow* your argument', or even,
etymologically considered, 'I comprehend'). It does not follow that
such irreducibly metaphorical discourse is thereby unintelligible,
devoid of cognitive meaning, or that it fails to be referential. And as
for eliminating as insignificant any metaphor whose referent was
unspecifiable apart from metaphor, this would eliminate a great
part of physical theory which relies on metaphor and concomitant
models to discuss entities and states of affairs beyond direct observation, a point we shall discuss at length in the following chapters.

There is one kind of irreducibility which all metaphors share by
virtue of their relational nature. No metaphor is completely

reducible to a literal equivalent without consequent loss of content, not even those metaphors for which one can specify an ostensive referent. When we speak of the camel as 'the ship of the desert', the relational irreducibility of the metaphor lies in the potentially limitless suggestions that are evoked by considering the camel on the model of a ship: the implied corollaries of a swaying motion, a heavy and precious cargo, a broad wilderness, a route mapped by stars, distant ports of call, and so on. Saying merely 'camel' does not bring in these associations at all, and the difficulty with the position of those, like Hobbes, who suggest that we should replace our metaphors with 'words proper' is that the words proper do not say what we wish to say. In so far as a metaphor suggests a community of relations (and all active metaphors do), its significance is not reducible to a single atomistic predicate. This same relational irreducibility characterizes other forms of figurative speech common to religious writings and is especially noteworthy in the case of parable. Rather than irreducibility being a flaw, it is one of the marks of the particular conceptual utility of metaphor. The demand for complete redescription is, in fact, a stipulation that only those metaphors which are direct substitutes for literal descriptions (those which are the least interesting and most dispensable sorts of metaphors) have cognitive significance. But there is no particular virtue in literal language for literal language's sake; we may need to use metaphor to say what we mean and particularly so, as Bruno Snell's book demonstrates, when we are seeking terminology to deal with abstract states of affairs, entities, and relations.

In understanding this one goes a long way towards understanding the irreducibility of a great many religious metaphors, especially in the language of the mystics. Despite their reputation for speaking of the trans-empirical, a good number of the mystics' figures are attempts to describe human experiences, albeit experiences of religious import. A good example of this is Teresa of Avila's descriptions of the prayer of quiet in The Way of Perfection:

The soul is here like a babe at the breast of its mother, who, to please it, feeds it without its moving its lips. Thus it is now, for the soul loves without using the understanding. Our Lord wishes it to realise, without reasoning about the matter, that it is in His company.[55]

Teresa's difficulty in giving account of the life of prayer, the main theme of The Way of Perfection, is not that she is talking of the transcendent God, but that she is describing human experiences which few have had and for which, consequently, there is no established set of literal terms. She is attempting to guide novices into experiences they have not yet had, by means of situations which are already familiar to them, hence her constant use of metaphor, particularly those sanctioned by biblical or mystical tradition; the life of prayer is described in terms of the flowing of rivers, rivulets, and fountains; as the return of bees to a hive; as a journey made across the sea. St Teresa's difficulty is in many respects similar to that of the ancient Greeks who made use of metaphor to chart the unexplored reaches of the mind, and in other ways her reliance on metaphor can be compared to that of the psychologist who speaks of 'streams of consciousness' or the political scientist who speaks of the 'cold war' or the wine taster trying to differentiate two clarets. There are many areas where, if we do not speak figuratively, we can say very little.

The arguments we have provided may meet the demands of someone who claims that metaphors in general, to have cognitive significance, must be reducible to literal expression; but it might be argued that they do not answer the difficulties of one who is troubled specifically by irreducible metaphors in the theist's talk about God. This person is not troubled by the fullness of significance which makes metaphor irreducible to literal equivalents without loss, nor by the fact that when dealing with abstractions like the 'cold war', 'inflation', 'understanding', or even the 'soul', one must rely on figurative terminology and forgo ostensive reference. His problem is rather with the radically elusive nature of our subject-matter when we claim to speak about God, with the fact that when the believer is asked to explain what he means by God's 'fatherly kindness' or his 'just wrath' he must use expressions equally metaphorical or say nothing at all. And this is not, the critic insists, just a quibble with overtly metaphorical language, because even the so-called literal terms we are accustomed to use such as 'infinite' and 'transcendent' and 'one' can be seen on examination to be oddly used when used of God. Put this way, the sceptic's problem is not a problem with metaphor as such when employed in religious language, but with the possibility of language about God at all. His difficulty is not with the way in which religious metaphors are significant or intelligible, but with the problem of how, even granted the existence of a transcendent God, we can possibly claim to talk about him in finite language.

VI

MODEL AND METAPHOR IN SCIENCE AND RELIGION: A CRITIQUE OF THE ARGUMENTS

BEHIND the foregoing discussion of the meaning and use of metaphor have been questions of reference and of truth, questions concerning the way in which language may mirror or fit the world. Indeed, theoretical assessments of metaphor are often dependent on broader intuitions about the relation of language to the world; in this connection, we have already indicated a considerable breadth of opinion, ranging from the scepticism of Nietzsche and Derrida to the neo-empiricism of Turbayne. Some discussion of the relation between metaphorical language and 'the world that is the case' is thus necessary. More, it is crucial to any account of the cognitive uses of metaphor, particularly in religious language of which criticism so often takes the form: 'Indeed these figures are full of human significance, but how can they refer?' Since the terms 'truth' and 'reference' have been used in so many disparate senses in theories already discussed, we shall discuss the problem of the purchase of metaphorical religious language as one of 'reality depiction.'[1]

As we have already noted, the reference of some metaphors is not problematic. A metaphorical form does not mean that an utterance makes a peculiar metaphorical reference; 'gnawing pain' is metaphorical but clearly and straightforwardly referential under the right circumstances, despite its irreducibility, and so is 'that old dragon'. In cases where reference can be established by ostension, metaphorical appellations are no more referentially problematic than their non-figurative counterparts; that is why they easily and frequently do lapse into literal speech—for example, 'eye of a needle', or 'ballast' (of an argument). Reference, and with it reality depiction, does become an issue with metaphors such as 'moral vision', 'stream of consciousness', and 'magnetic field', not simply because these figures are concerned with less tangible entities or states of affairs, but also because they entail a way of speaking about them and hence of describing them. To speak of moral 'vision' is to suggest that one may 'envisage' correct courses of action, that these are fixed and need only be 'seen', and that anyone can see them. Similarly, to speak of light as 'particles' is to bring in mechanical descriptive vocabulary such as 'bouncing', 'colliding', 'accelerating', and so on. It is not just the one metaphorical designation which is problematic, but whole 'systems of metaphorical predicates to which they give rise. To enquire into the nature of metaphor and reality depiction is thus to broach wider problems of the nature of explanation.

Here, positions tend to be influenced by the focus of concern; for instance, the referential or reality-depicting status of figurative speech has not seemed a problem to those literary critics who have tried to concern themselves with meaning alone and have happily surrendered any claims to reference or to truth. Thus C. K. Ogden and I. A. Richards, faced with positivist accounts of meaning, attempted to formulate a theory of 'emotive meaning' in which, for poetic language at least, questions of truth and reference had no place.[2] Doubtless, the literary critic is in a better position to exalt the autonomy of 'meaning' and discard the claims of reference than is the physicist, the cognitive psychologist, or even the theologian. The same tendency to make meaning autonomous recurs in literary theory more recent than that of Ogden and Richards. Karsten Harries, discussing metaphor and citing, not surprisingly, Jacques Derrida, goes so far as to argue that the purpose of some of the poet's metaphors is to weaken and break down the referential function of language in order to let us become absorbed in the poem. The poet's object is to direct us away from reality and to escape from the referentiality of language into the 'world' opened up by the aesthetic object.[3]

Similar approaches to meaning, though not indebted to Derrida, have been adopted in recent treatments of the New Testament parables in the tradition of E. Fuchs and J. Jeremias. Such accounts, influenced directly by theologians associated with the 'New Hermeneutic' and indirectly through these by Heidegger, see the parables primarily as pure units of meaning. The only world which is of importance is the 'world' entered into and shattered by the parable, a pre-eminently existential world. By implication, questions of reference are unimportant.[4]

Theologians have, quite rightly, been influenced by literary criticism, though in view of the scepticism implicit in some literary approaches to meaning and metaphor, one cannot but wonder if those theologians who uncritically take over their mode of analysis may find they have made a bad alliance. But metaphor and model in explanation have been topics of considerable interest in recent years to scientists and philosophers of science, although the latter have not turned as readily as the literary critics and some theologians to non-cognitivism. For balance, then, we shall consider the debate in philosophy of science over metaphor and what we are calling reality depiction. We will see here, too, metaphor and model are closely linked.

1. METAPHOR IN SCIENTIFIC LANGUAGE

Only someone completely unacquainted with the language of the natural sciences could believe that it contains no metaphors at all; even the most uninformed has run across phrases such as 'time warp', 'particle charm', or 'black hole' whose use he realizes to be figurative, although he may not be certain what they signify. A less naïve and more widespread opinion among non-scientists is that, while scientists do use metaphors, they do so only to explain their complex and essentially formal theories to the layman. Cleanth Brooks and Robert Penn Warren give voice to this opinion in their *Modern Rhetoric* where they take it as a given that "though metaphor is not necessary to purely scientific statement, the scientific writer very often needs to go beyond such stringently limited discourse, and then for him too, metaphor, employed as illustration, may be highly useful".[5] To illustrate their point, they cite a passage from *The Scientific Outlook* where Bertrand Russell describes what happens when we 'see' someone:

Little packets of light, called 'light quanta' shoot out from the sun, and some of these reach a region where there are atoms of a certain kind, composing Jones's face, and hands, and clothes. . . . Some of the light quanta, when they reach Jones's atoms, upset their internal economy. This causes him to become sunburnt and to manufacture Vitamin D. Others are reflected, and of those that are reflected some enter your eye. They there cause a complicated disturbance of the rods and cones, which, in turn, send a current along the optic nerve. When this current reaches the brain, it produces an event. The event which it produces is that which you call 'seeing Jones'.

To this account Russell added the concluding illustration:

To say that you see Jones is no more correct than it would be, if a ball
bounced off a wall in your garden and hit you, to say that the wall had hit
you. Indeed the two cases are closely analogous. [6]

Brooks and Penn Warren comment that most readers will be
grateful for this last analogy since the 'ball and wall' metaphor adds
an easy-to-grasp summary to an otherwise technical account. But if
their object had been to show that technical language is replete with
metaphor (rather than the opposite), they could not have done
better than to cite this passage, for talk of 'little packets' of 'light
shooting out', 'upsetting internal economies' and 'sending' a
'current' along the optic nerve is metaphorically constituted talk.

A more plausible view argues not against the presence of metaphor in scientific language, but against the necessary presence of
metaphor. Austin Farrer says in 'Poetic Truth':

As grammarians may break up sentences into words and words into letters,
so the scientist analyses the world into the factors which in his view compose
it. When in science we ask, What is such-and-such a thing? we really mean,
into what pattern of parts or system of factors can it be analysed? For this
purpose metaphors are not particularly useful. Many technical scientific
terms are metaphors, but that doesn't really help the scientific quest.
When the scientist goes further and substitutes English or Greek letters
instead of the names of his physical elements and functions, these letters do
just as well as the hideous words for which they stand. [7]

The argument is that while metaphorical terms may be introduced
into scientific language, once introduced these are simply technical
terms with the status of ciphers and not necessary to the scientific
quest.

There are certainly dead metaphors in scientific language which
fit this description, simple neologisms which, having been metaphorically introduced, then play no explanatory role as active
metaphor. Particle 'charm' might be an instance of this. It is
misleading, however, to suggest that all the metaphors of scientific
explanation are dispensable ciphers of this sort; if they were, it
would be difficult to see why the presence of metaphorical terms in
descriptive accounts has engendered so much debate amongst philosophers of science. It is clear that the most interesting, both
linguistically and scientifically, of the metaphors in theoretical
language are not those whose function is simply catechretical, but

those which suggest an explanatory network and hence are, as W. V. Quine says, "vital . . . at the growing edges of science and philosophy'.[8]

We must recall the manner in which we have suggested that metaphor is related to model. An object or state of affairs is a model when it is viewed in terms of its resemblance, real or hypothetical, to some other object or state of affairs; a miniature train is a model of the full-scale one, a jam jar full of cigarette ends is seen as a model for the lungs of a smoker, the behaviour of water is seen as a model for the action of electricity.

It should be noted that an entity, occurrence, or state of affairs is not a model in itself but 'it functions as a model when it is viewed as being in certain relationships to other things'.[9] Things become models by 'projective conventions', when characteristics read off the model's source are predicated of the model's subject. The billiard ball is a model only when viewed as sharing aspects or properties of behaviour with another entity, such as a molecule of gas. A model, then, is defined by its use as a model.

Conflation of the categories of 'model' and 'metaphor' is a common move and one usually made to the detriment of an account of metaphor. Max Black tends to conflate the two, as does Ian Barbour who (following Black) discusses models as 'systematically developed metaphors' and treats the difference between the two as largely a matter of degree. Similarly, Frederick Ferré says that models are a kind of metaphor.[10] Ferré and Barbour take this position because they see both model and metaphor as proposing analogies; metaphor, Barbour says, "proposes analogies between the familiar context of a word and a new context into which it is introduced".[11] The difficulty here, of course, is that by saying that both model and metaphor propose analogies we are in danger of lapsing once again into a comparison theory of metaphor. But while we have argued that metaphor and model are closely linked for general purposes, it is better to keep the two categories distinct.

As we have already said, a model is distinguishable from metaphor which is a *speaking* about one thing or state of affairs in terms suggestive of another; a model need not be linguistic at all, as with a model train. None the less, model and metaphor are closely linked. Metaphors arise when we speak on the basis of models; so if we are using the computer as a model for the brain and consequently speak of neural 'programming', 'input', and 'feedback', we are speaking metaphorically on the basis of the computer model; the intelligibility of these terms depends, initially at least, on their being related to this particular model of the brain.

While keeping in mind that 'model' and 'metaphor' are distinct categories, it should also be noted that the presentation of a model, its *linguistic* presentation, that is, can take the form of a metaphor as in the sentence, 'The brain is a computer.' Metaphors which propose a model in this way are sometimes called 'conceptual metaphors', but a more exact if more cumbrous title is 'theory-constitutive metaphors'.[12] These 'theory-constitutive metaphors' (metaphors which propose a model) should further be distinguished from metaphors which are the linguistic projections of such a model; for example, the cybernetic model of the brain referred to earlier is developed by discussion of neural 'programming', 'output', and 'feedback'. Terms like these will be called 'metaphorically constituted theory terms' or simply 'metaphorical terms' where context makes that usage clear.

Our distinction between the 'theory-constitutive metaphor' and a 'metaphorically constituted theory term' is important, for it allows us to focus on the individual metaphorical terms which a particular theory-constitutive metaphor suggests, and these individual terms are important to the debate about reality depiction in the philosophy of science. If this focus on the individual metaphorical term seems inconsistent with our earlier insistence that metaphor is not a phenomenon of the word, but of the complete utterance, we would point out that we take it as established that construal is made at the wider level of the complete utterance; the problem of reference is one that arises after construal has been made.

Following Harré, we can distinguish the 'source' of a model (whatever it is the model is based upon) from its 'subject' (whatever it represents or is a model for). The source of the cybernetic model which we have cited is the computer and its subject is the brain. On the basis of the relationship between model source and model subject, we can further distinguish two main types of models: homeomorphic models are those in which the subject of the model is also its source (e.g. a model aeroplane or a dummy used to teach life-saving skills), and paramorphic models are those where source and subject differ (e.g. the use of billiard balls to provide a model for discussion of the properties of gases). This distinction is sometimes described as one between models which are models 'of' a state of affairs, and models which are models 'for' one.[13]

The models used by the sciences for theoretical purposes are primarily paramorphic models, for while a homeomorphic model may have certain applied uses (a model aeroplane may be used in a wind tunnel to test the aerodynamic properties of its source), the task of theory construction itself is customarily the task of constructing models to explain better what we do not yet fully understand, rather than that of building models of states of affairs whose nature is clear to us.

Rather than demonstrating clear parallels, the paramorphic model suggests candidates for similarity and gives form to deliberation on unfamiliar subject matters, whether they be considerations of light as waves, or of linguistic competence as guided by innate structures, or of God's relation to man as that of a father. In science, social science, ethics, theology, indeed the whole realm of abstract theorising, it is the paramorphic models which are used in attempts to speak about the 'mysterious overplus'.[14]

2. THE COMPARISON OF MODELS IN SCIENCE AND RELIGION

The notion that religious and theological language is rich in models was popularized by Dr Ian Ramsey. He, and others following him, also noted that theology is not alone in being dependent upon models to give form to its reflections; science too considers one entity in terms of another and speaks, for example, of the hypothetical light 'wave' or magnetic 'field' which lies beyond experience. Furthermore both science and religion, theologians have been quick to note, rely on a multiplicity of models, each having a partial adequacy in describing the subject, and all being held in tension as a control against taking any one model as descriptively privileged. Religious apologists have further remarked that models are used in both domains to make sense of complex areas, to build up discourse, to speak of what eludes us, and that in both science and religion a given model must be comprehensive, consistent, and coherent if it is to be of any use.[15]

Such general points have been used to explain apologetically the presence, indeed the ubiquity, of models in religious thought, particularly in Jewish and Christian thought. The argument in this apology tends to be *de facto*, to suggest simply that there are these similarities in the use of models in science and religion and that therefore religion need not be ashamed to use models or even to rely on them, since natural science proceeds in the same way.

For the most part, any deeper examination of the problems involved in the use of models to describe the unobservable or transcendent has not been undertaken by theologians and philosophers of religion, who have contented themselves with drawing superficial parallels in use. More questionable still is the not uncommon practice of lifting a particular model from its context in the physical sciences and transplanting it whole into theological ground, without giving sufficient account to the qualified, theoretical status that the model may have, even on its home ground.

Despite the drawing of these parallels of use and function, theological apologists have been cautious, often at the expense of consistency, about equating the use of models in the two areas. The resulting positions are oddly hybrid, advocating on the one hand a hearty and uncritical realism as regards the models in science (in order to confirm their importance to science, and thus to justify their presence in theology), but on the other hand collapsing into an 'emotive meaning' argument when faced with religious models.

Frederick Ferré's discussion of metaphor and models in *Basic Modern Philosophy of Religion* is a good case in point. In discussing the cognitive possibility of theistic language, he suggests that the theist's models have a good deal in common with those of science; they provide ideational definiteness, conceptual unity, overall coherence, and so on. However when faced with the question of the appropriateness of theistic models (a question which holds concealed the question of reality depiction) his comparison breaks down and his argument collapses into the rather uninteresting conclusion that "religious imagery is above all a supremely intensive value phenomenon by which, for the sake of comprehensiveness, men also try to think".[16] Later he concludes

that the theistic model, as religious imagery, is a kind of symbolism which may function, for those who adopt it, to overcome the threat of the arbitrary on its valuational side as well as to meet the cognitive challenge of strangeness and disconnection on its theoretical side.[17]

Ferré's difficulty, and that of many others, is that while he wishes to say that the theist's models and metaphors guide our thought about

God and are in some sense descriptive and explanatory, he faces the alleged impossibility of specifying their referent in a way independent of further models and metaphors. At the critical stage for his comparison of the cognitive use of theistic models with the cognitive use of models elsewhere, Ferré is constrained to say that theistic models cannot be assessed in terms of truth and reference but only in terms of their valuational significance. The critical issue, that of reality depiction, is prescinded.

A slightly different response to the same difficulty of specifying a referent for the theist's claims, and one which has a certain popularity in discussions of parable and metaphor, retains reference as an issue but suggests the real referents of theistic models are certain kinds of human experiences, and not any transcendent states or relations. David Tracy takes this line in 'Metaphor and Religion' where he associates metaphor and model with parable. He says:

The referents of the parables are . . . certain specifically Christian religious-as-limit experiences: a style of life formed by what Christians call radical faith, fundamental trust, and agapic, non-self-serving, unsentimental love. Those possibilities are disclosed by the redescription of human possibility in a metaphor which uses a narrative form to serve as a model (a heuristic fiction). Then that model is joined to a strong qualifier ('The kingdom *of God* is like . . .') to disclose a limit use of the original metaphor, a use backed by the clues in the story itself of extravagant actions set into a realistic narrative. [18]

Though some of Tracy's language is reminiscent of Ramsey's, he is indebted in his handling of parables to theologians of the New Hermeneutic like Robert Funk, and via the New Hermeneutic to existentalism in the Bultmannian tradition. His phrase 'limit use' of metaphor is intended to indicate that they make no transcendental claims. But let us consider his comments in the light of particular parables, for instance, that of the Unrighteous Judge. It reads:

In a certain city there was a judge who neither feared God nor regarded man; and there was a widow in that city who kept coming to him and saying, "Vindicate me against my adversary." For a while he refused; but afterwards he said to himself, "Though I neither fear God nor regard man, yet because this widow bothers me, I will vindicate her, or she will wear me out by her continual coming." And the Lord said, "Hear what the unrighteous judge says. And will not God vindicate his elect, who cry to him day and night? Will he delay long over them? I tell you, he will vindicate them speedily. Nevertheless, when the Son of man comes, will he find faith on earth?'' (Luke 18: 1–8.)

The difficulty with saying that the referent of this parable is Christian experience or life-style, and with saying the same of the many parables which begin ''the kingdom of heaven is like . . .'', is that these parables do purport to tell us of God, and of our relation to Him. In this parable, the reader is told to be diligent in prayer and that God will vindicate him. By speaking of the referents of the theist's models as Christian experiences of radical faith and fundamental trust, we do not resolve the problem of reference but simply force it to a different level. Faith in what? Trust in what?

Are we being fair to Ferré and Tracy? It could be argued that reality depiction is only a problem for certain kinds of accounts (those we will call realist) which see Christian worship as directed towards ''a cosmos-transcending absolute being'' who is the creator of all there is.[19] But the theologian, it might be argued, need not retain this realism. He might find it more satisfactory both philosophically and theologically to abandon any consideration of reality depiction with its realist overtones and devote himself to an account of the structures of 'significance' in religious language. He could concern himself simply with questions of meaning in the text, in the same way a literary critic might, though the theologian would be concerned with 'meaning' in a more personalistic sense. This radical but consistent alternative would involve the redefinition, perhaps along existentialist lines, of central concepts like 'truth' and 'reality', and even of 'God' and 'man'. In this refashioned treatment, talk of 'reference', 'truth claims', 'reality depiction', and 'cognitive employment of models' would drop out altogether. Such an approach to religious language would be perfectly consistent. What is not consistent is the hybrid position in which a theologian continues to speak of the *cognitive* use of models in religious language and to insist on parallels between the use of models in science and religion, and yet fails to take sufficient account of the problem of reality depiction. The conclusion that theistic models are descriptive and representational, but that what they describe and represent is the human condition, is not only disappointing when it comes at the end of a comparison of models in science and religion, but makes the whole comparison a nonsense. It would be better to abandon talk of models in religious language altogether, as well as any hope for an illuminating comparison with the models of science.

Thus, if there is to be any valuable comparison of models in science and religion it must be one with realist assumptions, and traditional Christian belief has been characterized by these in any case. The Christian theist typically has not taken models like 'God is the father' or 'the kingdom of God' as merely evaluative phenomena or redescriptions of human experience, but as speaking, albeit obliquely, about states and relations which he knows himself not fully to understand but which he takes to be more than simply human states and relations. Christian theism has been undeniably realist about these models, whether it has a right to be or not.

Can this realism be defended? We suggest that it can, and that a comparison of models in science and religion is useful for this purpose, but that the comparison is of value only if it goes beyond the comparison of superficial similarities to a consideration of the nature of explanation in the two domains.

Before turning to this, we should examine several points at which theological apologists have suggested, and even stressed, that the use of models in science differs from their use in religion. A composite argument of points typically made on this score runs as follows:

There are, indeed, models in both scientific and religious language which are used to speak of things beyond our immediate experience, but there are these differences: scientific models are used to explicate and schematize a theory, they are projective, that is, they suggest new possibilities of understanding and most importantly they do so with the aim of accounting for causal mechanisms. Religious models, on the other hand, do not embody theories or explanations but serve to evoke a response from the listener, and to call to his mind or present before him an issue with forcefulness. Consequently, while the models of science are abstract and objectifying, the models of religious language are personal; while the models of science are used with precision, their entailments tightly constrained by the formal theory they illustrate, the models of religious language are vague, non-assertive, and always 'qualified'. And, finally, whereas in scientific thought the subservience of the model to the theory means that the model is a useful but dispensable heuristic, in religion there can be no comparable retreat into pure theory, for in religion the models are all that we have, trapped as we are within what Ronald Hepburn has described as a "wheel of images".

These putative differences in the use of models in the two areas can be reduced to two; the first is that, whereas the models of science are structural and causally explanatory, the models of religion are evocative and affective. The second is that, whereas the models of science are aids to theorizing which can be replaced at any time by a pure theory or mathematical formulation, those of religion are irreplaceable or, at least, replaceable only by another equally unsubstantiated model. If these two claims hold, it would be reasonable to conclude that the religious apologist has little to gain from studying the use of the model in scientific explanation. What is then surprising is that theologians, convinced that the use of models in science and in religion differs in such significant ways, should feel there was any value in the comparison at all! We suggest that religious apologists have conceded a sharper demarcation than in fact exists.

(A) 'That the models of science are explanatory and those of religion affective.'

The non-cognitivist thesis that, whereas the models of science are used explanatorily, the function of the religious models is affective draws its strength from the indisputably emotive character of religious imagery. A glance at the Psalms or the Prophets will light on passages such as this:

> For my sword has drunk its fill in the heavens;
> behold, it descends for judgement upon Edom,
> upon the people I have doomed.
> The LORD has a sword; it is sated with blood,
> it is gorged with fat . . . (Isaiah 34: 5–6.)

The chronicles, prophecies, allegories, and stories of the Bible are replete with figures whose role seems, particularly to the modern reader, primarily evocative. Whether the modern reader is justified in regarding as much of biblical imagery as he often does as simply evocative is another matter, and one for the hermeneutically inclined exegete to ponder. Consider, for example, the cognitive significance of 'kingship' to a people whose history was that of Israel and compare this with the flaccid notions the modern reader is likely to associate with the term.

The natural tendency to see biblical imagery as essentially evocative in function has been given theoretical grounding by writers influenced by the New Hermeneutic such as Funk and Crossan. These writers see the narrative unit (whether that be the story, the parable, or the metaphor) as a 'language' or 'speech event' and see its importance, *qua* event, in the impact it has on the reader; in its ability to shock, to shatter, and to reshape the 'world' in which the reader lives. Importantly on this count, and Crossan stresses this, the imagery is not only misunderstood if taken as reality depicting, but becomes totally misleading, for, according to Crossan, "reality is the world we create in and by our language and our story so that what is 'out there,' apart from our imagination and without of language, is as unknowable as, say, our fingerprints, had we never been conceived"; and, "the classical mind says, that's only a story, but the modern mind says, there's only story." [20]

From this point of view, those who cling to a realist position appear not only unmodern and confused but also unspiritual. But this is so only if the dilemma which seems forced on us at this stage is a real one. It appears that either the theists' models and metaphors are taken to be explanatory and descriptive, or they are being treated as affective and compelling commitment. And by virtue of God's transcendence and the limits of human reason, we know that these figures cannot be explanatory, so it must be that they are affective. But this dichotomy will not stand. A model in religious language may evoke an emotional, moral, or spiritual response but this does not mean that the model has no cognitive or explanatory function. In fact the reverse is true; the model can only be affective because it is taken as explanatory. Even the bloody imagery we have cited from Isaiah, while no doubt intended to prompt reform, has its power to do so because it purports to be some kind of a description of God, a God who is in some sense angry. The cognitive function is primary.

By definition, all paramorphic models suggest an explanatory grid between model source and model subject, so prior to considering any specific model in religious language, we can say that if they are indeed paramorphic models, they must purport to be structural and explanatory; if they were not, we would have no right to call them models at all. It would be much better in this case to abandon the idea of religious models altogether. If we wish to maintain that there are structures in theistic reflection which can legitimately be called models, we must take them as purporting to be explanatory. It does seem that, for example, regarding God as the heavenly father is a model in our sense, since it proposes a set of relations between the subject, God's dealings with man, and the source, fathers' dealings with sons. It evokes a response from the theist because it is regarded by him as in some sense explanatory. The issue is, in what sense?

One possibility is that they are explanatory only in a personal sense. Not all those who favour an affective treatment of religious models deny the theistic model an explanatory character. More common is a middle position which preserves a superficially cognitive aspect while emphasizing the affective side. Religious models are thus thought of as in some weak sense explanatory, but not as reality depicting . . . not, that is, if the reality to be depicted is thought of as other than the reality of human experience and response. This is ultimately the position of Sallie Te Selle's *Speaking in Parables*, a book which draws heavily on literary critical studies, and also of Thomas Fawcett's *The Symbolic Language of Religion*.

Fawcett's book well exemplifies this middle position, since it discusses directly the issue of models in science and religion. Fawcett argues that, whereas science requires models for explanation, religion values them primarily for their existential content. Science's interest is in physical objects, but religion deals with spiritual being and hence, "for religion the only adequate kind of language is that which derives from the personal. It is therefore *the phenomenon of man* which has always provided the control model for religious language."[21] What exactly he intends by this notion of 'control model' is never made sufficiently clear; sometimes it means that "primitive religion . . . speaks of virtually everything in human terms", sometimes that God is spoken of as a person, sometimes applying the 'control model' seems to mean assessing everything in personal, as opposed to scientific, categories.[22] In contrasting religious and scientific models, Fawcett says,

The scientist requires models which will ultimately prove of technological value . . . The theologian, however, requires models which are primarily valuable for their existential contents. Religious models exist to give a symbolic picture of reality of such a kind as to provide man with a way of orienting his life in the world. The control model of religion . . . exists precisely for this purpose. It furnishes men with such a way of looking at the universe that they can relate themselves to it meaningfully.

To this he adds that religious symbols "do not exist simply for the enlightenment of the soul'', they also entail an attitude towards life and a secular implementation. [23]

Fawcett then turns to the ''cognitive value of models'' where, interestingly enough, he criticizes the view of religious language as strictly functional or as ''making statements solely about the inner life of man'', for

If positions such as these are maintained . . . we would have to say that religious language is not what it has purported to be. There can be no doubt that the scriptures of world religion have all intended to make assertions about the nature of reality. [24]

While insisting that ''Religion stands or falls by the answer to the question concerning the cognitive value of religious language'', and criticizing those who make talk about God into talk about man, Fawcett in the end does not avoid this position himself. ''Religious symbols'', he says,

do not assert a reality other than that which is also assumed by scientific man. What they do assert is that the one reality has a dimension which is not exhaustively described in the objectifying language of science. It asserts that in addition to being apprehended as an It the world may also be apprehended as Thou. The cognitive assertion of religious symbol therefore is that what the scientist describes in quantitative terms must also be reckoned with in qualitative terms. [25]

One is left feeling puzzled as to how this amounts to much of a ''cognitive assertion'' at all.

None the less, the appeal of this position is clear; .t avoids all the difficulties of the reality depicting aspects of religious models, since their aim is not to provide information but to call forth and direct response; what information and explanation they provide does not concern a transcendent referent but the human condition. Religious language ceases to be of concern to theology and becomes a topic of philosophical anthropology. But to employ the 'person' model in such a way as to suggest that speaking of God in terms appropriate to man is either self-justifying or not in need of justification is illegitimate unless we can show how any model, including this privileged 'control model', can be regarded as saying anything about God at all.

The criticisms we levelled at the stronger non-cognitivism apply equally to the anthropocentric approach exemplified by Fawcett; if these models provide a way of orientating oneself in the world, they can do so only if they also provide reasons for that orientation. If they explain nothing, they provide no basis for any response, religious or moral. Typically, Christians respond to the models of their religious tradition not because they take them to be elegant and compelling means of describing the human condition, but because they believe them in some way to depict states and relations of a transcendent kind. As David Edge has remarked, the cognitive function of religious assertions is not only to recognize patterns in facts, but to recognize them as significant.[26] We could consider the way many Christians, in fact, regard models such as that of the 'kingdom' of heaven, Christ as the 'physician', and God as 'judge', but the model of God as the 'father' must be the central one with which to demonstrate the explanatory and projective use to which religious models are put. This is particularly so since we take this model of God as father in the personal sense (as opposed to father of the race or creator) as distinctive of the teaching of Jesus. The implications of this model used by Jesus were drawn out in the Gospels and Epistles and continue to be drawn out; if God is our father, he will hear us when we cry to him; if God is our father, then as children and heirs we come to him without fear; if God is our father, he will not give us stones when we ask for bread. It should be noticed not only that these convictions are based on the projections of the model, but also that the model is action guiding. How shall we come to God? Without fear, because he is our father. And the model is only action guiding in virtue of its claim to be reality depicting, namely, this is how it is with our relationship to God.

There seems to be no way of avoiding the conclusion that, whether they have a right to or not, in practice Christians tend to regard their models as both explanatory and reality depicting; and, although the basis from which a model may claim to depict reality differs between religious models and scientific ones, their application as explanatory is not as different as has been suggested.

(B) 'That the models of science are dispensable whereas those of religion are not.'

It is the conviction of some writers who discuss the similarities between the use of models in science and in religion that one big difference is the autonomy which scientific theory enjoys with regard to the models used to give form to it. Ramsey, speaking of paramorphic models in science (and citing R. B. Braithwaite's

Scientific Explanation) says of scientific models that scientists and philosophers of science "wished to play safe by subordinating the new kind of model to the mathematical and deductively structured theorizing with which in one way or another it is associated, and to which it gives rise".[27] Ferré (citing Ernst Nagel's *The Structure of Science*) spells this out more fully:

A theory 'uninterpreted' by any model is liable to be a highly arbitrary set of symbols held together by formal rules to compose what is sometimes called an 'abstract calculus'. This abstract calculus has a definite formal structure, and when its symbols are connected somehow to specifiable elements of experience it can have vastly important applications. This is the theoretical matrix; it can, if need be, exist and function without interpretation by a model.[28]

The issue in the philosophy of science is not so straightforward as these two quotations suggest. Ramsey seems to have imported Braithwaite's empiricism about models without questioning it. And Ferré's précis of Nagel uncritically takes over a number of assumptions about the relation of model to theory which stand in need of a justification Ferré never offers; for example, how is this abstract calculus to be connected to specifiable elements of experience? does the theoretical model precede the development of the abstract calculus or follow it? and is the theoretical matrix to which Ferré alludes predictive and if so how? Neither Ferré nor Ramsey could be expected to resolve the debate in the philosophy of science over the status of models, but they could be expected to acknowledge that there is such a debate. In particular, they can be criticized for not making clear, or perhaps for not being clear, that the accounts of model culled from Braithwaite and Nagel are not simply neutral accounts that all scientists and philosophers of science are agreed upon, but highly contested ones.

In fact, the notion that models are dispensable to the workings of the independent and formal theory works from within a particular view of scientific explanation associated with logical empiricism and is a notion which, in the post-logical positivist era, has proved increasingly difficult to defend. The ideal of physical theory as a "mathematical system with a deductive structure" has been successfully attacked from a number of quarters.[29] A theory that can be formulated without a model, J. J. C. Smart argues, is a dead theory. It contains no more explanatory or predictive powers; it no longer

suggests any possibilities, and its implications can be found by
mathematical logic alone. Yet theories do not apply by mathematical logic alone, they must also 'fit' with received experience,
and it is the role of the model (or analogy as it is sometimes called in
this context) to suggest how this fit might take place.[30] N. R.
Campbell states that such analogies are not just aids but "utterly
essential" to the theory, like the melody to the sonata.[31] The view
that analogies could be dispensed with once the theory is formulated could only be true, he says, if physical science were a purely
logical science with its object to establish a set of all true and all
logically connected propositions, but no other feature. In that case,
he points out, there would have been no need for an analogy in the
first place since anyone could solve the problems using only logic;
"a schoolboy in a day's work could solve the problems at which
generations have laboured in vain by the most trivial process of trial
and error."[32]

The same view is echoed by Harré in the statement that this "bit
of nonsense" has created nearly all the difficulties of classical
philosophy of science, "that the sense of theoretical terms is a
product of the sense of the observation terms to which they are, à la
Carnap, reducible, plus their logical rôle as calculating devices".[33]

The fertility of a theory lies in its ability to suggest possibilities of
explanation which, while not inconsistent with, are more than
simply the logical extensions of mathematical formulas. Dr Mary
Hesse argues that it is this suggestive capacity which constitutes the
fruitfulness of a theory, and gives the theory the predictive nature
which is its *raison d'être*. A good model suggests possibilities. The
comparison of the action of billiard balls to that of light considered
as particles will result in some positive analogies; for example, both
have properties of reflection, in some negative analogies, such as
that billiard balls are made of plastic or ivory and particles of light
are not, and in some neutral analogies, those aspects of the activity
of the billiard ball analogue which we do not know to be shared by
the analogate, light. These neutral analogies suggest areas where
work might continue. If we had only a purely abstract expression of
a theory we could have no reason other than random surmise for
choosing one interpretation of a model rather than another. Dr
Hesse says that in practice there *are* reasons for examining a hypothetical interpretation and these reasons are drawn from the
model.[34]

Harré concurs that the "generation of the concept at the heart of the theory . . . is a matter of analogy".[35] Building a theory is a matter of constructing a proper analogy and this analogy is provided by a model. Furthermore, the model is the source of metaphorical theory terms; the corpuscular model of gases prompts the terminology appropriate to the mechanical relations between billiard balls; velocity, impact, refraction, and so on. Harré contends that these projections are useful not only for the description of entities or relations not presently observable, but also for the discussion of entities and relations which we could not possibly observe but which, none the less, we might wish to say are real entities or states of affairs. They are the 'transcendentally real' objects of science, a category into which he would place both the nature of electromagnetism and the workings of the subconscious.

On any satisfactory account of scientific practice, it seems we cannot easily separate the model from the theory. The model or analogue forms the living part of the theory, the cutting edge of its projective capacity and, hence, is indispensable for explanatory and predictive purposes.

This strengthens the comparison with religious models. Ferré has argued that in scientific explanation the model must be subservient to the theory and always alterable and dispensable in favour of pure theory. Theistic models, he says, do not meet this criterion. But if the above account of Campbell, Smart, Harré, and Hesse is correct, then precisely what one cannot do with any living and valuable scientific theory is to make the model separate from and subordinate to it. In important cases, it is true to say that the model or analogue is the theory. Therefore, to say that in scientific explanation a model is alterable and dispensable means only that, first, any model is open to revision and subject to replacement (where revising and replacing the model can mean revising or replacing the theory), and second, that these models make no claim to be descriptive in an absolute sense. But these characteristics are in any case inherent in the notion of paramorphic model and hence apply to paramorphic religious models as well. It is true that theists are less willing than scientists to revise or replace their models, but this is not because the reflective theist thinks his models are completely adequate to their subject-matter but because he thinks they are the most adequate he has. Furthermore, many of these (consider "our God is a Rock") are embedded in Scripture and tradition, and the subject of innumerable glosses and reinterpretations. However, even the most thoroughgoing traditionalists could not reasonably deny that the central Christian models, too, are potentially revisable and dispensable in the sense that other models might take their place, though he might wish to argue that no individual nor even the Church has the right to dispense with the models given to us by the biblical writings. Indeed, the limited applicability and potential dispensability of our models is re-affirmed each time we acknowledge that what we now think of God is but a crude reflection of what we shall know when we see God 'face to face'.

This point suggests another one to do with Ramsey's account of religious models. He says that it is part of the 'logical oddness' of the theists' models that they are always hedged about by 'qualifiers' such as 'eternal', 'all-knowing', 'infinite', and so on, and also that they lead to absurdity if pushed too far. [36] But these are not characteristics of religious models alone; *all* paramorphic models are qualified; if they were not they would be, not models, but replicas of the modelled subject. By the same token, no paramorphic models can be pushed too far without consequent absurdity; Christian presuppositions make it absurd to extend the model of God's fatherhood so far as to say that he has a wife; scientific presuppositions make it absurd to push the billiard ball model for gas molecules so far as to suppose that gas molecules might be composed of plastic. Furthermore, along with suppressing developments which lead to absurdity, both groups of model users assume properties not provided by the model's source; for example, the kinetic theory of gases assumes billiard balls to be perfectly elastic spheres, the theist assumes the 'heavenly father' to be perfect in love and knowledge. The development of a paramorphic model is always constrained by received experience and theoretical assumption or bias in science as well as in religion.

To conclude, we have argued that religious apologists tend to concede a sharper demarcation in the use of models in the two areas than in fact exists; in both, models are used as explanatory and in both, models are indispensable. Why, then, have theologians and philosophers of religion been so quick to postulate differences in the use of models in the two areas which, if actual, would undercut the validity of any comparison between them? We suggest that they are motivated by a mixture of theological intuition and philosophical assumption. The theological intuition is an intuition that the creature cannot claim to describe the Creator as he is in himself; the utter transcendence of God is an embarrassment to apologists who have wished to discover parallels between models in scientific and religious thought. The philosophical embarrassment is that if we admit that Christians handle their models as though they are explanatory, we seem obliged to provide an explanation of how the terms of our model refer, and, in view of the precarious and tentative nature of anything we say about God, this problem of reference seems great indeed.

VII

METAPHOR, REFERENCE, AND REALISM

RONALD W. HEPBURN puts his finger directly on the most important problem for the cognitive and explanatory use in religious thought of models, analogues, and metaphors when he says:

The question which should be of greatest concern to the theologian is not whether this or that myth may be re-expressed in language less flagrantly pictorial, more abstract in appearance, but whether or not the circle of myth, metaphor and symbol is a closed one: and if closed then in what way propositions about God manage to refer. [1]

This question of reference, or as we would prefer to say, reality depiction must now be addressed.

We suggested in the last chapter that comparisons of the use of models and metaphors in science and in religion are toothless at the superficial level at which generally they have been made. In great part this is because, in commenting on the comparison, theologians and philosophers of religion have failed to note that the debate about the place of models in scientific theory is in essence a debate about the nature and purpose of scientific explanation. Let us see if a more detailed examination of the foundations on which model and metaphor are variously welcomed or rejected in science enables us to see more clearly the ways in which metaphor is essential to the project of reality depiction. As a starting point, we might ask why the positivists were so eager to limit the function of models in science, and what the consequences of an undermining of the positivist position might be.

The least satisfactory account of models, whether in science or religion, is that based upon a naïve realism. On that account models are viewed as providing a description of how things are in themselves, and science is seen as a process of making immediate the hitherto invisible structures of the world. Mary Hesse has isolated two assumptions of naïve realism particularly as manifested in seventeenth-century science; the first is its assumption that true theories could be attained in practice, and the second

that the hidden entities and processes of nature that are to be discovered by science are of the same kinds as observable entities and processes, and hence describable in the same descriptive vocabulary and satisfying the same laws. [2]

A theological naïve realism would assume there to be no difficulty in describing God by the same terms we use of observables; that God simply and truly gets 'angry', 'hardens his heart', or is the 'king of heaven'. We will assume that the inadequacy of a naïve realism concerning models, whether those of science or religion, needs no further discussion here.

It was the inadequacy of naïve realist assumptions about scientific explanation, particularly in the face of the increasing complexity and plurality of theory in the eighteenth and nineteenth centuries, which fathered the positivism of the twentieth. The move towards positivism such as that of the logical empiricists has been characterized as a 'retreat to the observables', for in the positivist account of physical theory it is these observables, rather than any unobservable 'real' structures, that provide the ultimate objects of scientific knowledge. [3] This position was reflected in their view of theoretical statements: logical empiricism, like empiricism in general, gave priority to observation statements and made the concomitant assumption that there existed a readily available 'observation language' on which science was firmly based and the meaning of whose terms was clear. 'Theoretical language', in contrast, was seen as having a parasitic nature and the meaning of its terms (e.g. electron, electromagnetic wave) was "held to be obscure". [4] Theoretical terms lacking specifically observational correlates could only, on this account, be viewed as logical and psychologically useful devices, that is, as heuristic aids. Given this general position, it is hardly surprising that model-generated metaphorical theory terms should be, in the positivist's eye, prime examples of terms lacking adequate observational correlates. Thus, while it is often said that the positivists viewed models and metaphors as mere heuristic aids, this must be understood in the context of their stipulation that all non-observational terms had this status. What was at issue was the status not of metaphor in particular, but of all non-observational theoretical terms in general.

As numerous critics of positivism have pointed out, it is precisely because the positivist regards statements as genuinely scientific only if they do not involve commitment to unobservable entities and states that the positivist account fails to provide an objective basis for science.[5] A great many scientific terms designate not observable entities and events, but hypothetical entities and relations, such as electric, magnetic, and gravitational fields, sub-atomic particles, and kinetic energy. Hence the rise of critical (as opposed to naïve) realism in the philosophy of science. The critical realist argues that to make sense of the way these terms function, not only within individual theories but also trans-theoretically, one must regard them not as logical ciphers but as terms which putatively refer to possibly real entities, relations, and states of affairs. The conviction that to make sense of scientific practice one must regard certain non-observational theoretical terms as about 'things' and their powers and not simply, in the instrumentalist fashion, as convenient fictions for the ordering of observables, is the impetus for a critical scientific realism the basic principle of which is that scientific investigation gives us access to structures that exist independently of us. Although the critical realists concede that these powers and structures may never be susceptible to direct observation by us and, in that sense, remain 'transcendent', they none the less regard scientific explanation, even in its reliance on models or analogues, as being reality depicting.

The debate over models is not exhausted by these positivist and realist positions. In a more consistently idealist position, as in a realist account, models and metaphors are seen as vital to the scientific enterprise, but with quite different implications. Sketching a broadly idealist position in the philosophy of science, Roy Bhaskar says that for such idealists:

the objects of scientific knowledge are models, ideals of natural order etc. Such objects are artificial constructs and though they may be independent of particular men, they are not independent of men or human activity in general . . . Knowledge is seen as a structure rather than as a surface. But the natural world becomes a construction of the human mind or, in its modern versions, of the scientific community.[6]

For this sort of idealist, the structure of human knowledge is a function of human need and the structures discovered in nature depend on human thought; hence models are important and even indispensable to the scientific enterprise, but not as descriptions of any external reality. No difficulty arises as to the reference of metaphorically constituted theory terms since no external reference is claimed, and no truth sought beyond one which we impose.

It should be pointed out that Bhaskar's idealist is in some sense a straw man, for few contemporary philosophers of science would fit, wittingly, into the position he sketches. The category does, however, include a fair number of philosophers of religion and can not unreasonably be stretched to include historical relativists like Paul Feyerabend and Thomas Kuhn (in some of his phases) whose writings, despite disclaimers, incorporate idealist assumptions. [7]

The idealist position sketched above seems at first to be the antithesis of the positivist position, and it is, in so far as the positivist views the models in scientific language as dispensable and the idealist sees them as integral; but the shared assumptions of the two positions are worth marking. In both, non-observational theory terms, and hence most metaphorical terms, have the basic status of heuristic fictions; consequently, the criteria for theory construction and elaboration must be formal or logical and not empirical. Furthermore, both the positivist and the idealist positions are linked to a nominalism, inherited from Locke, in terms of which the scientist *can only* deal with atomistic events or with nominal essences, because the real structures and tendencies of things are assumed to be unavailable. So it is that Hilary Putnam has suggested that positivism was based on an idealist world view, and the positivistic cut between 'observable things' and 'theoretical entities' (and hence between observation and theory language) was first introduced as a substitute for the thing/sensation dichotomy of the idealists. [8]

Realists argue that, for these reasons, the idealist is no better able than the positivist to make sense of scientific practice; a good case in point is the history of the term 'gene'. This term was initially introduced to designate the unknown bearer of acquired characteristics and was discussed by means of metaphors of the linguistic code: as bearer of 'information', medium for 'communications', etc. Subsequent genetic work developed the notion of the gene as the bearer not of acquired but of inherited characteristics, and technological advance has made it possible to locate the bearers of genetic information in the chromosomes. But, the realist argues, if scientists had regarded the concept 'gene', as no more than a useful fiction, as both positivist and idealist accounts say they must, there could have been no impetus for them to ask whether the gene did, in fact, have an independent existence, and to continue the research which now enables us to carry out genetic surgery. Similarly, if scientists had truly regarded the sub-atomic particle known as the 'neutrino' as only a useful fiction, they would not have constructed experiments to determine whether the neutrino had mass. Or, to use an example cited by Irving Copi, if scientists had not considered the theory of chemical weights and valencies to be not merely useful but also somehow true, they would have had no justification for projecting, on the basis of characteristics of known elements, not only to the existence of but also to the characteristics of further elements, which they were subsequently able to construct.[9] Putnam sums up the typical realist argument against idealism, of which he considers positivism to be a variant, thus: ''it makes the success of science a *miracle*.''[10]

So, the realist agrees with the positivist in saying that science aims at explanatory and predictive knowledge of the world, but takes issue with the positivist's assertion that knowledge can only be of observed regularities and not of underlying structures. He agrees with the idealist in saying that science must involve creative model building, but parts from idealism in thinking that the mechanisms and structures so conceived need not be fictions but may sometimes be regarded as real. The realist, then, is committed not to any one particular account of the world or even to the possibility that a perfect account could be provided, but to the intelligibility of what is essentially an ontological question, 'What must the world be like for science to be possible?'[11]

The scientific realist's argument is that the success of science means that its practitioners must assume not only that the world, its structures, and relations exist independently of our theorizing but also that our theorizing provides us with access to these structures, limited and revisable as that access may be at any given time. Bhaskar suggests a consideration of two sorts of scientific objects, the transitive and the intransitive. The transitive objects of scientific enquiry include raw materials of scientific practice such as theories, models, and methodologies—these may be supplanted in the course of investigation but they may not be dispensed with, for it is these transitive objects which provide access to the intransitive. The intransitive objects of science are those things which are not produced by men at all; the specific gravity of mercury, the process of electrolysis, mechanisms of light propagation, and so on. But just as we cannot conceive of science without transitive objects like revise-able models, we cannot conceive of it without the intransitive substrata which the models purport to describe. In Bhaskar's words, "the intelligibility of the scientific activities of perception and experimentation already entails the intransitivity of the objects to which, in the course of these activities, access is obtained."[12] The notion of 'access' coupled with the notions that theoretical terms can be referential and that scientific explanation is cumulative in its insights, is fundamental to a realist position, though many critical realists like Mary Hesse (and Hilary Putnam in recent writings) would exercise more caution than does Bhaskar in discussing the ultimate objects of scientific study and others, like Richard Boyd, would wish to discuss the matter more in terms of an 'epistemic access' than the ontological access preferred by Bhaskar.[13] None the less, Bhaskar seems correct in saying that nominalism, whether in positivist or more crudely idealist guise, seeks to rule out ontology without success. Inevitably the question arises: 'What must the world be like for science to be possible?' Each time a model invites an existential question like 'do viruses exist?' or 'does the neutrino have mass?', and every time answers to such questions are provided by a further technological advance, we are furnished with vindications of the realist thesis that scientific practice itself can only be understood as realist in intent and ontological in presumption. Bhaskar says:

To discover the independently existing and transfactually active machinery of nature is not, it should be stressed, the aim of an independent inquiry of metaphysics. Rather, it is the end to which all the empirical efforts of science are directed. Ontology has been vindicated not as providing a set of necessary truths about a mysterious underlying physical realm, but as providing a set of conditionally necessary truths about our ordinary world as investigated by science.[14]

Realist arguments like these have a direct bearing on the issue of models, for in the elaboration of a scientific theory it is models and the web of metaphor they give rise to which commonly constitute the means by which to speak of transcendent, but putatively real, entities or relations. The existential hypotheses which realists suggest it is the nature of scientific study to generate are in many instances generated by the models used in theory construction and elaboration. Harré suggests that models are used to generate hypotheses of four kinds: the billiard ball model of gases, for instance, suggests not only the existential hypothesis 'do molecules exist?'

but also hypothetical mechanisms like 'molecules are in motion'; causal hypotheses, such as 'is gas pressure caused by the impact of molecules?'; and, finally, modal transforms such as 'is gas temperature really only another way of looking at the mean kinetic energy of the molecules?'[15] For the true positivist, model-generated questions are largely improper and unanswerable; for the idealist, they have no referential and trans-theoretical import; but for the realist, they constitute the stuff of scientific investigation, representing to thought the possible if necessarily unobservable structures and relations of the world.

We move the argument a stage further in turning explicitly from model to metaphor. Metaphors, it is now clear, can by no means be treated as ornamental adjuncts to scientific descriptions by any account which concedes the centrality of models or analogues to explanation precisely because the theory terms which the model generates are metaphorical. Regarding the human brain as a computer is of value because it generates metaphorically constituted theory terms such as 'input', 'feedback', and 'programming' which serve as a hypothetical explanatory grid. This both a realist and an instrumentalist could accept, but for any position which claims to be realist there is a further problem: how can metaphorical theory terms, or any non-observational terms in the theory, be regarded as reality depicting, especially since we have said that in the cases which interest us (in both science and religion) we are using models to discuss that which we cannot possibly fully comprehend? Metaphorical theory terms seem open to the criticism of lacking specifiable referents and of being irresolvably vague. Boyd puts the problem in this way:

. . . a referential treatment of theoretical terms—and a treatment which explains how reference is possible prior to definitive knowledge—is apparently essential to any adequate treatment of the role of theoretical considerations in the assessment of scientific evidence.[16]

Putnam says succinctly: "Realism depends . . . on blocking the disastrous meta-induction that concludes 'no theoretical term ever refers'."[17]

It is here that the theories about reference advanced by Saul Kripke, Hilary Putnam, and Keith Donnellan, amongst others, provide an interesting buttress to the realist position, for they emphasize that reference need not involve unreviseable description. To see the impact of these treatments of reference, one must consider the theories of meaning and reference with which they take issue.

Richard Boyd makes the point that traditional empiricist accounts of meaning and reference rest, as do empiricist accounts of science in general, on a Lockean nominalism in which real essences are unknowable. Hence general terms like 'gold' and 'water' must be viewed as referring to kinds specified by 'nominal essences' and established by definitional convention. "We are to understand the kinds referred to by general terms to be specified by definitional conventions because—so the argument goes—knowledge of unobservable underlying 'powers' or 'inner constitutions' is impossible."[18] This traditional position in turn entails certain views about the meanings of general terms which Putnam has summarized as follows:

On the traditional view, the meaning of, say, 'lemon,' is given by specifying a conjunction of *properties*. For each of these properties, the statement 'lemons have the property P' is an analytic truth; and if P_1, $P_2, \ldots P_n$ are all of the properties in the conjunction, then 'anything with all of the properties $P_1 \ldots, P_n$ is a lemon' is likewise an analytic truth.[19]

On the traditional view, then, meaning determines reference because the meaning of the word is the basis on which speakers use it to refer.

This 'traditional view' Putnam criticizes is related to Locke's idea that "general terms must refer to kinds specified by 'nominal essences', that is, by criteria of membership fixed by definitional convention", a position which, Boyd says, has "formed the basis for all subsequent empiricist discussions of meaning and reference".[20] Indeed, it is not suprising that Locke is so vehement in his condemnation of the 'figurative application of words' when discussing 'things as they are' (see our first chapter). It is tempting to see in this a premonition of the damage these same figures could do to more general theories of naming and reference, for it must be pointed out that to allow inexact figures lacking fully specifiable referents into descriptions of 'things as they are' is to threaten the nominalist base of empiricist accounts of meaning and reference.

The empiricist position is one which, in any case, has major problems to resolve, at least if we are considering the strict form which has had some play in the philosophy of science. In so far as the empiricist sees the extension of general terms as fixed by unrevisable definitions, he faces a difficulty in accounting for theory change, for if the same term is defined in two successive theories by conflicting definitional stipulations it cannot, on the strict empiricist account, be regarded as referring to the same entity. For example, if the term 'gene' was initially introduced (as it was) to refer to that mechanism responsible for the transference of *acquired* characteristics, and if subsequent genetic theory, though calling the mechanism by which traits were transferred the 'gene', comes to deny that acquired characteristics can be genetically transferred, then the term 'gene' in the two stages of theory development cannot be regarded by the empiricist as referring to the same thing at all. Yet continuity of reference across theories (coreferentiality) is presupposed by the activity of genetic scientists who, having postulated the existence of this mechanism, went on to clarify its function. This highlights a point made by Boyd, that although the empiricist account of general terms may be construed as a theory of reference, in important ways it is a non-realist, non-referential account, since in it extensions are "largely fixed by arbitrary and empirically unrevisable definitional conventions" and hence cannot guarantee to be "referring to independently existing kinds or magnitudes".[21]

The similarities between this empiricism and the kind of historical relativism associated with Kuhn's 'paradigm shift' now becomes apparent (Boyd indeed refers to Kuhn's position as one of 'empiricist relativism').[22] It is not clear how changes in scientific theory which involve new critical definitions for entities like 'gene' or 'mass', (say, between Newtonian mechanics and special relativity) can, on either the more traditional empiricism or the historical relativist account, be regarded as new discoveries about, or new advances on old understandings of, the subject-matter. Instead, we face the unpalatable suggestion that these are theories concerning new subjects. The trouble is that there can be no continuity of reference centreing on the thing itself because reference is determined by continually changing definition, not by the essential properties of things which, according to the empiricist, are not available as possible objects of scientific study.

In the light of the cumulative nature of scientific explanation, this strict empiricist treatment of the meaning and reference of theory terms has become increasingly unsatisfactory. Yet the undeniable fact that scientific accounts do change, and sometimes radically, that Lavoisier's oxygen is different from Priestley's dephlogisticated air, has made reference and co-referentiality a problem for realist accounts of science, too. How, then, can theory terms be judged as in some sense referential prior to definitive knowledge?

Beginning from studies concerned with proper names, some theorists have come to challenge traditional theories as to how natural kind terms like 'cow', 'tiger', and 'lemon', and physical magnitude terms like 'heat' and 'electricity' refer. They suggest that terms can refer independently of unrevisable definitions and that reference can take place even where the identifying descriptions associated with a name or a natural kind term fail to be true of the individual in question; in Kripke's example, a speaker who knows of Columbus only that he was the man who discovered that the world was round or that he discovered America really refers when he mentions Columbus, even though Columbus did neither of these things.[23] The reason the speaker refers here, even though all his particular beliefs about Columbus are incorrect, is because the relevant linguistic competence does not involve an unequivocal knowledge, but rather depends on the fact that the speaker is a member of a linguistic community which has passed the name from link to link. Kripke argues that the definite description theory of determining reference is fundamentally mistaken. For example, we do not determine the reference of a proper name by having some properties which qualitatively uniquely pick out the subject but rather "it's in virtue of our connection with other speakers in the community, going back to the referent himself, that we refer to a certain man".[24] Interesting as the 'proper name' examples are, more important for our purposes is the application of these arguments to natural kind terms like 'gold' or 'tiger' and to physical magnitude terms like 'heat' and 'electricity'. The descriptions associated with these terms need not, on this revised treatment of meaning and reference, obtain of each or indeed of any member of the extension. Putnam says:

It is not analytic that all tigers have stripes, nor that some tigers have stripes; it is not analytic that all lemons are yellow, nor that some lemons are yellow; it is not even analytic that tigers are animals or that lemons are fruits. The stereotype is *associated* with the word; it is not a necessary and sufficient condition for membership in the corresponding class, nor even for being a normal member of the corresponding class.[25]

This is because descriptions associated with a term do not determine what it is to be of a kind; what it is to be of a kind is determined by the essential properties of things, *whatever these might be*. This is the reasoning, too, behind Kripke's elaboration of Putnam's initially bizarre-seeming suggestion that it is not even analytic that cats are animals;

cats might turn out to be automata, or strange demons . . . planted by a magician. Suppose they turned out to be a species of demon. Then on his [Putnam's] view, and I think also my view, the inclination is to say, not that there turned out to be no cats, but that cats have turned out not to be animals as we originally supposed. The original concept of cat is: *that kind of thing*, where the kind can be identified by paradigmatic instances. It is not something picked out by any qualitative dictionary definition.[26] [My bracket.]

To demonstrate how this is possible Donnellan and Kripke point out that one can refer to some one or some thing without providing an exhaustive or unrevisable definition of that person or thing. We may, for example, fix a reference simply by 'dubbing' or 'baptism', as in 'Electricity is that which is responsible for these effects'. We can even fix a reference by means of a description which is false of its object, for example, 'the man drinking the martini', when in fact he is drinking water, or when we say 'Phosphorus is the morning star' and it turns out that Phosphorus is not a star at all but a planet.[27] What we do here is provide a description which enables the audience to pick out some one or some thing, and if our purpose is simply a referential one, it need not matter that this description turns out not to hold of its object.

Putnam expands the point that reference may be separated from unrevisable description in terms of physical magnitude terms. A scientifically ignorant individual and a physicist can both use the term 'electricity', he says, without there being any discernible intension (in the form of a necessary and sufficient condition) that they both share. The reason they can do so is:

that each of them is connected by a certain kind of causal chain to a situation in which a *description* of electricity is given, and generally a *causal* description—that is, one which singles out electricity as *the* physical magnitude *responsible* for certain effects in a certain way.[28]

Putnam says, "if Benjamin Franklin gives me even an approximately correct description of a physical magnitude term like electricity, this constitutes an introducing event and·I can use the term."

The suggestion is that we can introduce a term like 'gold' or 'electricity' prior to any certain or unrevisable knowledge of its essential properties and yet claim that, when we use the term, we are referring to the kind as constituted by those properties, whatever they may be. It is this aspect of the new theories concerning meaning and reference which have been seen both as a support to a realist interpretation of scientific practice, and a stimulus to a new interest in metaphysics. Kripke makes this point: "In general, science attempts, by investigating basic structural traits, to find the nature, and thus the essence (in the philosophical sense) of the kind."[29]

Dramatic as these proposals are, the so-called "causal theories" of reference are not themselves free of problems, and both Kripke and Putnam have been criticized as far more successful in attacking the traditional theory of meaning and reference than in establishing a coherent "causal" alternative. For example, the causal basis of reference they espouse needs clarification, since it is clear that 'baptism' and 'dubbing' are fictive rather than actual processes. Similarly, there must be difficulties in generalizing from proper name examples like 'Columbus' to natural kind terms, and the treatment of natural kind terms described above stands in need of refinement on how one determines what is to count as a 'kind' in the first place.[30] Furthermore, if the traditional theory left one with some odd notions of reference, the causal theory implies some odd theories about meaning. Jerrold Katz makes the point that, if the traditional theory erred in implying that meaning determines reference, the 'causal theory' errs in its opposite assumption that all criteria of application are grounded in extra-linguistic matters of fact—concepts about empirical science, information about baptismal ceremonies, and so on.[31] As Katz points out, Putnam's assumptions seem to commit him to taking the meaning of 'cat' to be some inductive generalization from what uses of 'cat' have referred to in everyone's experience; so if all cats turned out to be robots, 'cat' would mean and refer to a sort of robot. But something is clearly amiss here. As Katz points out, the word 'witch' up to a certain time "was used to refer to ugly, frightening women—and never to refer to women with supernatural powers acquired in a pact with the devil—yet the referent of 'witch' is not ugly, frightening women". [32] When we came to disbelieve in witches, we did not say 'witch' really means ugly, frightening women just because the term had consistently been used to refer to such; instead, we say witches do not exist. The meaning of 'witch' remains much the same as it always was and when we have a witch in a fairy story, we do not have simply an ugly frightening woman, but a woman with sinister supernatural powers.

The causal theory, then, also has its limitations, but this is not say that both classical and causal theories of reference are simply wrong. It is rather that they are both partially right and this because reference is more complex a phenomenon than it appears at first. As Katz points out, both classical and causal treatments of reference fail to take sufficient note of an important distinction, that between the referent of a word or expression in the language, and the referent of an expression or a use of an expression in a context. [33] For example, the term 'witch' in standard English refers to a woman with sinister, supernatural powers, but many individual uses of 'witch' in their context were used to refer to ugly, frightening women. Katz's distinction is thus similar to that we made in Chapter III between individual terms of a language which have both sense and denotation, and complete utterances in their contexts of use which have meaning and reference; so, for example, the term 'dragon' may have the sense in the language of giant, fire-breathing reptile, but in particular instances of use may refer to large but ordinary lizards, or even figuratively to crabby, objectionable persons.

However one wishes to delineate this distinction, when dealing with meaning and reference it is necessary to make it, and having done so, much is clarified. At the level of reference or denotation of a term in the language, it may be argued that meaning does, as the traditional theory suggests, affect reference; but at the level of the use of an expression in its context, all kinds of factors, including stereotypes, causal relations, and so on, are the determinants of reference. What seems to occur in scientific language is an accomodation between the fixed senses and denotations of terms in the language, and the more flexible referential uses to which they are put in investigative procedures. Terms like 'gene' are introduced with fixed senses (say, "the mechanism responsible for the inheritance of acquired characteristics") but this sense, while guiding investigations, does not necessarily determine what it is that, in practice, the term is used to refer to. As the theory is improved, the original sense of the term may be altered (say by deleting 'acquired'), or in some cases (e.g. 'phlogiston') it may be decided that a term fails to refer. So the sense of the terms is important, not in tying one to a direct and exhaustive description of the referent, but rather in providing access to a referent, which access it is then the task of science to refine. We can still agree with Kripke that the possibility of new discovery and refinement of description was "part of the original enterprise", an enterprise which is fundamentally realist. [34]

Before going any further we must emphasize several points. First, the critical realism we are advocating does not commit us to viewing certain theories as privileged accounts of the world as it is, or even to the idea that it could coherently be the aim of a realist practitioner of science to provide such. What we are committed to is something more like Boyd's idea that some general terms "afford epistemic access to kinds which are 'natural' in the sense of corresponding to important causal features of the world". [35] And, secondly, it is a very important feature of this realism that it has a social and context-relative nature. The divisions we make, and even the 'kinds' we isolate, will themselves be relative to the context of the enquiry. [36] The classic example here is that of fish and whales since originally whales were classed as fish, but subsequent study of their mammalian structure resulted in their being reclassified as 'non-fish'. We can conceive, however, that a reclassification might have taken place along different lines for different purposes, say, if our main focus of interest was animal locomotion. In that case, whales might be still classified as fish (perhaps as 'mammalian fish') whereas some fishy creatures with non-fishy movements would be classed as 'non-fish'. [37] The way in which we divide up the world is not the only way this might adequately be done, nor need the realist aim for such exclusiveness. The important point, however, is that it is a way guided by the cumulative access of the investigating community (in this case, scientists) to important causal features of the world. The world informs our theory, although our theory can never adequately describe the world. We shall be expanding on the role of these social and contextual features later.

The realism here advanced is a cautious realism, but one which meets the three conditions which, Mary Hesse says,

ought to be satisfied by an account of science that claims to be realistic in anything like the traditional sense. These are: (1) Theoretical statements have truth value. (2) It is presupposed that the natural world does not change at the behest of our theories. (3) The realistic character of scientific knowledge consists in some sense in the permanent and cumulative capture of true propositions corresponding to the world. [38]

The last condition is the one most distinctive of realism; the conviction that our statements provide an 'epistemic access' (Boyd's term) to the world, and that, in so far as they facilitate a science which is cumulative in its insights, they must be regarded as in some manner reality depicting. Again, this is not to say that any one account could ever be regarded as ultimately privileged, nor even does it entail ''the realism of its primary entities and their properties as described in any given theory'', and in this sense it is not a 'metaphysical realism'. [39] On the contrary, it is part of the attraction of the critical realism we have been discussing that it need not hold that the terms of a mature science mirror the world in an unrevisable fashion. Its terms are seen as representing reality without claiming to be representationally privileged.

To recapitulate, we have made use of the arguments of Donnellan, Kripke, and Putnam more for their criticisms of the traditional theories, where meaning determines reference, than for their own 'causal' alternatives. The meaning of terms in a language, or as we prefer, their sense, does have a part to play at one level of reference, but at another, reference is determined by speakers in contexts of use, and not simply by individual speakers but by communities of speakers whose language provides access to the states and relations which are of interest to them. Reference, then, of the kind that interests us is social and is concerned with access. Senses of terms are important not so much for determining reference as for guiding access. It is because senses are important but not fully definitive that metaphor becomes extremely useful in the project of reality depiction, which is as we shall see a realist project.

From what we have said, there are three immediate consequences for the issue of metaphorical theory terms; first, as we have already noted, the discussion above provides theoretical support for the suggestion that the metaphorical predicates which a model generates can, prior to definitive knowledge, be seen as denoting candidates for real existence and enables one to say that the employment of metaphorical theory terms, while not exhaustively descriptive, may be 'partially denoting' or reality depicting.[40] Second, the account elaborates criticism of the demonstrably inadequate notion that metaphors, since they are vague, play only an ancillary role in science. In fact, the opposite is true—the vagueness of metaphorical terms, rather than rendering metaphors unsuited to scientific language, is just what makes them indispensable to it. If the task of the scientist, or more properly that of the scientific community, is as Boyd has it,

the task of *accommodation of language to the causal structure of the world* . . . the task of introducing terminology, and modifying usage of existing terminology, so that linguistic categories are available which describe the causally and explanatorily significant features of the world[41]

then in this task the theory-constitutive metaphor is particularly useful. It is useful because it provides a network of partially denoting terms, and it is just that vagueness inherent in the newly introduced metaphorical terminology, the lack of strict definitional stipulation, which *allows* for the revisability necessary to any account that aims to adapt itself to the world. The third consequence for our assessment of metaphorical theory terms flows from this revaluation of vagueness and is also discussed by Boyd. Scientific realists characteristically feel it necessary to speak not only of theoretical entities but also of states and relations, and these not as incidental to a realist description but as integral to it.[42] The utility of a model and the metaphorical terminology which it generates is that not only does it provide a set of terms to designate theoretical entities but also to depict relations. Boyd's favoured example here is the employment by cognitive psychology of language based on a computer model; hence, neural 'programming', 'storing', 'indexing', 'labelling', and so on; but Boyd's suggestion is that, in any young science, one will find theory-constitutive metaphors working after this fashion. Indeed, the same fashionable computer model is deployed by educationalists, linguists, and physiologists, amongst others, to provide a mapping of their particular domains.

Arguing along the lines of Boyd, this metaphorically constituted and relational language comes in for the same realist appraisal as has been given to more substantive terms. The relational terminology, too, can be seen as attempting to depict ''causally and explanatorily significant features of the world'' without claiming exhaustive or definitive knowledge.

These three points, that metaphors are allowable, their vagueness valuable, and their relational structures useful to theoretical accounts contribute to a more comprehensive point about metaphor which we can now define. Given that metaphors are permissible in theoretical explanation, why are they necessary to it? An answer is as follows: we have mentioned that, in treating some general terms in science, reference can be separated from unrevisable description and that, at the level of use, one can use terms to refer to little-understood features of the natural world without laying claim to unrevisable knowledge about them. This, in its theoretical stages, scientific explanation hopes to do. But how are new and potentially referential terms to be introduced? It is inconceivable that they should be terminological pinpoints without any concomitant sense whatsoever; if they were, they could scarcely be explanatory or action guiding. As we have said, it is unsatisfactory to suggest, as Putnam and Kripke at times seem to, that the senses of terms have no part to play in the whole referential act, even if they are not the whole story. Clearly, some semantic placing, some 'sense', must be associated with theory terms, even if it is then to be qualified, and this sense is most easily and commonly provided by locating the new theory terms within a model or theory-constitutive metaphor. A term like 'neural programming' is given semantic placement in terms of the model upon which it depends. Hence, the term (for instance, 'neural programming') relies on the associative network generated by its underlying model (that of the computer). But the fact that, in its context of utterance, the term is predicated not of the computer but of the brain indicates its extension to be different. It is the project of a scientific enquiry to explore what neural programming might be. Here we have the two levels at work in the referential process: the initial one in which sense does circumscribe the denotation of a term in a language, and the secondary one at which a term with a specifiable sense can be used by speakers or a community of speakers to refer to states and relations we only partially understand.

It is because, in the last analysis, it is not words which refer but speakers using words *who* refer that this is possible; we speak of neural 'programming', 'indexing', 'feedback', and so on relying on the significance these terms have in discussing the computer, while at the same time the speaker and the context of utterance make clear that we are speaking not of the computer but of the brain. To reintroduce the terms used in an earlier part of our study, we can say that in such a metaphor the currently inadequately comprehended 'tenor' of brain activity is mapped on the semantic points appropriate to the 'vehicle' of computer function.

The mistake of those who maintain that each metaphor has two distinct subjects can now be seen to arise from an implicit reliance on a 'building-block' theory of semantics which, despite Black's claim to focus on the sentence as the unit of metaphor, gives priority to the individual word. On the building block view, each term brings to the sentence its connotation and denotation, its sense and reference: hence in 'Man is a wolf' 'man' refers to man or men and brings with it (in Black's version) those associations one has with men, and 'wolf' refers to wolf or wolves, and brings those associations one has with wolves. The totality of terms, names, predicatives, connectives, and so on go to determine the meaning of the whole; and since terms of the sentence refer to both men and wolves, it seems to follow that this is a sentence about men and wolves, hence a sentence with two subjects. But to reason thus (and it seems that something like this must lie behind the notion that each metaphor has two subjects) is to confuse an account of sense and denotation for individual general or kind terms with an account of reference at the level of complete utterance. We may say (in the abstract) that the term 'wolf' refers to one of the set of wolves, but this does not mean that, whenever the term 'wolf' is present in an utterance, the *utterance* refers to (in the sense of 'is speaking about') wolves. The speaker who says when a cad enters the room 'That wolf is here again' is not speaking about a particular wolf any more than someone who asks 'Are you dining with that old battle-axe?' is, in this figurative application, speaking about some medieval instrument of warfare. At this point, one can agree with Donald Davidson's suggestion,[43] though for reasons different from his own, that the notion of reference is not a useful notion in a theory of meaning, if we mean by reference some freestanding relation supposed to obtain between individual proper names and what they name, complex singular terms and what they denote, and predicates and that of which they are true. When dealing with meaning, we must see that ''Words have no function save as they play a role in sentences . . .''; and so, too, words make no reference beyond that which speakers employ them to make in sentences. It is the fact that it is not strictly words which refer but speakers using words, which makes metaphor possible, and enables us to speak about one thing in terms which are seen as suggestive of another.

It is our suggestion that this account of meaning and reference goes some way to block what Putnam has called ''the disastrous meta-induction that concludes 'no theoretical terms ever refer' ''. In doing so, it supports the realist view that the metaphorical terminology which a model or analogue generates, while not necessarily directly descriptive, may despite their limitations be reality depicting. This provides us with at least the beginnings of an answer to Hepburn's challenge about religious language, with which we began this chapter. However, before applying this account of realism to theology, two things need re-emphasizing. First, it is a cautious realism, even in its scientific form. It does not hold that certain theories can be regarded as providing privileged accounts of the world 'as it is', nor that it could coherently be the aim of a realist to construct a theory which did so. On the contrary, it is part of the attraction of the above account of reference that it facilitates a realism which need not hold that the terms of a mature science mirror the world in unrevisable fashion. And, second, this realism has a significantly social aspect, particularly since the notion of membership of a linguistic community is an important feature of the new theories of reference. It is not words which refer, but speakers using words who refer. So Putnam says, ''The realist explanation, in a nutshell, is not that language mirrors the world but that *speakers* mirror the world; i.e. their environment—in the sense of *constructing a symbolic representation of that environment.*''[44]

The question remains how the foregoing account of metaphor, reference, and realism applies to the theological case. As Michael Dummett indicates, there is no point in being a realist *tout court*. One is realist about particular matters or, more exactly, one is realist about particular classes of statements, whether statements about the physical world, or mental events, or the past, or mathematical statements; so, being realist about certain classes of statements in scientific description does not commit one to be realist about mathematical ones, or historical or theological ones.[45] Our argument is not that, because realism is the most coherent stance *vis-à-vis* a class of scientific statements, it must be the most coherent stance about a class of religious ones. Such an approach is neither necessary nor desirable and it is certainly no part of our objective to make religious statements a subset of scientific ones. The suggestion is rather that, having examined ways in which metaphorical language can be judged to be reality depicting apart from definitive knowledge in the case of science, we might find analogies for the admittedly very different task of reality depiction in theology. A form of critical realism is advocated for theology, not because it is the only cogent position, but because so much of the Christian tradition has been undeniably realist in sensibility, and because it is important to defend a version of theological realism, given the anti-realist drift of so much modern philosophical theology.

There are at least two kinds of argument we can make as regards theology: the first is causal and treats of the way we use the term 'God'; the second is social and treats of the referential access provided more generally by religious language. We will examine the second of these in the next chapter.

How then do we speak of 'God'?[46] The causal theory of reference provides one alternative for examining the way in which terms refer apart from definitive knowledge. In the non-theological applications, that to which one refers can always be indicated in some way. In the case of natural kind terms, this, imaginatively, takes place at an initial ceremony of dubbing or baptism; 'whatever this is, is gold'. For proper names, there is ostension or historical chains of usage connecting the speaker to an initial 'baptism' or naming of the individual in question. For physical magnitude terms, it is often an observable concomitant which grounds reference; hence, 'whatever made the needle jump is electricity'. This last shows that it is not always direct ostension which is needed to ground the reference, it is only necessary that we be able to say that at some stage that to which we refer enters into causal relations with us. Someone must be able to say, for this kind of a dubbing ceremony, that 'x is that which caused this state of affairs'. It is this causal link which Boyd uses in his application of the non-definitional theories of reference to theory terms like 'gene', so 'genes are that which is responsible for these traits'.

Since we take it as given that no eye has seen God, and no finger pointed Him out, the theological application must rest on the theist's claim that we are causally related to God, a claim that Christians have tended to insist upon in any case. There are various points at which one might wish to forge this causal link. One, with initial plausibility because it is seemingly analogous to the scientific case, is to argue that God relates causally to men in religious experience; thus one could say 'God is that which on such and such a date seemed more real to John Henry Newman than his own hands and feet' or 'God is that which Moses experienced as speaking to him on Mount Sinai', and so on. The difficulty here, and the disanalogy with the scientific case, is that since such experiences cannot be replicated, fixing reference by means of them demands commitment to the validity of the experience as reported by the experient. But those who judge themselves to have experienced God may be mistaken, as theists freely admit. Few are likely to find it acceptable to fix a reference to God by someone's claim that 'God is whatever caused me to determine to murder my Member of Parliament'. This is not to eliminate the possibility that reference to God might be made by means of religious experience, but simply to point out that attempts to fix a reference in this way may fail to be widely convincing, given the contested nature of religious experiences themselves.

An initial tack, then, is to seek a designation on which there is general agreement that, if it designates anything, it designates God. A striking attempt at such is Anselm's formula in the Proslogion, "God is that than which nothing greater can be conceived", a formula which in its spare eloquence comes very near to the kind which we are seeking. It is found on examination to be extremely agnostic, for it attempts to indicate what a God must be, and not to describe God. Most especially, Anselm says nowhere that God is the greatest 'thing', or the greatest 'being', or even a being or thing greater than which cannot be conceived, as many writers, despite Anselm's reply to Gaunilo, persist in saying. Nor yet is God held by Anselm to be conceivable—He is "that than which nothing greater can be conceived", but He himself, as Anselm says, cannot be conceived. So the definition does not describe but rather gives a designation which, if it designates anything, designates only that which is called God. The task of Anselm's proof is to show that it must have a designation.

Anselm's proof is customarily regarded as unsuccessful. This does not matter for our purposes since our object is not a proof of the existence of God but simply a designation which, without claiming to define God, designates that which, if it existed, Christians would be obliged to say was God. To this end Anselm's definition is unsatisfactory, not because it fails in the proof, but because its formal nature deprives it of any means of linking God causally to the world. To employ an argument analogous to that which we have employed in the scientific case, we must claim to point to God via some effect and a more satisfactory way of doing so is to follow the more experiential lead of Aquinas and say that 'God is that which is the source and cause of all there is'. This does not demonstrate that there is a unified source nor that, if there is, it meets any description preferred by theists. As in the scientific case, to be a realist about reference is to be a 'fallibilist' about knowledge of the referent. Speakers may refer and yet be mistaken, even quite radically mistaken, as to the nature of that to which they refer. So the theist may be mistaken in his beliefs about the source and cause of all and assume it to be something of which one can appropriately predicate personalistic terms when one cannot, or assume it to be a unified source when it is not, and so on. This fallibilism should not trouble the Christian realist if he acknowledges that he may simply be wrong in his various beliefs and that some of these are so central that, if he is wrong concerning them, his whole structure of belief is gravely flawed. If that which the Christian refers to as the source and cause of all bears no conceivable resemblance to God as conceived by Christianity, then he must admit himself to be so deluded as to the nature of the referent that his faith must be lost. This possibility of being in error is the risk such a realist takes.

This said, it is important that we re-examine the attempt to ground a reference to God by means of religious experience, for although it is unlikely to persuade the sceptic, the 'pointing' to God through religious experience is of considerable importance to the faithful, particularly because religious communities put varying degrees of weight on accounts of religious experience. If an individual judged saintly by those who know him is convinced of the authenticity of his experience, he may persuade others that his experience is 'of God'. Hence, more confidence is likely to be placed in the belief that Newman's experience was of God than that the experience of the would-be murderer of the MP was, more yet in the belief that what Moses experienced on Mount Sinai truly was of God, more yet in the belief that whatever was responsible for the empty tomb of Jesus was God. These cases are controversial, certainly, for they rely on complex historical and hermeneutical issues—for example, the existence of Moses, or the historical reality of the empty tomb. We need not rely on these to fix a reference, yet the Christian may well feel that on some of these his belief stands or falls. Perhaps few would abandon their convictions if it could be demonstrated that Newman's experience was wholly the result of a sleeping draught, but more would be affected if, given an empty tomb, that which was responsible for it was man or simple confusion, more yet if, given a physical resurrection of Jesus, that which was responsible was radically unlike anything which one would wish to call God. The Christian realist must concede that there is a point, theoretically at least, at which one would be committed to abandoning theism, at which one would say, 'I judged that a God as conceived in a Christian way was responsible for these events or states of affairs, but I was wrong'.

This may seem extremely crude and, in a sense, the realist position is crude because it depends upon the belief that God is causally related to the world, at its origin or perhaps even in specific events and experiences within human history. But where this position is not crude is with respect to the criticism customarily levelled at the theological realist, that he claims to describe God. The agnosticism of our formulations preserves us from this presumption, for we do not claim to describe God but to point through His effects, and beyond His effects, to Him. It is, hence, of the utmost importance to keep in mind the distinction, never remote in the writings of Anselm or of Aquinas, between referring to God and defining Him. This is the fine edge at which negative theology and positive theology meet, for the apophatic insight that we say nothing of God, but only point towards Him, is the basis for the tentative and avowedly inadequate stammerings by which we attempt to speak of God and His acts. And, as we have argued, this separation of referring and defining is at the very heart of metaphorical speaking and is what makes it not only possible but necessary that in our stammering after a transcendent God we must speak, for the most part, metaphorically or not at all.

Let us reconsider Hepburn's challenge,

The question which should be of greatest concern to the theologian is not whether this or that myth may be re-expressed in language less flagrantly pictorial, more abstract in appearance, but whether or not the circle of myth, metaphor and symbol is a closed one: and if closed then in what way propositions about God manage to *refer*.

This contains an extremely radical criticism, not simply of metaphor, but of any claim to speak of God. Initially, the passage may seem to demand a proof for the existence of God but, whether or not this is what Hepburn wanted, what he is asking for here is not a proof but an account of how any finite and figurative speaking can ever claim to refer to a transcendent Deity. The intimation is that the theist can *only* claim to refer to God at the cost of making God finite, of making Him a thing amongst the things whose qualities we delimit and describe; in short, Hepburn seems prey to the bogey that reference must involve unrevisable or exhaustive description. But the theist need not share his fate nor his empiricism, for he can coherently claim that his language is referential or, as we prefer, reality depicting, without claim to definitive knowledge. We are not, of course, saying that the 'objects' of a theological study can also be the objects of a scientific theory; nor are we arguing that the theist is right in any of his claims about the Divine Other and his relationship to man. Rather, we are saying that the theist can reasonably take his talk of God, bound as it is within a wheel of images, as being reality depicting, while at the same time acknowledging its inadequacy as description. This, we believe, is the position a critical theological realist must take.

VIII

METAPHOR AND THEOLOGICAL REALISM

THE naïve theological realist, according to Don Cupitt, is one who maintains that Christian worship "is undeniably addressed to one other than the worshippers, a King of the universe who makes all things, knows all things and rules all things . . . a cosmos-transcending absolute being". The crucial objection to religious realism, he says, "is that insofar as it succeeds in being realistic it necessarily ceases to be religious".[1] This objectifying and meta-physical theism is, according to Cupitt, spiritually vulgar, morally suspect, and philosophically indefensible. Not only do the tradi-tional proofs for the existence of God fail, we cannot even know what it means to speak of a being who is omniscient, pure spirit, and beyond the realm of experience.[2] In *Taking Leave of God*, Cupitt cites Schleiermacher, Kierkegaard, and Feuerbach, but we suggest that his greater and unspoken debt is to Locke, Hobbes, and Hume, for his position, like that of many of his British and American contemporaries, is in the main stream of traditional empiricist assessments of religious language and is of interest to us in so far as it draws the conclusions that others shrink from. Whether they attack traditional theism as does Cupitt or attempt to defend it as do Ramsey and Ferré, few contemporary English-language writers on religious language are free from a residual empiricism which, whatever the intentions of its proponents, is fundamentally incompatible with traditional, transcendental Christianity.

Let us compare some of Cupitt's arguments with those of a noted modern empiricist openly hostile to religious belief. One cannot intelligibly believe in God, says A. J. Ayer, <u>unless one can give some account of what it means to say 'God exists'</u>. It is, he argues, customary for the theist to maintain that these words express a true proposition, "though they do not know what this proposition is; it is one that surpasses human understanding."[3] But until we have an intelligible proposition before us, there is nothing for faith to get to work on and it is only when those who understand (or think they understand) something by the phrase 'God exists' find their own account of it unworthy of credence, that they take refuge in saying that it falls short of what the words really mean. But words have no meaning beyond the meaning that is given them, and a proposition is not made the more credible by being treated as an approximation to something that we do not find intelligible.[4]

The theist must explain what he means if he wishes to be taken seriously. To say that words are inadequate and approximate does not help, for, since words have only the meanings we give them, if we do not know exactly what they mean, we cannot genuinely claim to mean anything. Cupitt is even more explicit; the word 'spirit', he says, is a human word and indicates a capacity of human beings. We do not know what it would mean

to suppose that there can exist a being that is pure spirit and nothing else. For how can there be a pure subsistent relation of transcending without any 'matter' or nature that is transcended? It seems not to make sense to say that the transcending *is* the nature. So it appears that we are forced back to the point from which we began, namely that for us there is no god but the religious requirement: the imperative *Become spirit!* is the presence of God within us, and for us it is God, it is the goal as well as the requirement.[5]

Here are all the traditional empiricist stipulations: if a claim is to be genuinely cognitive, there must be strictly applicable definition, clarity, certainty, and significant description. Above all, we must not 'abuse' words by claiming to use them in senses other than their 'given' and stipulated ones. We hear echoes of Locke here, and even stronger ones of Hume.

In Part III of Hume's *Dialogues Concerning Natural Religion*, Demea speaks of God's utter incomprehensibility to man. In Part IV, he is criticized by Cleanthes for insisting that God

"has no manner of likeness or resemblance to human creatures" . . . [for] (. . . "if our ideas, so far as they go, be not just and adequate and correspondent to his real nature, I do not know what there is in this subject worth insisting on. Is the name, without any meaning, of such mighty importance? Or how do you mystics, who maintain the absolute incomprehensibility of the Deity, differ from sceptics or atheists, who assert that the first cause of all is unknown and unintelligible?"

Demea objects to being called a 'mystic' and retorts "that *anthropomorphite* is an appellation as invidious, and implies as dangerous consequences, as the epithet of *mystic* . . .".[6]

This lays the ground on which Cupitt and others less outspoken, or perhaps simply less consistent, now stand; the would-be theist must claim to know too much of God, or claim to know nothing of him at all. He must be an "anthropomorphite" or a sceptic. For the philosophically refined, this is no choice, and the conciliatory Philo has only to remind us of the inability of our ideas to be "just and adequate and correspondent" to God's real nature to make the sceptic's case. If we cannot, as theists willingly admit, make statements which are just and adequate and correspondent to God's real nature we have no right, with tentative and approximating statements, to claim to speak of him at all—this is Hume's version of the empiricist line of argument which concludes, 'no theory term ever refers'. Similarly, Ayer states:

> to say that something transcends the human understanding is to say that it is unintelligible. And what is unintelligible cannot be significantly described . . . If one allows that it is impossible to define God in intelligible terms, then one is allowing that it is impossible for a sentence both to be significant and to be about God. If a mystic admits that the object of his vision cannot be described, then he must also admit that he is bound to talk nonsense when he describes it. [7]

If we are to judge from the frequency with which he mentions them, the mystics are particularly objectionable to Ayer. Certainly he objects to their reliance on 'non-literal speech'. In so recent a book as *The Central Questions of Philosophy*, a work which begins and ends with criticisms of metaphysics and religion, Ayer says of the mystical claim that, "If what they are said to establish does not make sense or, on any literal interpretation, is obviously false, then at the very least the case for their being cognitive has not been made out." [8]

On the basis of what we have said in the previous chapters, it is not surprising that empiricism should lead to religious scepticism— what is surprising is that contemporary theologians and philosophers of religion should cling to an empiricist framework at a time when the same empiricism has been shown to be bankrupt in other areas of philosophy. [9]

We have said that criticisms of metaphor in religious language often conceal a more radical critique of the possibility of any talk of God, of any traditional theologizing at all. This is so because the traditional empiricist criticisms of 'non-literal' speech are, as the quotations above demonstrate, in the end, attacks on the possibility of any metaphysics. The plan of our counter-argument has been to show that models and metaphorical theory terms may, in both the scientific and religious cases, be reality depicting without pretending to be directly descriptive, and by doing so to support the Christian's right to make metaphysical claims.

[margin note: DEPICTING REALITY W/OUT DESCRIBING IT DIRECTLY]

In the theological case as in the scientific one, assessment of the cognitive place of metaphor and model is tied up with the relative acceptability of empiricist, idealist, and realist appraisals of their role in theory constructions. These three categories fit the theological discussions even better than they did the scientific debate. For example, we mentioned that few scientists or philosophers of science are willing to commit themselves to a thoroughgoing idealism in which the scientist's models are simply fictive constructs. Some theologians, on the other hand, do not hesitate to say that the theist's models are fictive constructs without any pretension to depict a reality independent of the human condition.[10]

We have already seen that empiricism has its theological advocates, especially in the English-speaking world, and it is with these that we are chiefly concerned.[11] D. Z. Phillips's theory of 'religious language-games', for example, though purportedly Wittgensteinian, is very much in the spirit of twentieth-century linguistic empiricism. According to Phillips, the religious use of a term such as 'faith', 'hope', or 'prayer' can be empirically grounded by means of the place it has in a system of religious utterances or in an individual's 'religious language-game'. Sense is given, in an acceptably empiricist way, 'from the bottom up' and, as Phillips takes pains to mention, without relying on transcendental metaphysics.[12] From Phillips's point of view, this rejection of metaphysics is all to the good, but we may wonder about the value of grounding religious claims 'from the bottom up', if that means that the bottom is all one *can* speak of. If we reject transcendental questions, we must jettison much of what is traditionally involved in the use of terms like 'prayer', 'faith', and 'God'.

A more satisfactory and still putatively empiricist account of religious language and one which, moreover, deals explicitly with model and metaphor in religious language, is Ian Ramsey's "Christian Empiricism". Ramsey objected very much to suggestions that his treatment of theistic models in *Religious Language* rendered them little more than a matter of subjective picture preference. His object, he insisted, was to show them to be fully cognitive and hence to contribute to the rehabilitation of metaphysics.

In his later writings, Ramsey acknowledges that, if one wished to say that the theist's models were genuinely cognitive, it was not enough simply to mark their presence in religious language, note their qualified status, their inter-dependence, and so on—it was necessary to give some account of reference. "Christian assertions must be a clearer objective reference. Somewhere or other they must encourage us to appeal to 'what is the case'."[13] His suggestion was that the models could be grounded in 'cosmic disclosure', hence, "The claim for 'objectivity'—'objective reference'—is grounded in the sense I have of being confronted, of being acted upon, in the discernment I have of some claim impinging on me."[14] In his 1972 Address to the Aristotelian Society, he develops this in order to argue that reliance on disclosures does not "deprive religious statements of any objective reference and *a fortiori* of any transcendent claim". He cites an example from Locke: Suppose we see two figures shrouded in mist. We may be disposed to say that one is a statue and the other a man but, even when we lack reliable labels, something can be said with certainty, "viz. that in each case 'something exists'". We may be mistaken in our articulation of that which is given but, "we certainly cannot be mistaken about the objective reference, the objectivity which has been disclosed. We cannot be mistaken about that 'something' which is other than ourselves."[15]

This last point is not, perhaps, as certain as Ramsey suggests, yet for the purposes of our argument we can concede it him. Even so, it is unclear how he will then be able to move, as he wishes, from the fact of disclosure to the elaboration of disclosure by means of a model or of a plurality of models. His difficulty is this—he relies on his empiricism to ground his reference (the object is simply given in disclosure, like Locke's figures in the mist), but he is not justified in terms of the same empiricism in developing the 'disclosure-event' with models of God as husband, king, landlord, shepherd, or judge. The disclosure is simply a point of reference with no content and, to be consistent with his empiricism and with the spirit of Locke's example, Ramsey should restrict his claims to what is observable, but this he plainly does not wish to do. Furthermore, he does not wish to justify the use of just any model in speaking of God, but specifically those traditionally employed by Christians— spirit, father, king, and so on—models which, as Ramsey demonstrates in *Models for Divine Activity*, grow and change at the hands of the worshipping community. But even were these models 'given' in some disclosure event, on his own empiricist basis, the enrichment of sense over the generations would be without justification. Ramsey can elaborate his account in terms of models only by dispensing with his empiricism, yet he can ground the disclosures in which the models theoretically are based only by retaining it. Many of the inconsistencies of his programme arise from this desire to incorporate metaphysical claims in an empiricist framework.

It is more genuinely consistent with empiricism to take the theist's assertions or parables, as does R. B. Braithwaite in 'An Empiricist's View of the Nature of Religious Belief', in a conative way. Theistic assertions are regarded "as being primarily declarations of adherence to a policy of action, declarations of commitment to a way of life".[16] This position is free from the trans-empirical tendencies of Ramsey's models and disclosures, but it is correspondingly, as Braithwaite's critics have been quick to point out, much more agnostic. Indeed, it is not far from the scepticism which Philo advocated and to which Cupitt adheres. This, of course, is not surprising, for an empiricist theology consistently executed has little scope for the cognitive employment of models and gives no basis for trans-empirical claims.

Perhaps this is the reason why so many theologians and philosophers of religion have shown a preference for what are essentially idealist interpretations of models, suggesting that models have primarily or even exclusively an emotive value. This is not so far from the empiricist position as might at first be thought, for if we recall how much empiricist and idealist have in common in the appraisal of scientific models, we can see that the same is true in the theological case. Both the Christian empiricist and the Christian idealist must see the theist's models at best as useful fictions, and when the empiricist, too, adopts a conative or emotive theory, there remains little to separate him from the Christian idealist as we describe him. Hence, Braithwaite can cite with approval the comment of the idealist philosopher, J. M. E. McTaggart, that religion is "an emotion resting on a conviction of a harmony between ourselves and the universe at large",[17] and it is not surprising that Ramsey's account of models in terms of 'Christian empiricism' should be developed by others into positions which, in one degree or another, regard the theist's models as principally evaluative phenomena. Ramsey's purposes would have been better served had he rid himself of ''Christian empiricism'' and turned to a theological realism.

SUM OF 6 & 7

In the last two chapters, we have argued that the empiricist and idealist accounts of scientific models fail because they cannot account for actual scientific practice or for the predictive and cumulative success of investigations which are model-based, and that a cognitive treatment of such models adequate to actual practice is possible only on realist presuppositions. By providing an account of how the metaphorical theory terms which a model generates may be referential without being tied to unrevisable description, we have tried to facilitate a realism which is neither dogmatic nor presumptuous. Similarly, we suggest that any account which treats the theist's models as fully cognitive must be realist in orientation; the Christian empiricist should have no place for models at all, and the idealist, while he may retain them, cannot consistently say that they in any way depict transcendent states and relations. Empiricist or idealist analyses of model and metaphor in religious language are only really attractive if it is judged that realism has failed—indeed, *Taking Leave of God*, a book we take as symptomatic of the empiricist – idealist fusion which we have described, makes its argument precisely on the ground that realism has failed, both by being philosophically indefensible and religiously puerile.

THE BASIC POSITION TO BE DEFENDED

In defending theological realism, we defend the theist's right to make metaphysical claims, but we have stressed that it is not our object to prove the existence of God, still less to prove that the models and metaphors which Christians use in speaking of God have a special validity. Our concern is with conceptual possibility rather than proof, and with a demonstration that we may justly claim to speak of God without claiming to define him, and to do so by means of metaphor. Realism accommodates figurative speech which is reality depicting without claiming to be directly descriptive. Despite claims to the contrary, a reflective theological realism (even of the kind which holds that Christian worship ''is undeniably addressed to one other than the worshippers, a King of the universe who makes all things, knows all things'', etc., for the realism we defend is the very sort that Cupitt attacks) need not do violence to genuine religious conviction by vulgar anthropomorphism— indeed, it is particularly well suited to a theology which wishes to preserve the sense of God's transcendence.

But this realism has even more to commend itself to the Christian than this, for it emphasizes, in a way that neither an empiricist nor an idealist position does, the importance to Christian belief of experience, community, and an interpretive tradition. Even in its scientific application, the realism which we have defended brings these three factors into play. Experience is essential, for ultimately it is in experience that reference is grounded—thus, without being empiricist, this realism is an empirical theory. Community is essential because each speaker is a member of a particular community of interest, which provides the context for referential claims. A great part of our referential activity depends on what Putnam has called a "division of linguistic labour", that is, we rely on authoritative members of our community to ground referring expressions. We refer to Columbus when we mention his name, because we have heard the name from others, who heard it from others, etc., going back to Columbus himself. In a different example, we claim to refer to neutrinos when we speak of them, not in virtue of knowledge and experience which each of us has of them, but because we are members of a linguistic community containing experts whose experience is judged sufficiently immediate to ground a reference. Putnam's claim that it is not words which refer, but speakers using words who refer, bears the gloss that each speaker is a member of a particular linguistic community and thus connected by means of other speakers to a range of experience far exceeding their own.

The descriptive vocabulary which any individual uses is, in turn, dependent on the community of interest and investigation in which he finds himself, and the descriptive vocabulary which a community has at its disposal is embedded in particular traditions of investigation and conviction; for example, the geneticist will assume that it is a biochemical mechanism which is responsible for trait inheritance and not magical spells or curses. Descriptive language is forged in a particular context of investigation where there is agreement on matters such as what constitutes evidence, what are genuine arguments, what counts as a fact, and so on, and while claims may be genuinely referential, this does not mean that they escape from this contextuality. The realist position is not that we dispense with theoretical contexts or wider frameworks of assumption, but that the world informs our theory even though our theory may never adequately describe the world. This is behind Boyd's interesting observation that reference is linked to the context of enquiry, a puzzling claim until we recall that it is not words but speakers using words who refer, and that speakers use words according to established patterns of investigation and interest.[18]

The point that speakers use language according to precedents and established belief is not a new one (it was Vico's point and Thomas Kuhn's, too), but commonly it has been taken to imply a relativism like that of Nietzsche.[19] What is different about the reassessment of reference we have given is that it allows that reference does indeed occur within a context of enquiry, within a particular tradition of investigation with its own descriptive vocabulary, yet insists that this contextuality does not deprive the descriptive vocabulary of its referential status—this is the point of the claim that terms can be coreferential across theories, and in this way it reinforces a realist, rather than relativist, argument.

Corresponding to the scientific communities of interest, there are religious communities of interest (Christians, for example) which are bound by shared assumptions, interests, and traditions of interpretation, and share a descriptive vocabulary.

The Christian, too, makes claims on the basis of experience which, although different from the kind on which scientific judgements are based, is experience none the less. It is important to clarify what we mean by 'experience' in this context; it is a portmanteau term to cover two sorts, the first being the dramatic or pointed religious experiences of the kind which might prompt one to say, 'whatever appeared to me on the mountain was God', or 'whatever caused me to change my life was God'. The second are the diffuse experiences which form the subject of subsequent metaphysical reflection, the kind on which Aquinas based his proofs for the existence of God; for example, the experience of contingency which prompts us to postulate the non-contingent, the experience of cause which prompts us to postulate the uncaused, the experience of order which prompts us to postulate an ordering agent, and so on.[20] On this view, even the abstractions of natural theology are based, in the long run, on experience—although of a diffuse kind. When an individual, or the wider religious community, decides upon a particular model or image as a means of elucidating experience, pointed or diffuse, they do so as heirs to an established tradition of explanation and a common descriptive vocabulary. This insight is too often deprived of its value by being linked to the relativist arguments which vitiate the 'religious language-games' approach, but it is our suggestion that in the religious case as in the scientific one, although claims are made within a context of enquiry, this does not deprive them of their referential value. This realist argument is possible because we dispense with the empiricist dogma that reference is fixed by unrevisable description and adopt instead a social theory where reference is established partly by senses of terms, but largely by speakers' use of those terms in particular situations. Experience does remain vital, but it is admitted to be experience assessed in the categories used by a particular community of interest and within a particular tradition of evaluation.

Consider accounts of religious or mystical experience; the mystic, as we have noted, often feels a crisis of descriptive language because there do not seem to be words and concepts in the common stock adequate to his or her experience. This straining of linguistic resources leads to the catachretical employment of metaphor, of phrases like 'the dark night', 'the spiritual marriage', and 'mystic union'. But the significance of these terms can be assessed, even by other theists, only in terms of the contexts in which they arise. Often, indeed almost always, the mystical writer is influenced by a particular tradition of descriptive imagery and philosophical pre-supposition. John of the Cross, for example, uses scholastic terminology (although not always with the sense the scholastic writers intended) and the theme of 'mystic night' and 'cloud of unknowing' is itself a biblical theme, harking back to the Cloud of the Exodus and to the Night of the Song of Songs.[21] Often, too, it will be found that the mystic's remarks arise from particular patterns of devotional life; hence the common injunction that the neophyte follow a particular course of life, of reading and of prayer so that he may, by God's grace, be open to this 'night' or 'marriage'. Experience is vital to the mystic, but experience interpreted in the descriptive vocabulary of their particular community of interest and tradition of belief.

This emphasis on experience does not mean that only those privileged with mystical experiences can speak about them. The generality of Christians speak of the 'beatific vision' without having had experiences which they would describe as such. They do so because they belong to a community and tradition of faith which contains authoritative members for whom the term does denominate a particular experience. There is an element of trust involved in relying on others whose experience is wider than one's own, yet in almost all areas of life this is the perfectly rational enterprise of using the wider resources of the community to extend one's own, and necessarily limited, experience and expertise.

From our previous comments on metaphor and reference it should be clear that there is no reason why the mystics' claims, although qualified and couched in the language of their particular mystical tradition, should not be referential. The essential claim, the 'dubbing event', is something like 'Whatever caused this experience is God.' The referential value of the claim is not, then, affected by being articulated in theory-laden terms like 'spiritual marriage' or 'descent of the cloud', though it must be emphasized that to show that the use of terms like 'spiritual marriage', 'beatific vision', or 'dark night' refers does not guarantee that these are experiences of the sort Christians have taken them to be. It does not demonstrate that they are experiences of the Christian God, or of any god at all; but this is only to say that realism involves the possibility of error, as the theological realist is willing to admit. The mystics and those following them may be sadly misguided as to the cause of their experience and so, of course, may be the physicist who speaks of 'black holes in space'.

We discover perhaps to our surprise that the Christian mystic is of all theists the most likely to be a realist, aware of the presence and reality of God, yet aware at the same time of the inability of human speech and thought to contain Him. [22] To make sense of his experience the mystic has recourse to figures and images. Compelled by the strength of experience (or by religious superiors) to give account of it, she does so in the language of her time and tradition, using the language, perhaps, of Aquinas, or Cassian, or St Paul. But beneath this is the bedrock of her experience and it is here that her reference is grounded, and here ultimately that reference is grounded for those who take her account as authoritative.

[margin note: MYSTIC'S REFERENCE IS GROUNDED IN EXPERIENCE]

The mystic's case is a dramatic one, but in more commonplace theological reflections, and in the use of the more commonplace models and metaphors which Ramsey described, we see the same factors at work and the same realist presupposition. The religious teacher is not always privileged with experiences denied to the common run; he may equally be someone with the gift of putting into words what others have sensed. He may have the ability to find metaphors and choose models which illuminate the experience of others, for example, be the first to say that God's presence is like that of a powerful wind. The great divine and the great poet have this in common: both use metaphor to say that which can be said in no other way but which, once said, can be recognized by many.

A reflective realism is better suited to Ramsey's ends than his own empiricism precisely because, with its emphasis on linguistic community and tradition, it takes account of the fact that descriptive vocabulary and choice of models will arise within a context and within traditions of conviction and practice. That theological models must be understood contextually is shown admirably in Ramsey's discussion of the progressive development of the 'spirit' or 'wind' model for God's activity.[23] But it is not necessary to believe that, at one moment in the history of Israel, the model of God as spirit was given, by cosmic disclosure, in a fully elaborated state and immediately embraced by everyone. It is more likely that this was one of many stumbling approximations used to articulate experiences judged to be of God and that, over the years, this particular model was preferred to others by those attempting to describe similar experiences, that it was enriched by the association of wind with breath and gradually became so much a part of the community's descriptive vocabulary that to speak of God as 'spirit' became an accustomed manner of speech. In this way, over time, there comes into being a rich assortment of models whose sources may be unknown but which have been gradually selected out by the faithful as being especially adequate to their experience. This accumulation of favoured models, embellished by the glosses of generations, gives the context for Christian reflection and provides the matrix for the descriptive vocabulary which Christians continue to employ in attempts to describe their experience. This accretion of images, all of them hesitant and approximating, yet confirmed by generations of belief, constitutes much of what Christians call revelation. Thus, when Christians say that 'God is spirit' they are not, as Cupitt seems to think, giving a description of God, nor is the sense of their statement to be had by taking a definition of 'spirit' and applying it, *tout court*, to God as an instantiating case. Even the statement that 'God is spirit' is one which, on examination, the Christian feels compelled to qualify—hence the tendency to say that words fail to catch their subject which Ayer finds so provoking. This use of 'spirit' is one which sits in a particular context and tradition; its sense is not given by rigid definition, but by considering the way in which the term is variously used in the community and tradition, and importantly, the way it is used in Christianity's sacred texts. This is so much so that if someone wished to understand the sense of 'God is spirit' one might do well to say to him, 'read the Bible!'

Now it may seem that if we deal with murky definition, with a sense developed over centuries, and with a thousand innuendoes, we have the difficulty which the empiricist describes of not knowing exactly what we are saying, and hence not saying anything at all. The realist response to this complaint is that the claim that 'God is spirit' is not grounded in unequivocal knowledge. It denominates rather than describes God, or, more precisely, it denominates the source of thousands of experiences which Jews and Christians have spoken of, using the descriptive language at their disposal as the working of the spirit, and which they take to be God.

It is sometimes said that there is as much of Christian significance in the plays of Shakespeare as there is in the Old Testament; why not, therefore, regard the two equal as sources of revelation? Those who maintain this are greatly misled, not by irreverence for the sacred texts, but by insensitivity to the way texts are used within a literary tradition. In implying that revelation exists as a body of free-floating truths that can be picked up anywhere indifferently, they misunderstand the sense in which Christianity is 'a religion of the book'. This point can be made without recourse to Christian presupposition and any number of literary examples may be used to argue it, but a particularly striking one is that of Japanese Court Poetry.[24]

The body of poems known as Japanese Court Poetry spans the years 550–1500, a time when the Japanese sensibility was being distinguished from that of its neighbours, China and Korea. The poems were commissioned to be read at court and published in Court Anthologies; the topics were principally those which concerned the courtiers: courtly life, travel, and personal grievance. All this made it a literature particularly well suited to the use of literary conventions, not only stylistic ones, but conventions of significance. A writer, by the simple employment of a word or phrase, could call up the allusions of previous poems and use their significance to embellish his own. Earl Miner gives this example of the technique known as 'honkadori' (allusive variation):

In Episode CXXIII of *The Tales of Ise*, Narihira writes to a woman in the village of Fukakusa (which means 'deep grass'), saying he must leave her and wondering whether she will remain faithful. She replies with a protest of her fidelity and a plea for his constancy which is so moving that he resolves to stay . . . His poem runs:

> When I have gone
> From this village of Fukakusa,
> After all these years,
> Will its deep grass grow ever taller
> And it become a tangled moor?

She replies:

> Though it become a moor,
> Like the quails I will raise my plaintive
> cry
> As the long years pass,
> For can it be that you will not come back,
> If only briefly for the falconing?

That romantic exchange lies behind a poem . . . by Fujiwara Shunzei.

> As evening falls,
> From along the moors the autumn wind
> Blows chill into the heart,
> And the quails raise their plaintive cry
> In the deep grass of Fukakusa village.

Shunzei's is an autumn poem. It gains in resonance and significance by the romance implied in the allusion. The sense of beauty and desolation in autumn is heightened by allusion to a love affair between the dashing Narihira and a woman whose very name is lost and by locating the scene in a village that no longer existed.[25]

The image of the quails crying in the long grass is distinctive enough to stand even on its own. We do not need to recognize Shunzei's allusion to make sense of the poem, but for its intended readers the image did not stand on its own, it immediately recalled the previous application of Narihira. Two hundred years separate these poets, yet Shunzei could rely on his audiences' acquaintance with Narihira's image, and other writers writing later than both could, by using the same image, recall not only the original poem but the later gloss upon it.

This allusive formula is particularly successful because the corpus of poems is small and its readership restricted, but wherever a writer can rely on his readers' acquaintance with privileged texts, whether these are esteemed for their literary merit or because they are regarded as sacred, he can employ similar allusive techniques and, without the literary self-consciousness of 'honkadori', this is what has happened in the successive narratives, chronicles, poems, and prophecies which compose the sacred texts of Christianity and Judaism.

In St John's gospel, Jesus says to the woman at the well that, if she knew who he was, she would ask of him and he would give her 'living' (that is, 'running') water. It is perhaps enough for a minimal construal of the metaphor that we know that water is refreshing, cleansing, and life giving—any reader could tell you this. But this is not a metaphor used at random; in the prophetic literature 'living water' is associated with God as the source of life, hence the invitation,

> Ho, every one who thirsts,
> come to the waters; (Isaiah 55:1)

and the complaint,

> they have forsaken me
> the fountain of living waters, (Jeremiah 2:13)

and the eschatological promise that

> On that day living waters shall flow
> out from Jerusalem, (Zechariah 14:8)[26]

And these prophetic uses recall the Exodus where, when the Israelites were desperate with thirst, God bade Moses stand upon the rock in Horeb and smite it, that water might come out of it and the people drink. (Exodus 17: 5–6)

We can be sure that many of these allusions were apparent to the writer of the Fourth Gospel, and in John 7:37–38 we read that

On the last day of the feast, the great day, Jesus stood up and proclaimed, "If any one thirst, let him come to me and drink. He who believes in me, as the scripture has said, 'Out of his heart shall flow rivers of living water'."

We move from the Exodus to the prophetic promises, and from these to the water of John's baptism and the water from Christ's pierced side. (John 19:34). In the Book of Revelation, this water recurs, watering a renewed Paradise:

> Then he showed me the river of the water
> of life, bright as crystal, flowing from
> the throne of God and of the Lamb. (22:1)

The smitten rock, the riven side, the fountain of life, death by water in the flood and life by water in baptism and the resurrected Christ—these images appear again and again in liturgies, in homiletics, on baptismal founts, in church mosaics and friezes, on stained glass, and in countless paintings. They form an almost inescapable background to Christian thought, with each new reflection bringing to mind those that went before it. But this is not static—the image of living water can be renewed and embellished by each individual who reflects upon it—so Teresa of Avila, who as a child knelt before a picture of Christ at the Samaritan well and prayed "Lord, give me this water", says:

I cannot find anything more apt for the explanation of certain spiritual things than this element of water; for, as I am ignorant and my wit gives me no help and I am so fond of this element, I have looked at it more attentively than at other things[27]

and uses the image as the basis for a similitude comparing the contemplative's progress to the watering of a garden. Any who think that this use and re-use of figures is characteristic only of the early Church or the unreformed need only open an Evangelical hymnal of the nineteenth century where the same figures reappear:

> When Israel's tribes were parch'd with thirst,
> Forth from the rock the waters burst;
> And all their future journey through
> Yielded them drink, and gospel too!
>
> In Moses' rod a type they saw
> Of his severe and firy law
> The smitten rock prefigur'd Him
> From whose pierc'd side all blessings stream.
>
> John Newton, 'That Rock was Christ' (1772)

and the more familiar;

Rock of Ages, cleft for me,
Let me hide myself in Thee!
Let the water and the blood,
From Thy riven side which flowed,
Be of sin the double cure,
Cleanse me from its guilt and power. [28]

In Christian theology, this repetition of metaphor has often gone hand in hand with typological interpretation and the conviction that certain events in the Old Testament prefigure those in the New. We need not commit ourselves to this tenet of faith to make the essentially literary point that, in ways similar to the allusive techniques of any literary tradition, certain metaphors and models of God's presence and gracious acts, models which often can stand as significant in their own right without historical glosses, have been used and re-used in the central texts of Christianity and in subsequent expositions of those texts. So, to explain what it means to Christians to say that God is a fountain of living water, or a vine-keeper, or a rock, or fortress, or king requires an account not merely of fountains, rocks, vines, and kings but of a whole tradition of experiences and of the literary tradition which records and interprets them.

This, incidentally, is an answer to the frequently put question, 'on what basis are some of the Christian's models given priority over others?' Choice is not unconditioned; we do not choose the model of God as shepherd over that of God as poultry keeper or cattleman at random. A favoured model continues to be so in virtue of its own applicability certainly, but also because the history of its application makes it already freighted with meaning. To say that God is 'king' recalls a whole history of kingship and insubordination recorded in the biblical texts.

These metaphors retain their metaphorical nature but they have become more than simple metaphor—they are almost emblematic— and if one were to undertake a study, not of the use of metaphor as a conceptual vehicle in religious language, but of the specific senses of Christian metaphorical uses, it would, in a great part, be a study of gloss upon gloss, use and re-use of the figures which comprise an interweaving of meanings so complex that the possible readings are never exhausted.

For this reason, it is dull and misguided to suggest that Shakespeare and the Old Testament might be considered as religious texts of equal value to Christianity, if this is to suggest that the value of a text consists wholly in the set of moral or spiritual dicta which may be extracted from it. This is the crudest form of theological empiricism. The Old Testament's importance is not principally as a set of propositions but as the milieu from which Christian belief arose and indeed still arises, for these books are the source of Christian descriptive language and particularly of metaphors which have embodied a people's understanding of God.

From the literary observation we return to the philosophical one, for the touchstone of these chronicles of faith is experience, experiences pointed or diffuse, the experience of individuals and of communities which are believed to be experiences of the activity of a transcendent God. The language used to account for them is metaphorical and qualified, it stands within a tradition of use and is theory-laden, yet in so far as it is grounded on experience it is referential, and it is the theological realist's conviction that that to which it refers, the source of these experiences, is God who is the source and cause of all that is.

John Donne's 'Hymne to Christ, at the Authors Last Going Into Germany' begins in this way,

> In what torne ship soever I embarke,
> That ship shall be my embleme of thy Arke;
> What sea soever swallow mee, that flood
> Shall be to mee an embleme of thy blood;

The ark, the flood, death—death in Christ's blood—water, baptism, death and rising again—in four lines, Donne brings together the sacred past and the author's present in one image at the centre of which is Christ's atonement. The author's experience is interpreted by his sacred texts, his sacred texts are reinterpreted by his own experience, the whole is founded upon centuries of devotional practice. If there is one insight to be taken from philosophical hermeneutics, it is this—that we interpret texts and they interpret us. But something needs to be added to this formula, for it is not simply that texts interpret us, they interpret our experiences; and it is not simply that we interpret texts, for we also interpret the experiences which they more or less obscurely chronicle.

It is a commonplace that in the twentieth century we have lost the living sense of the biblical metaphors which our forefathers had. Sometimes it is suggested that this is a consequence of urban life where few have any contact with shepherds and sheep, kings, and vines. This simple view fails to see that the distinctively Christian reading of the metaphors of God as shepherd, or king, or vine keeper could never be had simply by knowing about sheep, kings, and vines, and forgets that the Scottish crofter of a previous generation who had no experience of grape vines or Temples had no trouble construing Jesus's claim to be the true vine or Temple. Other times, it is said that we have lost this living sense because we no longer read the Bible and there is much in this, yet it is not difficult to imagine that there are some Christians (extreme fundamentalists) who know the text word for word, yet for whom, precisely because they regard it as simply a book of historical fact, much of its allusive significance is lost. If it is true that biblical imagery is lifeless to modern man (and it is not obvious that this is so), this is more likely to be the legacy of historical criticism, of the search for the historical Jesus, and of attempts made by Christians both liberal and conservative to salvage his exact words and acts from the dross of allusion and interpretation with which the gospel writers surrounded them. It is the legacy of a literalism which equates religious truth with historical facts, whatever these might be. Christianity is indeed a religion of the book, but not of a book of this sort of fact. Its sacred texts are chronicles of experience, armouries of metaphor, and purveyors of an interpretive tradition. The sacred literature thus both records the experiences of the past and provides the descriptive language by which any new experience may be interpreted. If this is so, then experience, customarily regarded as the foundation of natural theology, is also the touchstone of the revealed. All the metaphors which we use to speak of God arise from experiences of that which cannot adequately be described, of that which Jews and Christians believe to be 'He Who Is'. The apophatic is always present with the cataphatic, and we are most in danger of theological travesty when we forget that this is so.

> Though thou with clouds of anger do disguise
> Thy face; yet through that maske I know those eyes,
> Which, though they turne away sometimes,
> They never will despise.

God, in Donne's poem, is beloved and dreaded, horribly absent and compellingly present. This is the beginning and end of theology. It comes as no surprise that this poem which begins with a barrage of imagery ends:

[handwritten margin note: IN ALL FAIRNESS, THIS PERSON DOESN'T EXIST.]

> Churches are best for Prayer, that have least light:
> To see God only, I goe out of sight:
> And to scape stormy dayes, I chuse
> An Everlasting night.

Prayer, darkness, silence, and in the silence all that can be said of God, and fullness. The poem's progress towards God is a progress from experience to images, and from images to prayer.

NOTES

INTRODUCTION

1 See, for example, George Caird, *The Language and Imagery of the Bible* (London: Gerald Duckworth & Co., 1980).

CHAPTER I

1 Stephen Ullmann, *Semantics* (Oxford: Basil Blackwell, 1962), p. 213 n.

2 R. H. Robins, *A Short History of Linguistics*, 2nd edn. (London: Longman Group, 1979), p. 18.

3 John Lyons, *Introduction to Theoretical Linguistics* (Cambridge: Cambridge University Press, 1968), p. 4.

4 Robins, p. 18.

5 John Lyons, *Semantics* (Cambridge: Cambridge University Press, 1977), I, 104.

6 Jonathan Barnes, *The Presocratic Philosophers* (London: Routledge & Kegan Paul, 1979), II, 166.

7 Lyons, *Introduction*, p. 4.

8 Plato, *Crat.*, 400b–c.

9 Ludwig Wittgenstein, *Philosophical Investigations* (New York: The Macmillan Company, 1953), para. 1.

10 Quoted in I. A. Richards, *The Philosophy of Rhetoric* (Oxford: Oxford University Press, 1936), p. 93.

11 Barnes, pp. 164–5.

12 Arist. *Poet.* 1457b; trans. M. E. Hubbard in *Ancient Literary Criticism*, ed. D. A. Russell and M. Winterbottom (Oxford: Oxford University Press, 1972), pp. 119–20.

13 *Poet.* 1457b. 4; see also *Rhet.* 1404b. 2.

14 Paul Henle, 'Metaphor', in *Language, Thought and Culture*, ed. Paul Henle, Ann Arbor Paperback edn. (Ann Arbor: The University of Michigan Press, 1965), p. 173.

15 Paul Ricoeur, *The Rule of Metaphor*, trans. Robert Czerny (London: Routledge & Kegan Paul, 1978), p. 16; Eberhard Jüngel, 'Metaphorische Wahrheit', in *Evangelische Theologie Sonderheft* (München: Chr. Kaiser Verlag, 1974), p. 88.

16 Ricoeur, p. 17.

17 Arist. *Poet.* 1457b 5–10 (Kassel).

18 Trans. Hubbard, p. 119.

19 Samuel Levin, *The Semantics of Metaphor* (London: The Johns Hopkins University Press, 1977), p. 85.
20 Samuel Ijsseling, *Rhetoric and Philosophy in Conflict* (The Hague: Martinus Nijhoff, 1976), p. 115.
21 See F. R. Palmer, *Semantics* (Cambridge: Cambridge University Press, 1976), p. 29.
22 See Thomas Aquinas, *Summa Theologica*, Ia. 13, 2 (London: Blackfriars, 1964), vol. III, hereafter *ST*. The 'hydrogen' example is used by the translator, Herbert McCabe, to bring out Aquinas's point.
23 Quintilian, *Inst. Or.* VIII. vi. 8.
24 Ibid. vi. 9–10; trans. H. E. Butler (London: William Heinemann Ltd., 1921), vol. III, pp. 305–7.
25 Ullmann, *Semantics*, pp. 214–18.
26 Max Black, 'More about Metaphor', in *Metaphor and Thought*, ed. Andrew Ortony (Cambridge: Cambridge University Press, 1979), p. 22.
27 Black, 'Metaphor', in *Models and Metaphors* (Ithaca: Cornell University Press, 1962), p. 31. Black is cautious about directly attributing the substitution view to Aristotle, though his comments do imply this. Others, influenced by Black, are not so cautious. So Andrew Ortony says that Aristotle believed the use of metaphor to be primarily ornamental, and that metaphors "are not necessary, they are just nice." ('Metaphor: A Multidisciplinary Problem', in *Metaphor and Thought*, p. 3.)
28 Black, 'Metaphor', p. 35.
29 Levin goes so far as to say that Quintilian "implicitly assumes the literal expression of a thought and then considers how the poet has in fact expressed it." (p. 84.)
30 Levin, p. 82.
31 Arist. *Poet.* 1457b.; trans. Hubbard, p. 120.
32 Ibid., 1459a.; trans. Hubbard, p. 122.
33 Levin, p. 86.
34 Quint. *Inst. Or.* VIII. vi. 74–5; trans. Butler, pp. 343–4.
35 Ibid. 2–3; p. 301.
36 See Lyons, *Intro.*, p. 406.
37 The hostility of 'philosophy' towards 'rhetoric' is discussed most suggestively by Ijsseling, and also by George A. Kennedy in *Classical Rhetoric and its Christian and Secular Tradition from Ancient to Modern Times* (London: Croom Helm, 1980).
38 Kennedy, p. 47.
39 Ibid., p. 48.
40 Cicero, *De Oratore* III. xvi. 60–1; trans. H. Rackham (London: William Heinemann, 1948), vol. II, p. 49.
41 Kennedy, p. 57.

42 Ibid., p. 20.

43 See Brian Vickers, 'Rhetoric and Renaissance Literature', in *Rhetorik: Ein Internationales Jahrbuch*, Bard 2 (Stuttgart: Frommann-Holzboog, 1981), pp. 107–8.

44 Hobbes, *Leviathan* (London: J. M. Dent & Sons, 1914), pp. 20–1.

45 John Locke, *Essay Concerning Human Understanding* (Oxford: The Clarendon Press, 1894), vol. II, pp. 146–7.

CHAPTER II

1 H. H. Lieb, cited by Ijsseling, p. 116.

2 Herbert Read, *English Prose Style* (London: G. Bell & Sons, 1928), p. 25.

3 Paul Ricoeur, following Leibniz, makes use of a distinction between a nominal and a real definition in his account of metaphor: "The nominal definition allows us to identify something; the real definition shows how it is brought about". (*The Rule of Metaphor*, p. 65) This parallels our distinction between nominal definition and functional account. However, Ricoeur's choice for a nominal definition is that metaphor is a "giving an unaccustomed name to some other thing, which thereby is not being given its proper name" loc. cit., a definition which he argues later in the book to be completely misguided. The nominal definition we have given, on the other hand, is partial rather than misguided and will be filled out in the next chapters.

4 See below, Chapter IV.

5 Colin Murray Turbayne, *The Myth of Metaphor* (New Haven: Yale University Press, 1962), p. 12; Nelson Goodman, *Languages of Art: An Approach to a Theory of Symbols*, 2nd edn. (Indianapolis: Hackett Publishing Company, 1976), p. 84. Allan Paivio falls into the same error when he says that "Postural cues, lines of motion, and the like, are essentially pictorial metaphors that elicit sensations, or images, of movement". ('Psychological Processes in the Comprehension of Metaphor', in *Metaphor and Thought*, ed. Ortony, p. 157.).

6 The complete poem is:

> The Sky is low—the Clouds are mean.
> A travelling Flake of Snow
> Across a Barn or through a Rut
> Debates if it will go—
>
> A Narrow Wind complains all Day
> How some one treated him
> Nature, like Us is sometimes caught
> Without her Diadem.

> *The Complete Poems of Emily Dickinson*, ed. Thomas H. Johnson (London: Faber and Faber, 1975), p. 488.

7 Marcus B. Hester, *The Meaning of Poetic Metaphor: An Analysis in the Light of Wittgenstein's Claim that Meaning is Use* (The Hague: Mouton & Co., 1967), p. 187; Marc Belth, *The Process of Thinking* (New York: David Mackay Company, 1977), p. 7; Monroe C. Beardsley, 'Metaphor', *Encyclopedia of Philosophy*, 1967 edn., vol. 5, p. 285.

8 The term metaphorical "focus" is Black's in 'Metaphor', p. 28.

9 'The Semantics of Metaphor', in *Metaphor and Thought*, ed. Ortony, p. 65.

10 Ullmann, *Semantics*, p. 213; Black, 'More about Metaphor', in *Metaphor and Thought*, ed. Ortony, p. 28.

11 *Semantics*, pp. 213, 216.

12 Dorothy Mack makes the same point that metaphor cannot be isolated in a single word, nor even in the single sentence. She cites J. L. Austin, "'what we have to study is *not* the sentence but the issuing of an utterance in a speech situation', or 'the total speech act'." Mack consequently discusses the production of metaphor, which she calls 'metaphoring', as a speech act. ('Metaphoring as Speech Act: Some Happiness Conditions for Implicit Similes and Simple Metaphors', *Poetics*, 4 (1975), p. 245.)

While agreeing that the metaphor is not constrained to the sentence unit, we do not use the terminology of 'speech act' because it suggests that metaphor is one amongst speech acts such as question, command, statement, and so on, whereas metaphor can be presented in any of these forms. Mack, on the other hand, does claim that 'metaphoring' is a speech act akin to stating or commanding, since it imposes a way of seeing or feeling as if the speaker were saying, 'I urge you to see it thus' or 'I suggest you see it thus'. (ibid., p. 248.)

13 Mack, p. 246.

14 Ricoeur, p. 44.

15 The 'cold coals' example is our translation of Cuddie Headrigg's "that's a cauld coal to blaw at, Mither". In Sir Walter Scott, *Old Mortality* (London: Macmillan & Co., 1901), p. 91.

16 Cited by Richards, *The Philosophy of Rhetoric*, p. 121.

17 Laurence Sterne, *The Life and Opinions of Tristram Shandy, Gentleman* (London: John Lehmann, 1948), pp. 24–5.

CHAPTER III

1 For summaries of the more common theories of metaphor, see Monroe C. Beardsley, *Aesthetics: Problems in the Philosophy of Criticism* (New York: Harcourt, Brace & Company, 1958), pp. 134–44, and his article 'Metaphor' in the *Encyclopedia of Philosophy*; also Max Black, 'Metaphor', and Israel Scheffler, *Beyond the Letter: A Philosophical Inquiry into Ambiguity, Vagueness and Metaphor in Language* (London: Routledge & Kegan Paul, 1979), pp. 79–130.

2 Richards, p. 90.

3 *ST*, Ia. 1,9. This is not to be taken as a summary of St Thomas's views on metaphor. For an account of these, see Herwi Rikhof, *The Concept of Church: A Methodological Inquiry into the Use of Metaphors in Ecclesiology* (London: Sheed and Ward, 1981), pp. 167–91.

4 Beardsley, 'Metaphor', p. 285. Both Beardsley and Max Black (in his 'Metaphor') credit Aristotle with the Comparison view.

5 Black, 'Metaphor', p. 35.

6 *Aesthetics*, pp. 134–5.

7 For example, R. B. Braithwaite, 'An Empiricist's View of the Nature of Religious Belief', in *The Philosophy of Religion*, ed. Basil Mitchell (Oxford: Oxford University Press, 1971), pp. 72–91.

8 Donald Davidson, "What Metaphors Mean", in *On Metaphor*, ed. Sheldon Sacks (Chicago: the University of Chicago Press, 1979), pp. 30–31.

9 Ibid., p. 31.

10 Ibid., p. 41.

11 Ibid., p. 30.

12 Ibid., p. 42, p. 36.

13 Ibid., p. 36.

14 For example, his unwillingness to speak of the 'meaning' of metaphor is linked with the nominalism which makes him reluctant to talk of 'meanings' altogether. Also, his project of making a theory of meaning dependent on a theory of truth, or of 'truth-in-a-language' means that it is important for him to be able to correlate the terms of a statement with criteria for its truth. Hence his objection to the idea that a blatant falsehood, such as he takes most metaphor to be (e.g. 'Man is a wolf'), should be adjudged to have a particular 'meaning'.

15 Ibid., pp. 29, 36, and 32 respectively. It should be noted that Davidson does mention metaphors in other forms, for example, on p. 40, he cites Shakespeare's description of Cleopatra's barge which "like a burnish'd throne Burn'd on the water". It would seem that he acknowledges such examples as metaphors, yet all the metaphors he cites in direct support of his thesis are of the form 'A is a B'.

16 Ibid., p. 44.

17 'How Metaphors Work: A Reply to Donald Davidson', in *On Metaphor*, ed. Sheldon Sacks, p. 184n.

18 Davidson, p. 30. For a theory of linguistic communication that attempts to explain metaphor by means of such distinctions, see Kent Bach and Robert Harnish, *Linguistic Communication and Speech Acts* (Cambridge, Ma. and London: The MIT Press, 1982).

19 Scheffler, p. 84.

20 Levin is concerned primarily with metaphorical construal and chooses

to treat metaphor as 'semantic deviance', that is, deviance "which results from an improper collocation of lexical items: viz, *Green ideas sleep furiously* where the deviance is an immediate function of the combined meanings, and where questions of reference, presupposition, intention, and coincident features of the non-linguistic setting are either secondary or do not arise". Levin, p. 4.

21 *Aesth.*, p. 138.
22 Ibid., p. 141; see also 'Twist', p. 299.
23 *Aesth.*, p. 125. It should be noted that this distinction between designation, denotation, and connotation is particular to Beardsley. Others have used the terms differently.
24 Ibid., p. 141.
25 Ibid., p. 143.
26 Ibid., p. 144.
27 See Scheffler, pp. 97–107. Scheffler calls Beardsley's programme, 'Intensionalism', "to emphasise the central role of connoted properties in his account". (p. 97n.)
28 'Senses', p. 8.
29 'Twist', p. 299.
30 'Twist', p. 299.
31 Ibid., p. 294.
32 Beardsley, 'Senses', pp. 3, 7.
33 Max Black, 'More about Metaphor', in *Metaphor and Thought*, ed. Ortony, p. 35.
34 'Twist', p. 299.
35 Beardsley concedes this much in 'The Metaphorical Twist' where he says: "Here is where the Object-comparison theory makes its contribution after all. For it is correct in saying that sometimes in explicating metaphors we must consider the properties of the objects denoted by the modifier. But those objects are not referred to for comparison: they are referred to so that some of their relevant properties can be given a new status as elements of verbal meaning." (p. 302.) It is not clear, however, that Beardsley can bring in properties of *objects* and yet retain the purely linguistic nature of his account as he wishes to do.
36 'Is Semantics Possible?', in *Naming, Necessity, and Natural Kinds*, ed. Stephen P. Schwartz (Ithaca: Cornell University Press, 1977). Furthermore, both Putnam and Saul Kripke have alerted us to the difficulties of establishing a set of 'necessary' properties even for the natural kind terms, and of making the meaning of a general term the set of such properties. We will return to this point later.
37 Black, 'Metaphor', p. 25.
38 Richards, p. 93.
39 Black, 'Metaphor', pp. 38–9.

40 Ibid., p. 27.
41 Donald Davidson implies this kind of criticism of Black in his (David-son's) 'What Metaphors Mean', pp. 29–33, and Max Black rebuts this in his article 'How Metaphors Work: A Reply to Donald Davidson', pp. 186–8 of the same volume, *On Metaphor*, ed. Sheldon Sacks. See also Black's "More about Metaphor", p. 443.
42 Black, 'Metaphor', p. 41.
43 Ibid., p. 41.
44 Ibid., p. 37.
45 Ibid., pp. 46, 44.
46 Black, 'More about Metaphor', p. 31.
47 Black, 'Metaphor', p. 35.
48 Black says ('More', p. 31) that "Looking at a scene through blue spectacles is different from *comparing* that scene with something else"; but one must respond that looking at a scene through blue spectacles is hardly the activity of recognizing an isomorphism of structure. Black is here vacillating between two conflicting theoretical notions.
49 Black, 'More', p. 39.
50 The problem of 'filtering' meanings seems just as acute for what we regard as literal utterances such as 'I love cricket', and 'I love my mother'. At some stage, one can fall back on the intuitions of the speaker of a language, and on formalizations of these intuitions such as Grice's notion of "conversational implicature". See H. P. Grice, 'Logic and Conversation', in *Speech Acts*, vol. III of *Syntax and Semantics*, ed. Peter Cole and Jerry L. Morgan (New York: Academic Press, 1975).
51 An exhaustive treatment would be, of course, not simply a theory of metaphor but a complete account of the inferential patterns in all linguistic communications. For an attempt at this see Bach and Har-nish, *Linguistic Communication and Speech Acts*.
52 Richards, p. 55.
53 Ibid.
54 Ibid., p. 93.
55 Black, 'Metaphor', p. 47n. Black criticized the terminology of 'tenor' and 'vehicle' as being "psychological language" in a discussion of his own theory of metaphor given in Oxford on 18 May 1978, but his own notion of "associated commonplaces" is potentially as psychological.
56 Cited by Richards, p. 102.
57 Ricoeur, *The Rule of Metaphor*, p. 85.
58 Virginia Woolf, *To the Lighthouse* (London: J. M. Dent & Sons, 1938), pp. 32–3.
59 Richards, p. 100.
60 Ibid.
61 John Lyons, *Semantics*, vol. I, p. 174.
62 Ibid., pp. 176–7.

63 See Keith S. Donnellan, 'Reference and Definite Descriptions', in *Naming, Necessity, and Natural Kinds*, ed. Schwartz, pp.42–65.
64 See Lyons, *Semantics*, vol. I, p. 207. It should be noted that this intension/denotation distinction is not the same as the traditional one between intension and extension, as Lyons points out (pp. 207–8).

CHAPTER IV

1 Ricoeur, *The Rule of Metaphor*, p. 44. Ricoeur's reason for wishing to avoid 'tropology' is that it can lead to a misguided focus on the word as the unit of meaning (in his phrase, "the hegemony of the word") and thus to analysis of metaphor simply in terms of deviant word meaning. We can however make distinctions between tropes without being misled in this way.
2 That this is so can be seen in cases where whole books are allegories or satire, like Dante's *Divine Comedy* and Orwell's *Animal Farm*, but incorporate within this textual form metaphor and other figures of speech. Of course, allegory and satire work only if the guise is really a semblance of a guise. It is the author's intention in these cases that the reader see through the guise.
3 For conflationary usages of this sort, see John Dominic Crossan, *The Dark Interval: Towards a Theology of Story* (Niles, Ill.: Argus Communications, 1975), especially the Epilogue.
4 Levin, p. 80.
5 See Black, 'More about Metaphor', especially the section "Metaphors and Similes", pp. 31–2.
6 Cited by Mark Platts on the frontispiece of his *Ways of Meaning: An Introduction to a Philosophy of Language* (London: Routledge & Kegan Paul, 1979).
7 A similar point is made by Stephen Ullmann who argues that "the difference between simile and metaphor . . . is at times of somewhat marginal importance." 'Simile and Metaphor', in *Studies in Greek, Italic, and Indo-European Linguistics offered to Leonard R. Palmer*, ed. Anna Morpurgo Davies and Wolfgang Meid (Innsbruck: Innsbruck Beiträge Zur Sprachwissenschaft, 1976), p. 429.
8 Henry James, *Portrait of a Lady* (Harmondsworth: Penguin Books, 1963), pp. 404, 432.
9 The popular etymology which suggests that 'nylon' arose from the conflation of 'New York' and 'London', alas, is spurious.
10 These cybernetic metaphors used to describe the brain are given special attention in Richard Boyd's 'Metaphor and Theory Change: What is "Metaphor" a Metaphor for?' in *Metaphor and Thought*, ed. Ortony; see esp. pp. 359–64.
11 The power of this particular example, 'body politic' and 'ship of state', in Puritan thought is discussed by Michael Walzer in *The Revolution of*

the Saints: A Study in the Origins of Radical Politics (Cambridge, Mass.: Harvard University Press, 1965).

12 K. Rahner and J. Ratzinger, *The Episcopate and the Primacy* (Freiburg: Herder Freiburg, 1962).

13 Cited by Brian Vickers, *Francis Bacon and Renaissance Prose* (Cambridge: Cambridge University Press, 1968), p. 153.

14 Goodman makes this claim for metaphor in his *Languages of Art* (Indianapolis; Hackett Publ. Co., 1976), p. 69. What we are calling 'linguistic analogy' should not be confused with what historical linguistics has traditionally called 'extension by analogy' which is an analogy (proportionality) of grammatical form, as in boy/boys, tree/trees; see John Lyons, *Introduction to Theoretical Linguistics*, p. 6. As we wished to use the term analogy in a sense similar to that of Aquinas, we referred to the phenomenon mentioned above as 'extension by parallel syntax'.

15 Such a category would be especially useful in discussing aesthetic terms. We find it in nascent form in Goodman's *Languages of Art*, when he says: "Every application of a predicate to a new event or new-found object is new; but such routine projection does not constitute metaphor. And even the earliest applications of a coined term need not be in the least metaphorical . . . But what is the difference between merely applying a familiar label to new things and applying it in a novel way? Briefly, a metaphor is an affair between a predicate with a past and an object that yields while protesting . . . Where there is metaphor, there is conflict . . .'', p. 69. It is surprising, given this position, that Goodman holds such terms as 'cold colour' and 'high note' to be metaphorical, when they would seem much more to be 'routine projections' in his terms, or analogous claims in ours, than conflict-generating metaphors.

16 For a detailed discussion of Aquinas' position, see Rikhof, pp. 167–71, especially his discussion of the *ratio propria* and the *ratio communis*.

CHAPTER V

1 Thomas Hobbes, *Leviathan* (London: J. M. Dent & Sons, 1914), p. 20–1.

2 J. L. Austin, *How to Do Things with Words* (Oxford: Oxford University Press, 1962), p. 104. See also John R. Searle, *Speech Acts* (Cambridge: Cambridge University Press, 1969), p. 78, where Searle develops the notion of parasitic forms of discourse, though not with special reference to metaphor.

3 A. J. Ayer, *Language, Truth and Logic* (Harmondsworth: Penguin Books, 1971), p. 152.

4 David Stacey, *Interpreting the Bible* (London: Sheldon Press, 1976), p. 16; John Hick, *The Philosophy of Religion* (Englewood Cliffs, N.J.:

Prentice-Hall, 1973), p. 92; Rudolph Bultmann, 'New Testament and Mythology', in *Kerygma and Myth*, ed. Hans Werner Bartsch, vol. I (London: SPCK, 1972).

5 Bach and Harnish, p. 33 and *passim*.

6 William Alston, *Philosophy of Language* (Englewood Cliffs, N.J.: Prentice-Hall, 1964), p. 102.

7 Stacey, p. 16.

8 Paul Edwards, 'Professor Tillich's Confusions', *Mind*, 74 (1965), pp. 198-9.

9 Ferdinand de Saussure, *Course in General Linguistics*, trans. Wade Baskin, ed. Charles Bally and Albert Sechehaye with Albert Reidlinger (London: Peter Owen, 1974), p. 68.

10 Black, 'More about Metaphor', p. 26.

11 Richards, p. 108.

12 Bruno Snell, *The Discovery of the Mind: The Greek Origins of European Thought* (Oxford: Basil Blackwell, 1953), p. v.

13 Ibid., p. 198.

14 See Isaiah Berlin, *Vico and Herder: Two Studies in the History of Ideas* (New York: Random House, 1977), pp. 42-52.

15 Owen Barfield, *Saving the Appearances: A Study in Idolatry* (New York: Harcourt, Brace & World, undated), pp. 116-22.

16 Berlin, p. 51.

17 James Edie, 'Ideality and Metaphor: A Phenomenological Theory of Polysemy', *The Journal of the British Society for Phenomenology*, 6 (1975).

18 Frederick Ferré, 'Metaphor in Religious Discourse', *Dictionary of the History of Ideas*, 1973 edn., vol. 3, p. 201.

19 Ibid., p. 201.

20 Ibid., p. 202.

21 Friedrich Nietzsche, 'On Truth and Falsity in their Ultramoral Sense', in vol. II of *Collected Works*, ed. Dr Oscar Levy (London and Edinburgh: T. N. Foulis, 1911), p. 180.

22 Wittgenstein, *Philosophical Investigations*, para. 303.

23 Gilbert Ryle, *The Concept of Mind* (Harmondsworth: Penguin Books, 1963), p. 40.

24 Ibid., p. 19.

25 Colin Turbayne, *The Myth of Metaphor* (New Haven: Yale University Press, 1962), p. 13.

26 Ibid., p. 22.

27 Ibid., p. 27.

28 Ricoeur, p. 253.

29 Belth, p. 80.

30 Jacques Derrida, 'White Mythology: Metaphor in the Text of Philosophy', *New Literary History*, 6 (1974), 10-11.

31 George Lakoff and Mark Johnson, *Metaphors We Live By* (Chicago: The University of Chicago Press, 1980).

32 James Barr, *The Semantics of Biblical Language* (Oxford: Oxford University Press, 1961), p. 109; see also pp. 70–1 and 217–38 where Barr discusses the excesses of biblical critics who have uncritically built great interpretive constructs upon etymologies or aspects of syntax.

33 Cf. the etymological definition of marriage given by Isadore of Seville, "Matrimonium quasi matris munium, i.e. officium quod dat mulieribus esse matrem", (*Etymol.*, IX, 8, 19 [PL 82, 366]), cited by E. Schillebeeckx in *Marriage: Secular Reality and Saving Mystery*, vol. II (London: Sheed & Ward, 1965), p. 80.

34 George Eliot, *The Mill on the Floss* (Harmondsworth: Penguin Books, 1979), p. 208–9.

35 *Semantics*, p. 65.

36 Nelson Goodman, 'Metaphor as Moonlighting', in *On Metaphor*, ed. Sacks, p. 175.

37 *ST* 1a.1,10.

38 Thomas Gilby in Appendix 12, 'The Senses of Scripture', to *ST*, vol. I, p. 140.

39 Ricoeur, p. 221.

40 Ibid., pp. 221, 230.

41 Ibid., pp. 224, 248–9.

42 Ibid., p. 255.

43 Sallie McFague, *Metaphorical Theology* (London: SCM Press, 1983), *passim*.

44 Donald Davidson, 'What Metaphors Mean', in *On Metaphor*, ed. Sacks, hereafter WMM; and Searle, 'Metaphor', in Ortony.

45 Donald Davidson, 'Truth and Meaning', *Synthese*, 17 (1967), 310.

46 Davidson, WMM, pp. 31, 39.

47 'Metaphor', in *Metaphor and Thought*, ed. Ortony, p. 92; Searle calls these two kinds of meaning "*word*, or *sentence meaning*" and "*speaker's utterance meaning*", p. 93.

48 Davidson, WMM, p. 39.

49 Searle, 'Metaphor', p. 112.

50 Ibid., p. 105.

51 See, for example, Stephen Ullmann's 'Simile and Metaphor', in Davies and Meid.

52 Davidson has claimed that it is his object to give an account of natural languages, so in 'Truth and Meaning' he says: "Tarski's second point is that we would have to reform a natural language out of all recognition before we could apply formal semantical methods. If this is true, it is fatal to my project, for the task of a theory of meaning as I conceive it is not to change, improve or reform a language, but to describe and understand it." (p. 314.) Metaphor, then, may prove the acid test for such a theory.

53 Edwards, pp. 199–200.

54 Andrew Burgess, 'Irreducible Religious Metaphors', *Religious Studies*, 8 (1972), 355.

55 Teresa of Avila, *The Way of Perfection*, trans. by the Benedictines of Stanbrook (London: Thomas Baker, 1919), pp. 182–3.

CHAPTER VI

1 I am grateful to Dr Mary Tiles for suggesting the phrase 'reality depiction' to me.

2 See C. K. Ogden and I. A. Richards, *The Meaning of Meaning* (London: Routledge & Kegan Paul, 1923).

3 Karsten Harries, 'The Many Uses of Metaphor', in *On Metaphor*, ed. Sacks, pp. 171–2. Levin makes a related point in his discussion of 'Metaphor and Truth' (Chapter VI of *The Semantics of Metaphor*), when he suggests that each poem evokes a 'possible world' of the poet's imagining.

4 See, for example, Crossan, *The Dark Interval*; Robert W. Funk, 'The Parable as Metaphor', in his *Language, Hermeneutic, and Word of God* (New York: Harper & Row, Publishers, 1966), pp. 133–62; Geraint Vaughan Jones, *The Art and Truth of the Parables* (London: SPCK, 1964); Sallie McFague TeSelle, *Speaking in Parables: A Study in Metaphor and Theology* (London: SCM Press, 1975); and Dan Otto Via, Jr., *The Parables: Their Literary and Existential Dimension* (Philadelphia, Pa.: Fortress Press, 1967), all of which emphasize the notion of the personal 'world' of the parable and skirt or deny the importance of the issue of reality depiction.

5 Cleanth Brooks and Robert Penn Warren, *Modern Rhetoric*, Shorter 3rd edn. (New York: Harcourt Brace Jovanovich, 1972), p. 319.

6 Bertrand Russell, *The Scientific Outlook*, cited by Brooks and Penn Warren, p. 320.

7 Austin Farrer, 'Poetic Truth', in *Reflective Faith: Essays in Philosophical Theology*, ed. Charles C. Conti (London: SPCK, 1972), pp. 29–30.

8 W. V. Quine, 'A Postscript on Metaphor', in *On Metaphor*, ed. Sacks, p. 159.

9 R. Harré, *The Principles of Scientific Thinking* (London: Macmillan & Co, 1970), p. 40. See also Harré's *The Philosophies of Science: An Introductory Survey* (Oxford: OUP, 1972), p. 174.

10 Ian G. Barbour, *Myths, Models and Paradigms: The Nature of Scientific and Religious Language* (London: SCM Press, 1974), pp. 42–3; Frederick Ferré, 'Metaphors, Models, and Religion', *Soundings* 2 (1968), p. 334.

11 Barbour, p. 42.

12 This term is from Richard Boyd, 'Metaphor and Theory Change', in Ortony, p. 360. In this extremely suggestive article, Boyd does not speak of 'models' or 'analogues' at all, his term 'theory-constitutive metaphor' doing the same duty.

13 Harré, *Principles*, pp. 38–40.

14 The term 'mysterious overplus' is Austin Farrer's.

15 Cf. Ian Ramsey, *Models and Mystery* (Oxford: OUP, 1964); *Models for Divine Activity* (London: SCM Press, 1973); Ian Barbour, *Myths, Models and Paradigms*; Thomas Fawcett, *The Symbolic Language of Religion* (London: SCM Press, 1970); Frederick Ferré, *Basic Modern Philosophy of Religion* (London: George Allen & Unwin, 1968) and *Language, Logic and God* (London: Eyre & Spottiswoode, 1962).

16 Ferré, *Basic Modern*, p. 381; see also his 'Metaphors, Models and Religion'.

17 Ibid., p. 395.

18 David Tracy, 'Metaphor and Religion', in *On Metaphor*, ed. Sheldon Sacks (Chicago: The University of Chicago Press, 1979), pp. 98–9.

19 This definition of the realist's God is from Don Cupitt, *Taking Leave of God* (London: SCM Press, 1980), p. 67.

20 Crossan, pp. 40, 45.

21 Fawcett, p. 80.

22 Ibid.

23 Ibid., pp. 85–6.

24 Ibid., p. 88.

25 Ibid., pp. 89–90.

26 David Edge, 'Science and Religion: An Analysis of Issues', in *Science and Religion: The Re-Opening Dialogue*, ed. G. Walters (Bath: Bath University Press, 1970), p. 23.

27 Ramsey, *Models and Mystery*, p. 13.

28 Ferré, *Basic Modern*, p. 375.

29 Mary Hesse in *Models and Analogies in Science* (Notre Dame: University of Notre Dame Press, 1966) attributes this ideal of a scientific theory to Duhem, a noted and outspoken opponent of the use of models in scientific explanation. The models to which Duhem objected, however, were the mechanical models more common in nineteenth-century science than they are now.

30 J. J. C. Smart, 'Theory Construction', in *Logic and Language: Second Series*, ed. A. G. N. Flew (Oxford: Basil Blackwell Mott, 1959).

31 Norman R. Campbell, 'The Structure of Theories', in *Readings in the Philosophy of Science*, ed. Herbert Feigl and May Brodbeck (New York: Appleton – Century – Crofts, 1953), pp. 297–8.

32 Campbell, p. 298.

33 Harré, *Principles*, pp. 49–50.

34 Hesse, *Models and Analogies*, p. 30. In this context, those who argue

for the autonomy of formal theory sometimes cite quantum theory where one has a self-consistent mathematical formalism but no single model adequate to give form to it (sometimes the wave model being the most useful, and sometimes the particle model). Does this not show that the model cannot be essential to the theory? Ian Barbour applies this to the theological case: ''there are also features of complementarity in atomic physics which are absent from theology. In atomic physics there is a unifying mathematical formalism which allows at least probabilistic prediction of particular observations. There is consistency at the level of *theory*, although not at the level of *models*. Theory specifies what is essential in the models by indicating the positive and negative analogies.'' (*Myths, Models and Paradigms*, p. 91.) This point, while valid in terms of the specific physical theory which Barbour's paragraph isolates, is misleading in a context where it suggests a general truth about the subordination of model to theory in scientific explanation. Even in the case of quantum physics, this argument does not mean that the models are dispensable; as Dr Hesse points out, the models are the means by which the theory is interpreted, they suggest new possibilities of explanation and are hence vital to the predictive enterprise. (Hesse, *Models and Analogies*, pp. 43–55.)

35 Harré, *The Philosophies of Science*, p. 171.
36 See Ramsey, *Religious Language: An Empirical Placing of Theological Phrases* (London: SCM Press, 1957), Ch. II.

CHAPTER VII

1 'Demythologizing and the Problem of Validity', in *New Essays in Philosophical Theology*, ed. Antony Flew and Alasdair MacIntyre (London: SCM Press, 1955), p. 237.
2 Mary Hesse, *The Structure of Scientific Inference* (London: The Macmillan Press, 1974), pp. 285–6.
3 Hesse, *Structure*, p. 286.
4 Hesse, *Structure*, p. 10.
5 See Russell Keat and John Urry, *Social Theory as Science* (London: Routledge and Kegan Paul, 1975), p. 18; also Roy Bhaskar, *A Realist Theory of Science* (Leeds: Leeds Books, 1975) and Harré, *The Principles of Scientific Thinking*.
6 Bhaskar, p. 25.
7 See Hesse, *Structure*, p. 290.
8 Hilary Putnam, 'Explanation and Reference', in *Mind, Language and Reality*, vol. II of *Philosophical Papers* (Cambridge: CUP, 1975), p. 209.
9 Irving M. Copi, 'Essence and Accident', in *Naming, Necessity, and Natural Kinds*, ed. Schwartz, p. 187. Copi here makes a similar critique of Lockean nominalism and its contention that real essences are

unknowable. He says: "Contemporary science, however, presents a quite different picture. Locke characterized the (allegedly unknowable) real essences of things as the '. . . constitution of their insensible parts; from which flow those sensible qualities, which serve us to distinguish them one from another . . .' Now modern atomic theory is directly concerned with the insensible parts of things. Through the use of his Periodic Table, . . . 'Mendeleev was enabled to predict the existence *and properties* . . .' of half a dozen elements whose existence had not been previously known or even suspected. And other scientists have subsequently been able to make similar predictions. Modern science seeks to know the *real* essences of things, and its increasing successes seem to be bringing it progressively nearer to that goal." (p. 187.) Copi, of course, acknowledges that "Our *notion* of what constitutes a real essence of a thing is relative to the science of our day." (p. 190), but it is still real essences with which science is concerned.

10 Hilary Putnam, 'What is "Realism"?', *PAS.*, 76 (1975–6), 177.
11 See Bhaskar, p. 23.
12 Bhaskar, pp. 23–4, 21.
13 See Hesse, *Structure*, especially Ch. 12, 'A Realist Interpretation of Science', pp. 283–302; and Putnam, 'Realism and Reason', in his *Meaning and the Moral Sciences* (London: Routledge & Kegan Paul, 1978). Also Richard Boyd, 'Metaphor and Theory Change: What is "Metaphor" a Metaphor for?', in Ortony.
14 Bhaskar, p. 52.
15 Harré, *Principles*, pp. 55–6.
16 Boyd, p. 386.
17 Putnam, 'What is Realism?', p. 194.
18 Boyd, p. 365; see also p. 364. Boyd's article is particularly suggestive and in much of what follows I am indebted to him.
19 Putnam, 'Is Semantics Possible?', in *Naming, Necessity and Natural Kinds*, ed. Schwartz, p. 103.
20 Boyd, pp. 364–5.
21 Ibid., p. 374.
22 Ibid., p. 398.
23 Kripke, p. 295.
24 Ibid., p. 301.
25 Putnam, 'Explanation and Reference', p. 205.
26 Kripke, pp. 318–19.
27 Ibid., p. 348, n. 34.
28 Putnam, 'Explanation and Reference', p. 200.
29 Kripke, p. 330.
30 This is not to say that Kripke's position, even as it stands in 'Naming and Necessity', cannot be defended on this point; but the defence goes beyond the scope of the present discussion.

31 Jerrold J. Katz, 'The Neoclassical Theory of Reference', in *Contemporary Perspectives in the Philosophy of Language*, ed. Peter A. French, Theodore E. Uehling, Jr., and Howard K. Wettstein (Minneapolis: University of Minnesota Press, 1979), p. 105.
32 Katz, p. 110.
33 Ibid.
34 Kripke, p. 330.
35 Boyd, p. 392.
36 Ibid., pp. 392, 407–8 n. 2.
37 Ibid., p. 395; Kripke, pp. 330–1.
38 Hesse, *Structure*, p. 290.
39 Ibid., p. 301. It should be pointed out that Dr Hesse's defence of realism does not make use of, or even discuss, non-definitional reference fixing. She says, "Theories about essences are neither stable nor cumulative, and are therefore not part of the realistic aspects of science." (p. 299.)
40 'Partial denotation', a term of Hartry Field's, is discussed by Boyd, pp. 396–7.
41 Boyd, p. 358.
42 See, for instance, Copi, pp. 190–1.
43 Davidson, 'Realism Without Reference'; *Dialectica*, 31 (1977), 247–58.
44 'Realism and Reason', p. 123.
45 Michael Dummett, 'Common Sense and Physics', in *Perception and Identity*, ed. G. F. Macdonald (London: The Macmillan Press, 1979), p. 3.
46 In what follows we do not comment on the interesting matter of whether or not 'God' is a proper name. This is because, for reasons too lengthy to be discussed here, we do not think a decision on this matter affects our argument.

CHAPTER VIII

1 *Taking Leave of God* (London: SCM Press, 1980), pp. 67, 45.
2 Ibid., p. 85, p. 90.
3 *The Central Questions of Philosophy* (Harmondsworth: Penguin Books, 1976), p. 211.
4 Ibid., pp. 211–12.
5 Cupitt, pp. 90–1.
6 David Hume, *Dialogues Concerning Natural Religion*, ed. Henry D. Aiken (New York: Hafner Publishing Co., 1948), p. 31.
7 *Language, Truth and Logic*, p. 156.
8 *The Central Questions of Philosophy*, pp. 4–5.
9 See our Chapters VI and VII.
10 The same movement of thought is particularly common in discussions of myth. Harold H. Oliver gives this analysis of the presumably mythic

claim, 'I trust (in) God': "we have to do, not with God-as-*the*-Other, but with the Eminent Other, that is, with God-Language. We are, in sum, dealing with myth, whether in the form of 'eminent literature' or of belief statements utilizing its prime categories . . . In myth, interpreted rigorously in terms of a relational paradigm, one has to do, not with God existing *beyond* (i.e., trans-) experience, but rather with the other of eminent imaging, that is, with a coaspectual imaging of experience-considered-as-a-Totality." 'Relational Ontology and Hermeneutics', in *Myth, Symbol and Reality*, ed. Alan M. Olson (Notre Dame: Notre Dame University Press, 1980), p. 84. Rudolph Bultmann's essay "New Testament and Mythology" is usually considered the locus classicus of this position.

11 We have no theoretical objection to an idealist-inspired theological programme which emphasizes that the truths of religion are of relational and personal nature, particularly if such a programme is consistently applied with no shrinking from its radical implications. What we object to are theories which claim to account for Christian religious language as genuinely cognitive in the way Christians have characteristically held it to be, but which at some critical point say that, because we cannot know God, the theist's claims must refer only to aspects of the human condition.

12 D. Z. Phillips, 'Religious Beliefs and Language Games', in *The Philosophy of Religion*, ed. Basil Mitchell (Oxford: Oxford University Press, 1971), pp. 121–42. See especially p. 131. The phrase 'from the bottom up' is our own.

13 *Models for Divine Activity* (London: SCM Press, 1973), p. 58.

14 Ibid., p. 61.

15 'Facts and Disclosures', Address to the Aristotelian Society, 24 January 1972, reprinted in *Christian Empiricism*, ed. Jerry H. Gill (London: Sheldon Press, 1974), pp. 159–76. Our citations: pp. 159, 172, 174.

16 In *The Philosophy of Religion*, ed. Mitchell, p. 80.

17 Ibid., p. 79.

18 Consider also Putnam: "The realist explanation, in a nutshell, is not that language mirrors the world but that *speakers* mirror the world—i.e. their environment—in the sense of constructing a symbolic representation of that environment." ('Realism and Reason', p. 123.) Mary Hesse comes to interesting similar conclusions concerning the contextuality of scientific claims in *The Structure of Scientific Inference*. See her Chapter Twelve, 'A Realist Interpretation of Science', especially pp. 298–9, where she discusses the 'witchcraft' and 'phlogiston' examples.

It is worth commenting on the marked similarity between the remarks of Boyd, Putnam, and Hesse, which arise within the analytic tradition of philosophy and of philosophy of science, and those of writers influenced by hermeneutic philosophy. Charles Taylor makes almost the same criticisms of empiricism and points about social contextuality (although without a discussion of reference) in his article "Interpretation and the Sciences of Man", (*Review of Metaphysics*, 25, No. 1 (1971), 4–51). In discussing vocabulary and social practice, he speaks of "the artificiality of the distinction between social reality and the language of description of that social reality. The language is constitutive of the reality, is essential to its being the kind of reality it is" (p. 24), and later: "What the ontology of mainstream social science lacks is the notion of meaning as not simply for an individual subject; of a subject who can be a 'we' as well as an 'I'. The exclusion of this possibility, of the communal, comes once again from the baleful influence of the epistemological tradition for which all knowledge has to be reconstructed from the impressions imprinted on the individual subject. But if we free ourselves from the hold of these prejudices, this seems a wildly implausible view about the development of human consciousness; we are aware of the world through a 'we' before we are through an 'I'." (p. 32.) See also Hans-Georg Gadamer, *Truth and Method* (London: Sheed & Ward, 1975), *passim*.

19 Viz. that since language structures the world, the structure which language imposes is all the structure that there is. See our Chapter V.

20 Aquinas holds that all our knowledge takes its rise from sensation; "we are of the kind to reach the world of intelligence through the world of sense". *ST* Ia. 1,9.

21 A. Léonard, OP, 'Studies on the Phenomena of Mystical Experience', in *Mystery and Mysticism: A Symposium* (London: Blackfriars Publications, 1956), p. 94. For St John of the Cross's use of scholastic categories, see Leslie Ross Collings, 'Passivity in the Spiritual Life: from the writings of St. Thomas Aquinas and St. John of the Cross', (D.Phil. thesis Oxford, 1978), especially Chapter 1, Part iii, 'Consequences in style: contrasting roles of image and concept', pp. 23–35.

22 Fr. Léonard explains this preference for realism with reference to the mystic's use of symbols (or imagery): "If, in fact, one denies to reality and to God existence in themselves, the symbol loses its representative function and substitutes itself for reality. Exterior reality becomes a symbol, and the symbol becomes the only reality. From an idealist point of view the symbol acquires an autonomous value; from a realist point of view it is bound to the reality it symbolizes." (p. 108.)

23 *Models for Divine Activity*, Chapter I, pp. 1–14.

24 See Earl Miner, *An Introduction to Japanese Court Poetry* (Stanford: Stanford University Press, 1968).

25 Miner, p. 24–5. We have deleted the original Japanese of the poems from Miner's text.

26 For a discussion of the use of the expression 'living water' in the biblical

texts, see Jean Daniélou, SJ, *Primitive Christian Symbols*, trans. Donald Attwater (London: Burns & Oates, 1964), esp. Chapter Three, 'Living Water and the Fish'.

27 Cited by E. Allison Peers in *Mother of Carmel: A Portrait of St. Teresa of Jesus*, p. 54. The similitude of watering the garden occurs in Teresa's own *Life*, Chapter XI.

28 These hymns are cited by George P. Landow in his *Victorian Types, Victorian Shadows: Biblical Typology in Victorian Literature, Art and Thought* (London: Routledge & Kegan Paul, 1980), pp. 66, 74. His Chapter Two is concerned entirely with the Victorian use of the type of the 'smitten rock'.

BIBLIOGRAPHY

Alston, William, *Philosophy of Language*. Englewood Cliffs, N.J.: Prentice-Hall, 1964.

Aristotle, *Poetics*. Greek text: R. Kassel, Oxford: Oxford University Press, 1965. English text: D. A. Russell and M. Winterbottom (eds.), *Ancient Literary Criticism: The Principal Texts in New Translations*. Oxford: Oxford University Press, 1972.

—— *Rhetoric*. In: Russell and Winterbottom, op. cit.

Aquinas, Thomas, *Summa Theologica*. London: Blackfriars, 1964.

Auden, W. H. and Louis Kronenburger, *The Faber Book of Aphorisms*. London: Faber and Faber, 1962.

Austin, J. L., *How To Do Things with Words*. Oxford: Oxford Univesity Press, 1962.

Ayer, A. J., *Language, Truth and Logic*. Harmondsworth: Penguin Books, 1971.

—— *The Central Questions of Philosophy*. Harmondsworth: Penguin Books, 1976.

Bach, Kent, and Harnish, Robert M., *Linguistic Communication and Speech Acts*. Cambridge, Ma. and London: The MIT Press, paperback edn. 1982.

Barbour, Ian G., *Myths, Models and Paradigms: The Nature of Scientific and Religious Language*. London: SCM Press, 1974.

Barfield, Owen, *Saving the Appearances: A Study in Idolatry*. New York: Harcourt, Brace & World, edn. undated.

Barnes, Jonathan, *The Presocratic Philosophers*, London: Routledge & Kegan Paul, 1979, vol. II.

Barr, James, *The Semantics of Biblical Language*. Oxford: Oxford University Press, 1961.

Beardsley, Monroe C., *Aesthetics: Problems in the Philosophy of Criticism*. New York: Harcourt, Brace & Company, 1958.

—— 'Metaphor', *Encyclopedia of Philosophy*. New York: Macmillan Publishing Co., Inc. & The Free Press, 1967 edn.

—— 'Metaphorical Senses', *Noûs* 12 (1978), 3–16.

—— 'The Metaphorical Twist', *Philosophy and Phenomenological Research* 22 (1962), 293–307.

Belth, Marc, *The Process of Thinking*. New York: David McKay Company, 1977.

Berlin, Isaiah, *Vico and Herder: Two Studies in the History of Ideas*. New York: A Division of Random House, 1977.

Bhaskar, Roy, *A Realist Theory of Science*. Leeds: Leeds Books, 1975.

Bible, The Revised Standard Version.

Black, Max, 'How Metaphors Work: A Reply to Donald Davidson'. In: Sacks, pp. 181–92.

―――― 'Metaphor'. *In Models and Metaphors: Studies in Language and Philosophy*. Ithaca: Cornell University Press, 1962, pp. 25–47.

―――― 'More About Metaphor', in: Ortony, pp. 19–43.

Boyd, Richard, 'Metaphor and Theory Change', in: Ortony, pp. 356–408.

Braithwaite, R. B., 'An Empiricist's View of the Nature of Religious Belief'. In: Mitchell, pp. 72–91.

Brooks, Cleanth, and Warren, Robert Penn, *Modern Rhetoric*, shorter 3rd edn. New York: Harcourt Brace Jovanovich, 1972.

Bultmann, Rudolph, 'New Testament and Mythology'. In: Hans Werner Bartsch (ed.), *Kerygma and Myth: A Theological Debate*, trans. Reginald H. Fuller. London: SPCK, 1972.

Burgess, Andrew J., 'Irreducible Religious Metaphors', *Religious Studies* 8 (1972), 355–66.

Burrell, David C. SC, *Analogy and Philosophical Language*. New Haven and London: Yale University Press, 1973.

Caird, G. B., *The Language and Imagery of the Bible*. London: Gerald Duckworth & Co., 1980.

Campbell, Norman R., 'The Structure of Theories', in: Herbert Feigl and May Brodbeck (eds.), *Readings in the Philosophy of Science*. New York: Appleton – Century – Crofts, 1953, pp. 288–308.

Cicero, *De Oratore*, trans. H. Rackham. London: William Heinemann, 1948, vol. II.

Collings, Leslie Ross, Passivity in the Spiritual Life: from the writings of St. Thomas Aquinas and St. John of the Cross. Oxford University D.Phil., 1978.

Copi, Irving M., 'Essence and Accident', in: Schwartz, pp. 176–91.

Crossan, John Dominic, *The Dark Interval: Towards a Theology of Story*. Niles, Ill.: Argus Communications, 1975.

Cupitt, Don, *Taking Leave of God*. London: SCM Press, 1980.

Daniélou, Jean, S. J., *Primitive Christian Symbols*, trans. Donald Attwater. London: Burns & Oats, 1964.

Davidson, Donald, 'Realism without Reference', *Dialectica* 31 (1977), 247–58.

―――― 'Truth and Meaning', *Synthèse* 17 (1967), 304–23.

―――― 'What Metaphors Mean', in: Sacks, pp. 29–45.

Derrida, Jacques, 'White Mythology: Metaphor in the Text of Philosophy', *New Literary History* 6 (1974), 5–74.

Dickinson, Emily, *The Complete Poems of Emily Dickinson*, ed. Thomas H. Johnson. London: Faber and Faber, 1975.

Donnellan, Keith S., 'Reference and Definite Descriptions', in: Schwartz, pp. 42–65.

Dummett, Michael, 'Common Sense and Physics', in: J. F. Macdonald (ed.), *Perception and Identity*, London: The Macmillan Press, 1979, pp. 1–40.

Edge, David, 'Science and Religion: An Analysis of Issues', in: G. Walters (ed.), *Science and Religion: The Re-opening Dialogue*. Bath: Bath University Press, 1970, pp. 15–35.

Edie, James M., 'Ideality and Metaphor: A Phenomenological Theory of Polysemy', *The Journal of the British Society for Phenomenology* 6 (1975), 32–41.

Edwards, Paul, 'Professor Tillich's Confusions', *Mind* 74 (1965), 192–214.

Eliot, George, *The Mill on the Floss*. Harmondsworth: Penguin Books, 1979.

Farrer, Austin, *Reflective Faith: Essays in Philosophical Theology*, ed. Charles C. Conti. London: SPCK, 1972.

—— *The Glass of Vision*. Glasgow: The University Press, 1948.

Fawcett, Thomas, *The Symbolic Language of Religion*. London: SCM Press, 1970.

Ferré, Frederick, *Basic Modern Philosophy of Religion*. London: George Allen & Unwin, 1968.

—— *Language, Logic and God*. London: Eyre & Spottiswoode, 1962; Fontana Library, 1970.

—— 'Metaphor in Religious Discourse', *Dictionary of the History of Ideas*. 1973 edn.

—— 'Metaphors, Models and Religion', *Soundings* 2 (1968).

Foss, Martin, *Symbol and Metaphor in Human Experience*. Princeton: Princeton University Press, 1949.

Funk, Robert W., *Language, Hermeneutic, and Word of God: The Problem of Language in the New Testament and Contemporary Theology*. New York: Harper & Row, Publishers, 1966.

Gadamer, Hans-Georg, *Truth and Method*. London: Sheed & Ward, 1975.

Gill, Jerry H., *Christian Empiricism*. London: Sheldon Press, 1974.

Goodman, Nelson, *Languages of Art: An Approach to a Theory of Symbols*. 2nd edn. Indianapolis: Hackett Publishing Company, 1976.

—— 'Metaphor as Moonlighting', in: Sacks, pp. 175–80.

Grice, H. P., 'Logic and Conversation', in: Peter Cole and Jerry L. Morgan (eds.), *Syntax and Semantics*. New York: Academic Press, 1975, pp. 41–58.

Harré, R., *The Philosophies of Science: An Introductory Survey*. Oxford: Oxford University Press, 1972.

—— *The Principles of Scientific Thinking*. London: Macmillan and Co., 1970.

Harries, Karsten, 'The Many Uses of Metaphor', in: Sacks, pp. 165–72.

Hayward, John (ed.), *The Faber Book of English Verse*. London: Faber and Faber, 1958.

Henle, Paul (ed.), *Language, Thought and Culture*. Ann Arbor: The University of Michigan Press, 1965.

Hepburn, Ronald W., 'Demythologizing and the Problem of Validity', in: Antony Flew and Alasdair MacIntyre (eds.), *New Essays in Philosophical Theology*. London: SCM Press, 1955, pp. 227–42.

Hesse, Mary B., *Models and Analogies in Science*. Notre Dame, Ind.: Notre Dame University Press, 1966.

—— *The Structure of Scientific Inference*. London: The Macmillan Press, 1974.

Hester, Marcus B., *The Meaning of Poetic Metaphor: An Analysis in the Light of Wittgenstein's Claim that Meaning is Use*. The Hague: Mouton & Co., 1967.

High, Dallas M., *Language, Persons and Belief: Studies in Wittgenstein's Philosophical Investigations and Religious Uses of Language*. New York: Oxford University Press, 1967.

Hick, John, *The Philosophy of Religion*. Englewood Cliffs, N.J.: Prentice-Hall, 1973.

Hobbes, Thomas, *Leviathan*. London: J. M. Dent & Sons, 1914.

Hume, David, *Dialogues Concerning Natural Religion*, ed. Henry D. Aiken. New York: Hafner Publishing Co., 1948.

Ijsseling, Samuel, *Rhetoric and Philosophy in Conflict: An Historical Survey*, trans. P. Dunphy. The Hague: Martinus Nijhoff, 1976.

Jakobson, R., and Halle, Morris, *Fundamentals of Language*. The Hague: Mouton & Co., 1956.

James, Henry, *Portrait of a Lady*. Harmondsworth: Penguin Books, 1963.

Jones, Geraint Vaughan, *The Art and Truth of the Parables*. London: SPCK, 1964.

Jüngel, Eberhard, 'Metaphorische Wahrheit'. *Evangelische Theologie Sonderheft*. München: Chr. Kaiser Verlag, 1974, pp. 71–122.

Katz, Jerrold J., 'The Neoclassical Theory of Reference', in: Peter A. French, Theodore E. Uehling, Jr., and Howard K. Wettstein (eds.), *Contemporary Perspectives in the Philosophy of Language*. Minneapolis: The University of Minnesota Press, 1979, pp. 103–24.

Keat, Russell, and Urry, John, *Social Theory as Science*. London: Routledge & Kegan Paul, 1975.

Kennedy, George A., *Classical Rhetoric and its Christian and Secular Tradition from Ancient to Modern Times*. London: Croom Helm, 1980.

Kripke, Saul A., 'Naming and Necessity', in: Donald Davidson and Gilbert Harman (eds.), *Semantics of Natural Language*. Dordrecht: D. Reidel Publishing Company, 1972, pp. 253–355.

Lakoff, George, and Johnson, Mark, *Metaphors We Live By*. Chicago: University of Chicago Press, 1980.

Landow, George P., *Victorian Types, Victorian Shadows: Biblical Typology in Victorian Literature, Art and Thought*. London: Routledge & Kegan Paul, 1980.

Léonard, A., OP, 'Studies on the Phenomena of Mystical Experience', *in: Mystery and Mysticism: A symposium*. London: Blackfriars Publications, 1956.

Levin, Samuel R., *The Semantics of Metaphor*. London: The Johns Hopkins University Press, 1977.

Locke, John, *An Essay Concerning Human Understanding*. Oxford: The Clarendon Press, 1894, vol. II.

Lyons, John, *Introduction to Theoretical Linguistics*. Cambridge: Cambridge University Press, 1968.

—— *Semantics*, 2 vols. Cambridge: Cambridge University Press, 1977.

McFague, Sallie, *Metaphorical Theology: Models of God in Religious Language*. London: SCM Press, 1983.

Mack, Dorothy, 'Metaphoring As Speech Act: Some Happiness Conditions for Implicit Similes and Simple Metaphors'. *Poetics* 4 (1975), 221–56.

Miner, Earl, *An Introduction to Japanese Court Poetry*, with translations by the author and Robert H. Brower. Stanford: Stanford University Press, 1968.

Mitchell, Basil (ed.), *The Philosophy of Religion*. Oxford: Oxford University Press, 1971.

Morgan, Jerry L., 'Observations on the Pragmatics of Metaphor', in: Ortony, pp. 136–47.

Nietzsche, Friedrich, 'On Truth and Falsity in their Ultramoral Sense', in: *Early Greek Philosophy and Other Essays*, trans. Maximilian A. Mügge, vol. II of *The Complete Works of Nietzsche*, ed. Dr Oscar Levy. London and Edinburgh: T. N. Foulis, 1911, pp. 173–92.

Ogden, C. K. and Richards, I. A., *The Meaning of Meaning*. London: Routledge and Kegan Paul, 1923.

Oliver, Harold H., 'Relational Ontology and Hermeneutics,' in: Alan M. Olson (ed.), *Myth, Symbol and Reality*. Notre Dame, London: University of Notre Dame Press, 1980, pp. 69–85.

Ortony, Andrew (ed.), *Metaphor and Thought*. Cambridge: Cambridge University Press, 1979.

Palmer, F. R., *Semantics: A New Outline*. Cambridge: Cambridge University Press, 1976.

Peers, E. Allison, *Mother of Carmel: A Portrait of St. Teresa of Jesus*. London SCM Press, 1945.

Perelman, Chaim and Olbrechts-Tyteca, L., *The New Rhetoric: A Treatise on Argumentation*, trans. John Wilkinson and Purcell Weaver. Notre Dame, Ind.: The University of Notre Dame Press, 1969.

Phillips, D. Z., 'Religious Beliefs and Language Games', in: Basil Mitchell (ed.), *The Philosophy of Religion*. Oxford: Oxford University Press, 1971.

Plato, *Cratylus*, in: *The Dialogues of Plato*, trans. B. Jowett, 3rd edn. Oxford: The Clarendon Press, 1892.

Platts, Mark de Bretton, *Ways of Meaning: An Introduction to a Philosophy of Language*. London: Routledge & Kegan Paul, 1979.

Putnam, Hilary, 'Explanation and Reference', in: *Mind, Language and Reality*, vol. II of *Philosophical Papers*. Cambridge: Cambridge University Press, 1975, pp. 196–214.

────── 'Is Semantics Possible?', in: Schwartz, pp. 102–18.

────── *Meaning and the Moral Sciences*. London: Routledge & Kegan Paul, 1978.

────── 'Realism and Reason', in: *Meaning and the Moral Sciences*, pp. 123–38.

────── 'What is Realism?' *PAS* 76 (1975–76), 177–94.

Quine, W. V., 'A Postscript on Metaphor', in: Sacks, pp. 159–60.

Quintilian, *The Institutio Oratoria*, trans. H. E. Butler. London: William Heinemann, 1921, vol. III.

Rahner, Karl and Ratzinger, Joseph, *The Episcopate and the Primacy*. Freiburg: Herder Freiburg, 1962.

Ramsey, Ian T., *Christian Discourse: Some Logical Explorations*. Oxford: Oxford University Press, 1965.

────── *Christian Empiricism*, ed. Jerry H. Gill. London: Sheldon Press, 1974.

────── 'Facts and Disclosures', Address to the Aristotelian Society, 24 January 1972, reprinted in: Jerry H. Gill (ed.), *Christian Empiricism*. London: Sheldon Press, 1974.

────── *Models and Mystery*. Oxford: Oxford University Press, 1964.

────── *Models for Divine Activity*. London: SCM Press, 1973.

────── *Religious Language: An Empirical Placing of Theological Phrases*. London: SCM Press, 1957.

Read, Herbert, *English Prose Style*. London: G. Bell and Sons, 1928.

Richards, I. A., *The Philosophy of Rhetoric*. Oxford: Oxford University Press, 1936.

Ricoeur, Paul, *The Rule of Metaphor: Multi-disciplinary studies of the creation of meaning in language*, trans. Robert Czerny with Kathleen McLaughlin and John Costello, SJ. London: Routledge & Kegan Paul, 1978.

Rikhof, Herwi, *The Concept of Church: A Methodological Inquiry into the Use of Metaphors in Ecclesiology*. London: Sheed and Ward, 1981.

Robins, R. H., *A Short History of Linguistics*, 2nd edn. London: Longman Group, 1979.

Ryle, Gilbert, *The Concept of Mind*. Harmondsworth: Penguin Books, 1963.

Sacks, Sheldon (ed.), *On Metaphor*. Chicago: The University of Chicago Press, 1979.

Saussure, Ferdinand de, *Course in General Lingustics*, trans. Wade Baskin, ed. Charles Bally and Albert Sechehaye with Albert Reidlinger. London: Peter Owen, 1974.

Scheffler, Israel, *Beyond the Letter: A Philosophical Inquiry into Ambiguity, Vagueness and Metaphor in Language*. London: Routledge & Kegan Paul, 1979.

Schillebeeckx, E., OP, *Marriage: Secular Reality and Saving Mystery*. London: Sheed and Ward, 1965. vol. II.

Schwartz, Stephen P. (ed.), *Naming, Necessity, and Natural Kinds*. Ithaca: Cornell University Press, 1977.

Scott, Sir Walter, *Old Mortality*. London: Macmillan and Co., 1901.

Searle, John R., 'Metaphor', in: Ortony, pp. 92–123.

—— *Speech Acts: An Essay in the Philosophy of Language*. Cambridge: Cambridge University Press, 1969.

Sherry, Patrick, 'Analogy Today'. *Philosophy* 51 (1976), 431–46.

Smart, Professor J. J. C., 'Theory Construction', in: A. G. N. Flew (ed.), *Logic and Language: Second Series*. Oxford: Basil Blackwell Mott, 1959, pp. 222–42.

Snell, Bruno, *The Discovery of the Mind: The Greek Origins of European Thought*, trans. T. G. Rosenmeyer. Oxford: Basil Blackwell, 1953.

Stacey, David, *Interpreting the Bible*. London: Sheldon Press, 1976.

Sterne, Laurence, *The Life and Opinions of Tristram Shandy, Gentleman*. London: John Lehmann, 1948.

Taylor, Charles, 'Interpretation and the Sciences of Man', *Review of Metaphysics* 25, No. 1 (1971), 3–51.

Teresa of Avila, *The Life of the Holy Mother Teresa of Jesus*, in: *The Complete Works of St. Teresa of Jesus*, vol. I, trans. and ed. E. Allison Peers. London: Sheed and Ward, 1972.

—— *The Way of Perfection*, trans. The Benedictines of Stanbrook. London: Thomas Baker, 1919.

TeSelle, Sallie McFague, *Speaking in Parables: A Study in Metaphor and Theology*. London: SCM Press, 1975.

Thiselton, Anthony C., *The Two Horizons: New Testament Hermeneutics and Philosophical Description with Special Reference to Heidegger, Bultmann, Gadamer and Wittgenstein*. Exeter: The Paternoster Press, 1980.

Tracy, David, 'Metaphor and Religion', in: Sacks, pp. 89–104.

Turbayne, Colin Murray, *The Myth of Metaphor*. New Haven: Yale University Press, 1962.

Ullmann, Stephen, *Semantics: An Introduction to the Science of Meaning*. Oxford: Basil Blackwell, 1962.

—— 'Simile and Metaphor', in: Anna Morpurgo Davies and Wolfgang Meid (eds.), *Studies in Greek, Italic, and Indo-European Linguistics offered to Leonard R. Palmer*. Innsbruck: Innsbruck Beitrage Zur Sprachwissenschaft, *1976, pp. 425–30*.

Via, Dan Otto, Jr., *The Parables: Their Literary and Existential Dimension*. Philadelphia, Pa.: Fortress Press, 1967.

Vickers, Brian, *Francis Bacon and Renaissance Prose*. Cambridge: Cambridge University Press, 1968.

—— 'Rhetoric and Renaissance Literature', in *Rhetorik: Ein internationales Jahrbuch*, Band 2 (1981). Stuttgart: Frommann-Holzboog, 1981, pp. 106–30.

Walzer, Michael, *The Revolution of the Saints: A Study in the Origins of Radical Politics*. Cambridge, Mass.: Harvard University Press, 1965.

Wittgenstein, Ludwig, *Philosophical Investigations*, trans. G. E. M. Anscombe. New York: The Macmillan Company, 1953.

Woolf, Virginia. *To the Lighthouse*. London: J. M. Dent & Sons, 1938.

INDEX

TeSelle, Sallie McFague 110
'Theory-constitutive metaphors' 102
Tracy, David 105–6
Tropes, Ch. 4
Turbayne, Colin Murray 17, 79
'Two subjects' thesis (that each
   metaphor has) 20, 38ff, 86–90

Ullmann, Stephen 7, 20, 59n
Vickers, Brian 12
Vico, Giambattista 74–6, 150

Walzer, Michael 62n, 74
Wittgenstein 2, 78–9, 82
Woolf, Virginia 47, 84

HHH6HO
2/24/2011